THINK, ENGAGE, RESPOND
Communicating for Citizenship

SECOND EDITION

Mohawk College of Applied Arts and Technology

Taken from:

Politics, Power and the Common Good: An Introduction to Political Science, Second Edition
by Eric Mintz, David Close, and Osvaldo Croci

Impact: A Guide to Business Communication, Seventh Edition
by Margot Northey and Joan McKibbin

Strategies for Active Citizenship
by Kateri M. Drexler and Gwen Garcelon

Critical Thinking: Learn the Tools the Best Thinkers Use, Concise Edition
by Richard Paul and Linda Elder

Keys to Success: Building Successful Intelligence and Achieving Your Goals, Fourth Canadian Edition
by Carol Carter, Joyce Bishop, Sarah Lyman Kravits, and Peter J. Maurin

The Right Choice: Making Ethical Decisions on the Job
by Jane Ann McLachlan

Writing: A Guide for College and Beyond, Brief Edition
by Lester Faigley

Custom Publishing

New York   Boston   San Francisco
London   Toronto   Sydney   Tokyo   Singapore   Madrid
Mexico City   Munich   Paris   Cape Town   Hong Kong   Montreal

Cover Art: Courtesy of Earl & Nazima Kowall/Corbis Images.

Taken from:

Politics, Power and the Common Good: An Introduction to Political Science, Second Edition
by Eric Mintz, David Close, and Osvaldo Croci
Copyright © 2009, 2006 by Pearson Education Canada, Inc.
Published by Prentice Hall
Toronto, Ontario
Canada

Critical Thinking: Learn the Tools the Best Thinkers Use, Concise Edition
by Richard Paul and Linda Elder
Copyright © 2006 by Richard Paul and Linda Elder
Published by Prentice Hall
A Pearson Education Company

Keys to Success: Building Successful Intelligence and Achieving Your Goals, Fourth Canadian Edition
by Carol Carter, Joyce Bishop, Sarah Lyman Kravits, and Peter J. Maurin
Copyright © 2007, 2004, 2001 by Pearson Education Canada, Inc.
Published by Prentice Hall

The Right Choice: Making Ethical Decisions on the Job
by Jane Ann McLachlan
Copyright © 2009 by Pearson Education Canada, Inc.
Published by Prentice Hall

Writing: A Guide for College and Beyond, Brief Edition
by Lester Faigley
Copyright © 2007 by Pearson Education, Inc.
Published by Longman
New York, New York 10036

Strategies for Active Citizenship
by Kateri M. Drexler and Gwen Garcelon
Copyright © 2005 by Pearson Education, Inc.
Published by Prentice Hall
Upper Saddle River, New Jersey 07458

Impact: A Guide to Business Communication, Seventh Edition
by Margot Northey and Joan McKibbin
Copyright © 2008, 2005, 2002, 1998, 1993, 1990, 1986 by Pearson Education Canada, Inc.
Published by Prentice Hall

Printed in Canada

10 9 8 7 6

2008160509

MH/LD

**Pearson
Custom Publishing**
is a division of

www.pearsonhighered.com

ISBN 10: 0-555-01593-9
ISBN 13: 978-0-555-01593-3

CONTENTS

Chapter 1
COMMUNICATING FOR CITIZENS   1

Pages 2–8, 24–34, 36–40, and 49–61 were taken from *Impact: A Guide to Business Communication,* Seventh Edition, by Margot Northey and Joan McKibbin.

Pages 9–23, 35, 41–42, and 45–48 were taken from *Writing: A Guide for College and Beyond,* Brief Edition, by Lester Faigley.

Pages 42–44 were taken from *Keys to Success: Building Successful Intelligence and Achieving Your Goals,* Fourth Canadian Edition, by Carol Carter, Joyce Bishop, Sarah Lyman Kravits, and Peter J. Maurin.

Chapter 2

EXAMINING YOUR PERSONAL VALUES   63

Taken from *Strategies for Active Citizenship,* by Kateri M. Drexler and Gwen Garcelon.

Chapter 3

CONSIDERING DIVERSITY   87

Taken from *Keys to Success: Building Successful Intelligence and Achieving Your Goals,* Fourth Canadian Edition, by Carol Carter, Joyce Bishop, Sarah Lyman Kravits, and Peter J. Maurin.

Chapter 4
DEFINING THE COMMON GOOD   97

Pages 97–124 were taken from *Politics, Power and the Common Good: An Introduction to Political Science,* Second Edition, by Eric Mintz, David Close, and Osvaldo Croci.

Pages 124–126 were taken from *Citizenship: Issues and Action,* by Mark Evans, Michael Slodovnick, Terezia Zoric, and Rosemary Evans.

Chapter 5
THINKING CRITICALLY   127

Pages 127–148 were taken from *Critical Thinking: Learn the Tools the Best Thinkers Use,* Concise Edition, by Richard Paul and Linda Elder.

Pages 148–160 were taken from *Keys to Success: Building Successful Intelligence and Achieving Your Goals,* Fourth Canadian Edition, by Carol Carter, Joyce Bishop, Sarah Lyman Kravits, and Peter J. Maurin.

Chapter 6

DEFINING AND APPLYING ETHICS   161

Pages 161–166 were taken from "Introduction to Ethics," by Robert C. Solomon, reprinted from *A Handbook for Ethics* (1995), Wadsworth.

Pages 167-184 were taken from *The Right Choice: Making Ethical Decisions on the Job,* by Jane Ann McLachlan.

Chapter 7

EVALUATING THE MEDIA   185

Taken from *Politics, Power and the Common Good: An Introduction to Political Science,* Second Edition, by Eric Mintz, David Close, and Osvaldo Croci.

FOREWORD

Mohawk College has a well-earned reputation for providing employers with highly skilled graduates. Our reputation is reflected in graduate employment rates and employer satisfaction scores that are consistently outstanding. Today, nine out of ten Mohawk students are working within six months of graduating from college and nine out of ten employers report being satisfied or very satisfied with the Mohawk graduates that they have hired.

A few years back, our industry partners told us they were looking for employees with a new set of skills. They not only wanted graduates with leading-edge technical expertise. They also needed graduates who had developed "soft skills" in leadership, teamwork, communication and facilitation. In short, they were searching for prospective employees who could quickly make their mark, make a difference and move into leadership roles within their organizations and in the communities where they did business.

At Mohawk, we have long recognized that meeting the needs of employers gives our students and graduates yet another competitive advantage in the workplace. So Mohawk became the first college in all of Ontario to develop and introduce an Active Citizenship Course.

Today, every one of our 10,000 full-time students is required to take the course. We have assembled a dedicated and passionate team of professors to help students explore issues related to ethics and citizenship in local, provincial and global contexts. Students are also encouraged to learn how to participate in public discourse, take action and demonstrate personal leadership on issues that matter. Learning happens both in the classroom and in the community. Through discussion, reflection and analysis, Mohawk students begin to build the foundation for highly sought-after communication, teamwork and leadership skills.

To celebrate the launch of Mohawk's Active Citizenship course, we hosted an official Swearing-In Ceremony in our auditorium where twenty-five newcomers to our country became Canadian citizens. The auditorium was filled with proud families, students and staff. The ceremony, which has since become an annual tradition at Mohawk, serves as a powerful reminder of why we are so privileged to learn, work and live in such a great country, province and city.

Our graduates are Mohawk's single greatest contribution to economic and social development. With our Active Citizenship Course, we are helping students to realize their potential and share in the responsibility for making our community an even better place in which to work, learn, live and play.

MaryLynn West-Moynes, President
Mohawk College of Applied Arts and Technology
Hamilton Ontario Canada

INTRODUCTION

ACTIVE CITIZENSHIP IN AN AGE OF FEAR AND APATHY

In the classic tale, The Once and Future King, Merlyn the magician turns the future King Arthur into an ant, so Arthur can understand how ants live. What he learns is that ants are unimaginative creatures that simply follow orders without thinking about their lives or their surroundings. Watching the ants bringing food to the nest, Arthur observes,

> The ants who had filled their crops to the brim were walking back to the inner fortress, to be replaced by a procession of empty ants who were coming from the same direction. There were never any new ants in the procession, only this same dozen, going backward and forward, as they would do during all their lives. (White, 1971, 124)

Life for them is a dull routine where individuals do nothing more than meet their obligations as servants of the colony and its queen. Arthur ultimately rejects the ants' political and social arrangement as unsuitable for human beings.

What about humans? What brings meaning to our lives? Are we content simply to learn the skills required to do our jobs as part of an organization or corporation? What kind of rights and responsibilities do we enjoy, not just as workers and consumers, but as citizens with common needs and desires? How can we make the most out of our total lives?

For many Canadians, the answer is 'active citizenship'. Active citizenship is about giving back to your local, national and global communities, and about reaping the benefits of living in a society where others do the same. Being an active citizen implies both rights and duties, and requires the knowledge, skills and opportunities to exercise such duties. However, as author Bernard Crick argues, these skills and opportunities are wasted if citizens lack a practical understanding of how power is wielded in society. In turn, understanding that power requires knowing something about the institutions that constitute the 'arena' of decision-making. In democratic societies, these institutions include

1. elected representatives
2. free, fair, and frequent elections

3. freedom of expression

4. access to alternative, independent sources of information

5. autonomous associations (i.e. interest groups, trade unions)

6. inclusive citizenship [Crick, 2002, 107-8]

How do individuals interact with these institutions? How do we determine the character of our society? In Canada, we engage in debates about issues that matter to us. These debates are reflected in our politics where two positions are represented in varying degrees: 1) that which favours the development of an 'activist' state with its redistribution of income and wealth to defuse discontent with the system (social democrats, social liberals), and 2) that which prefers a more individualist, profit-driven economy with minimal state interference in the market (neo-liberals/conservatives).

Crick's view is that the middle class ethos has reflected more recently the values of the latter position. He describes the middle class as being

> ...far more individualistic...more self and family-centred with less feeling for public service, less belief that rights entail duties and responsibilities....They will attack racism as, indeed, an affront to human dignity and any kind of democracy, but not face up to the root causes of discrimination – stark poverty, economic disadvantage, and even relative deprivation. [Crick, 2002, 111]

How then do we choose to address issues such as poverty? With politicians downsizing government activism since the 1990's, 'volunteerism' has been promoted as the alternative to government-funded social programmes. Thus government's role has been replaced by dependence on the good graces of those with the resources and time to volunteer and donate to charities and other local organizations. However, active citizenship can not and must not be reduced to volunteerism if it means that some citizens' security and welfare is subject to the whims and preferences of others.

Recent global events have had a significant impact on the practice of active citizenship in western democracies. Civil rights advocates maintain that since September 11, 2001, governments have used the 'war on terror' to justify the curtailment of constitutional and civil rights, and that critical thinking and tolerance for dissenting opinions is more restricted than prior to the attacks on the World Trade Center. We have become more reluctant to practise active citizenship. This change in attitude, along with a higher degree of public apathy, has resulted in a different kind of citizenship that apparently meets the approval of governing institutions in modern democracies. [Crick, 2002, 112]

> The very scale of the political and legal institutions of modern democracies seems to demand the **good citizen** more than the **active citizen**: the relatively smooth working of and security of democratic institutions can actually smother an active democratic spirit by appearing to diminish its need. Nearly all significant measures of public participation in political processes now show marked decline, not merely in election turn-outs. [Crick, 2002, 113]

The ants, observed by Arthur, are examples of good citizens who follow society's rules and laws. Yet citizenship is about more than good behaviour; it is about participating in the transformation of our communities, local, national and global. Active citizenship requires

> ...people to think of themselves as active citizens, willing, able and equipped to have an influence in public life and with the critical capacities to weigh evidence before speaking and acting; to build on and to extend radically to young people the best in existing traditions of community and public service, and to make them individually confident in finding new forms of involvement and action among themselves. [Crick, 2002, 114]

Active citizenship does not happen automatically; rather, it requires skills that must be learned and developed. Consequently, Crick sees an important role for schools in promoting an active citizenship agenda in students from an early age that includes

> ...discussion of controversial issues; participation in school and community affairs; learning skills of advocacy; the idea of 'political literacy' as a blending of skills, knowledge and attitudes; learning awareness of cultural diversities – [including] the different nations, religions and ethnic groups.... [Crick, 2002, 114]

Now, from the perspective of those in power, there are definite risks involved in promoting active citizenship, in addition to good citizenship. An active, politically literate citizenry asks more questions and makes more demands of government and non-governmental authorities. Citizens can no longer be counted on to go along with policies that are imposed from above. They may even demand an increased role in the planning and implementation of such policies.

Democracy is not simply a question of entitlement. Yes, living in a democracy comes with fundamental rights and freedoms, and we are entitled to make our case when we believe our rights have been denied. However, for democracy to be effective, citizens must understand how "the system" works, and must be prepared to be full participants in our society. Active citizenship is a right, a freedom, and a responsibility.

Geoff Ondercin-Bourne
Active Citizenship Team Member
Mohawk College of Applied Arts and Technology

Bibliography

Crick, Bernard. *Democracy: A Very Short Introduction.* (New York, New York: Oxford University Press), 2002.

White, T.H. *The Once and Future King.* (London, UK: Collins Fontana Books), 1971.

COMMUNICATING AS CITIZENS: ARE WE USELESS STONES OR DISCOVERED DIAMONDS?

By what strange law of mind is it that an idea long overlooked, and trodden under foot as a useless stone, suddenly sparkles out in new light, as a discovered diamond?

Harriet Beecher Stowe (*Uncle Tom's Cabin,* 2004 (1852), p. 406)

Today we are bombarded with images, ideas, stories, and marketing ploys intended to help us define who we are as individuals. This can make speaking up or even thinking of alternatives to what is the "norm" a fearful proposition. It will certainly take an epochal social movement to reverse the role (or at least equalize the role) that media, government, and the global economy play in shaping our society. This period of history, however, may find that movement slowly becoming a reality. One group that is beginning to pave the way toward a more unified sense of communal values and activities is called the "social innovation" movement. *Wikipedia*, one of the forerunners of this style of community based information systems, defines the term as one that

> refers to new strategies, concepts, ideas and organizations that meet social needs of all kinds—from working conditions and education to community development and health—and that extend and strengthen civil society (http://en.wikipedia.org/wiki/Social_innovation)

Social innovators focus on the intersection between the self and the workplace, the family and the government, the patient and the health care corporation, and everything (and everyone) in between. Social innovators ask people to be creative and to use their minds to start a revolution that revolves around being active citizens. In fact, "THE HUB," one of the hot websites devoted to "social innovators," says to its web-surfers,

> You could join our email list, it might help, but chances are it won't be enough. Why not just expose yourself to a world, a state, a bunch of people? You can get on and do your thing. And others will get on and do theirs. But before long, someone's bound to be asking. What would we do if we could? (http://www.the-hub.net/whynot/)

In our current Canadian climate, one of the most important ways that we can contribute to our community as social innovators and as active citizens is through our ability to communicate about the issues that concern us, to really ask what we "could" do if we just tried. To really ask the questions about what we would do if we could requires knowledge about how communications leads to more participatory involvement. These communications include reading, writing, speaking, and thinking. Reading a newspaper, writing a letter to a cultural organization, speaking out at a union meeting, and thinking about your own role on issues like climate change and violence in schools are only a few examples of what these communications might be.

The key to really making a difference with these types of communications is in using our ability to read, write, think and speak *effectively*. The question is, how can we measure the effectiveness of our communication? Frank Herbert, the writer who penned the *Dune* series, once wrote, "[p]eople, not commercial organizations or chains of command, are what make great civilizations work, every civilization depends upon the quality of the individuals it produces. If you overorganize humans, over-legalize them, suppress their urge to greatness—they cannot work and their civilization collapses" (Herbert, *Children of Dune*). What is this quality in individuals Herbert speaks of? It is the innovative ideas and questions that are latent within all individuals. But how does "over-organization" and "over-legalization" threaten innovative ideas? This textbook and the readings reproduced inside start a dialogue about this very issue.

If authentic citizenship is about communicating your own ideas effectively (one definition of which may be clearly and intelligently across a variety of local and global contexts)—then whatever those ideas are—we must be able to communicate creatively and critically in order to engage with our global community. We must also be able to analyze the information we are bombarded with from others, so that we can judge issues for ourselves without bias and with a consciousness of how the world works. When this type of communication happens then we can see the transformation that Harriet Beecher Stowe speaks of in the quotation above, where an unpolished stone suddenly becomes something much greater. It becomes a diamond. With a commitment to discovering what makes us effective communicators our work inevitably evolves, transmutes, and intensifies in such a way that we can only succeed in increasing our awareness and involvement in our global community.

The degree to which we attempt to engage with our society through our communications is how we become social innovators and active citizens. Advancing our skills in all of the above areas allows us to think, speak, and write in a non-biased and open way so that, as a community, we can share our ideas without prejudice. So that we unpolished rocks, once hidden at the bottom of the earth's streams, rivers, and oceans, can rise up and show ourselves as powerful and empowered members of every community we choose to become a part of.

Rhonda Dynes
Active Citizenship team member
Mohawk College of Applied Arts and Technology

Bibliography

Stowe, Harriet Beecher. *Uncle Tom's Cabin*, (Oxford U. Press, 2002 (1852)), p. 406.

Herbert, Frank. *Children of Dune*, (Ace, 1987).

PREFACE TO INSTRUCTORS

This textbook is augmented from the first edition, and includes more information about the communications frameworks required to really teach students about the process of participatory and responsible citizenship. The text still expects students to employ effective communications formatting skills: letter writing, argumentative communications, presentations, and report writing—the same things that are generally taught in Business, Technical or general Workplace Communications courses. Now, however, instructors and professors must also look to current events and media and use analytical skills to hone students' writing, reading, speaking, and thinking skills. Students must also learn how to communicate ideas in a more open and clear manner.

This textbook, and the course it accompanies, is designed to help students' work actively, through writing and speaking, to become more engaged citizens in our community.

Not only must students be able to speak about their ideas, they must also problem solve around communications issues and be able to function in group and individual settings where conflict may take place. Students' abilities to act in a leadership position and their ability to communicate effectively, will give students an edge not only in the workplace, but in the world and at home.

One major role instructors will have in teaching this course is setting up a community within their classroom that facilitates students' abilities to engage in a much more advanced form of communications than what they may have been a part of previously. In thinking about how that classroom may operate, some useful images from "The Hub," a website devoted to research in social innovation, may prove useful. This is a type of self reflective citizenship where values and an individual's own role in communicating effectively become fore-grounded. The Hub writes of its space:

> We've borrowed from the best of a professional office, friendly cafe, independent cinema and the comforts of home to create a new kind of social space.
>
> This is a space in which to move and be moved. To take risks and make mistakes. To collaborate and participate. To laugh and despair. To lead and to learn. It's a networked space, fertile space, social space. (http://www.the-hub.net/here/)

On that note, please check out the foreword to this book's organization. There you will find information about ways the textbook material can be organized and individualized to your course, and the way you can make the most of your student's time on their road to becoming more advanced communicators and more effective and involved citizens.

Rhonda Dynes
Active Citizenship team member
Mohawk College of Applied Arts and Technology

A READER'S GUIDE TO THIS TEXTBOOK

This short section is intended to give a general overview of the aims and organization of *Think, Engage, Respond: Communicating for Citizenship*. The various prefaces to this textbook are intended to familiarize students and professors with the goals and aims of a Communications or General Education course that focuses on Citizenship themes and ideas. The first Preface is from our current President and outlines the importance of looking at the issues inherent in being a responsible citizen in Canadian society. This general outlook is intended to form a general outline for the purpose of a course such as Active Citizenship. The second Preface is for Professors who find that they are teaching this type of course. It addresses the importance of communications as a framework for any discussion of citizenship and differentiates the aims and goals of the textbook as different from those texts that focus solely on politics or government. This textbook is not about "Civics." It is intended as a post-secondary level textbook that explains how effective communication about societal issues forms the foundation for "active" or participatory or responsible citizenship. To that end, each of the chapters of the text aim to lead the reader towards that outcome.

An introduction to the text gives readers their first look at the Canadian climate with regard to citizenship issues. The first part of the Introduction, "Active Citizenship in an Age of Fear and Apathy" focuses on a responsible citizen's role in a changing society where fear and apathy control many and where silence seems to be an acceptable way to live. This text challenges that belief and invites readers to think in a new way about how they might choose to act differently and actively participate in how their society functions. The second part of the introduction outlines the various ways that people can get involved in communicating about citizenship and about how their society functions. In this part of the textbook, readers are challenged to think about what effective communication is and how it fits into becoming a more responsible and socially innovative member of their various communities.

Chapter One, "Communicating for Citizens" provides readers with advanced communications ideas about how to begin reading, writing, speaking, and thinking about citizenship issues. Since this textbook assumes basic workplace or professional communications readers are asked to go beyond basic precepts and to ponder questions about intercultural communications practices, in depth listening skills, and contextual writing practice. Chapter One also includes information about argument and analysis, report writing, and presentation skills. This information is meant to provide a solid foundation for the communication skills required to become a responsible and participatory citizen.

Chapters Two, Three, and Four all provide readings on three important topics for Canadian citizens. Chapter Two focuses on Personal Values. Here readers are asked to think about their own beliefs and structures of expression. Chapter Three looks at Diversity and asks readers to consider how they work within diverse communities and varied contexts. Diversity is explored and expanded to include not only cultural diversity but also age, sexual orientation, gender, and economic diversity. Chapter Four is concerned with how our values and expressions of diversity come together for the Common Good. The concept of the common good is explored as it relates to our political and governmental structures. The focus here, though, is on how we can work toward expressing our selves and our beliefs so that our communities are strengthened rather than compartmentalized.

Taking the previous three chapters as "content" oriented, in the sense that each reading is focused on explaining and defining concepts, the next two chapters focus on exploring frameworks to aid in the discussion and analysis of that content. Chapter Five concerns Critical Thinking, the ability to "read" texts for messages, ideas, bias, and perspective. Chapter Six looks at Ethics and, through the use of case studies, gives readers the chance to actively apply a framework for understand how our ethical viewpoints actively change the way we interact in our social communities whether those be at home, at school, at the workplace, or anywhere else in the world.

Chapter Seven, the last in the textbook looks at Media, and the various ways that citizens can get informed (and misinformed) about the very issues that have previously been described in the textbook. This chapter is intended to present a balanced look at how media (whether it be through a website, a blog, a newspaper, a radio show, a podcast, a letter, or an advertisement just to name a few) impact our ability to make decisions as a citizen. Looking at the role of media touches on the creation of values, the expression of diversity, and the impact of the common good. It also stretches our abilities to think critically and to come up with ethical arguments. As such it is an appropriate way to end the text. Together, each of these chapters will enable readers to think more deeply and responsibly about their role as citizens. It is our hope that as our society grows and changes so will this textbook. For now we hope this brief explanation may help to guide you through these pages.

Rhonda Dynes
Active Citizenship team member
Mohawk College of Applied Arts and Technology

COMMUNICATING FOR CITIZENS

Thinking about the relationship between communications and citizenship requires a previous knowledge of the foundations of professional and business reading, writing, listening, speaking and thinking.

The opening section of this chapter is intended to stretch basic communications skills and knowledge from a local to a global level and from application in unique to broad range contexts. One common example is not just going to a business meeting at your local branch but having to travel to Germany for a meeting. In Germany there are a variety of different communications styles that are seen as professional. Knowledge of intercultural and diverse communications styles is one way of furthering your education in the workplace. Another example might be trying to write a letter not just to your local paper but to a national one: there are different standards and there may be a much different audience. The points keep coming back to knowing your audience and keeping your communications reader-centred.

The second part of this chapter includes three sections: analytical writing, report writing, and presentations. The first part examines ways not only to read and summarize communications but also to think about the process of reading and writing in a more *argumentative and analytical* way. The second section, on *report writing*, looks at the broader issues implied in writing a report. That is to say, the focus isn't so much on formatting (though we've included some tips as a refresher) but is on effectively and responsibly writing *and* citing material. The focus is also on how writers need to focus on the needs of their readers in order to be effective. The last section is on presentation skills, and again, the focus isn't just on doing a *presentation*, but about refining and building on previous experience. It's also about being part of a collaborative team. There is a short section on teamwork and working to effectively include all types of personalities and abilities when there are oral communications to accomplish.

In total, this chapter is meant to provide a framework for the reading, writing, speaking, listening, and thinking that is required for responsible and participatory citizens. The focus is on how effective communications is the foundation of an inclusive and diverse community.

Rhonda Dynes
Active Citizenship team member
Mohawk College of Applied Arts and Technology

THE ROLE OF INTERCULTURAL COMMUNICATION

Increased global opportunity in our increasingly multicultural society has resulted in a heightened awareness of the need to communicate effectively with people of different cultures. As businesses strive to compete in diverse environments, they have recognized the importance of intercultural communication skills for professional success. Resolving issues across cultural and ethnic differences requires an appreciation of cultural diversity and an awareness of intercultural practices. Each year, it seems, the technology improves and the costs decrease.

For instance, attitudes to time vary from culture to culture. North Americans are generally concerned about being on time. In business, "on time" means precisely at the scheduled hour, perhaps even at the scheduled minute. North American executives who have to cool their heels for an hour in the waiting room of a South American associate could be infuriated about "wasting time" if they didn't realize that their ideas about time are not always shared by others.

Attitudes to space also vary. Research in proxemics (the study of the space between people) shows that different cultural ideas of what is "private space" may cause communication problems. For example, South Americans and southern Europeans like to move close when they talk to each other. Northern Europeans and North Americans, by contrast, like to keep about a metre apart in business relationships, moving closer only if the relationship becomes more intimate. The British, with their customary reserve, have a reputation for being the most "standoffish." It's easy for people from these different cultural backgrounds to give offence unknowingly when talking to one another by moving in during a conversation or by backing away.

Attitudes toward the Internet can also reveal cultural differences. A request for digital photographs and biographies of business partners or staff may meet some resistance from Latin Americans who are reluctant to share personal information with people they do not know; North Americans, on the other hand, tend to see this type of exposure as a good promotional tool.

E-mail messages, too, can show cross-cultural differences. Asians tend to adopt a very formal tone, writing e-mail notes that are similar to written letters and include openings and closings. North Americans, with their commitment to speed and efficiency, often forego these formalities.

Different cultures practise varying business etiquette and communication styles when negotiating business deals. One study (Hung, 1994, Conclusion section, para. 2–3) identifies Canadian negotiating styles as individualistic, informal, and direct, with a sequential approach to the handling of tasks and a marked dislike of silence. According to this research, only 15 percent of the typical negotiating styles of Canadian business executives are appropriate in Pacific Asia, Canada's second most important trading partner after the United States.

Bridging cross-cultural differences has become a fundamental ingredient of successful business communication. When diversity issues are involved, the following guidelines will prove helpful in enhancing communication, both written and spoken.

Writing across Cultures

1. *Avoid the temptation to sound sophisticated or erudite.* Choose words that are common and may well be included in the English lexicon of a non-native speaker of English. For example, try *rank* instead of *prioritize* or *make* instead of *implement*.

2. *Stay away from any slang or colloquial expressions.* Terms such as *headhunter* or *bean counter* might create some unintended confusion.

3. *Avoid complex, inverted sentence structure.* Beginning a sentence with an introductory clause makes it harder for the reader to interpret the message. Try to use simple syntax that places the subject and verb at the beginning of the sentence.

4. *Remember not to use acronyms, contractions, or abbreviations.* What might be common knowledge to a North American may well be unknown to an Asian or European reader. Writing the phrase in full diminishes the need for any guesswork on the part of the reader.

Speaking across Cultures

1. *Watch for signs of confusion or lack of comprehension.* Use the nonverbal communication cues discussed below to assess whether your message is being understood.

2. *Be an active listener.* North Americans have sometimes been told that they have a tendency to talk too much. Be sure to allow ample opportunity for others to ask questions or verify information.

3. *Be a sensitive listener.* People from different cultures may have an imperfect understanding of English, but this is not a reflection of their thinking. Be sensitive to what is underneath their struggles with your language.

4. *Remember that gesture and facial expression are the most commonly understood means of communication.* A smile or a raised eyebrow can say a great deal, bearing in mind the cultural differences discussed below.

Assessing the Receiver in Context

Socrates' prescription for understanding is first to "Know thyself." For business communication, that wise dictum might be amended to read, "Know your audience." The most frequent and serious of all mistakes in business correspondence comes from an incorrect or inadequate assessment of the receiver. Too often people communicate as if to thin air or to some faceless machine, or else they assume that the receiver will think the same way they do. As a result they produce letters or reports that are *writer based* rather than *reader based* and speeches that miss their mark with the audience. (Flower [1993] discusses these terms in detail.) Don't fall into this communication trap;

spend time assessing your receiver. And since people don't exist in isolation, consider also the environment, or context, which may influence the receiver's response. Ask yourself the following questions:

1. *How will the receiver benefit?* In a routine memo, the benefit may simply be that the reader will be better informed, but in correspondence in which you are making suggestions you need to figure out specifically what benefit there is to following your proposal. By pointing out the benefit, such as increased savings, higher profits, or improved company morale, you have a better chance of interesting the receiver in what you are saying—and of getting results.

2. *What is the receiver's position and responsibility?* Is he or she your superior, your subordinate, or an associate? Considering the receiver's position may help you decide the level of formality to use. Determining the exact area of responsibility will help you decide the kind of detail to include.

   Suppose you have an idea for a new product and want to sound out others in the company about its feasibility. Clearly you would want to have a different emphasis and a different set of questions for the marketing manager than for the plant manager or the controller. Where one person would be most concerned with potential markets and sales, another might be concerned with production problems or costs. In the same way, if you are composing application letters you should stress different aspects of your qualifications, depending upon the different responsibilities of the people to whom you are writing.

3. *What is the receiver's knowledge?* Considering this question will help prevent you from being either condescending or confusing. Most business people have a specialized understanding of certain aspects of their business. If you give them information that they already know, you may annoy them. It would be condescending for a surveyor to write to a lawyer, "A survey by a registered surveyor has legal authority," or for a manager to send a memo to a new assistant saying, "I require my letters to be properly formatted and free of typographical errors." (The manager should speak to a new employee anyway, rather than send a memo.)

   On the other hand, you don't want to assume too much about a person's knowledge, giving information the receiver will not likely understand or issuing instructions the receiver will have difficulty following. Technical experts frequently make the mistake of giving highly specialized information to managers who are confused by it and, as a result, often get annoyed. By thinking about the receiver's field and level of knowledge before you begin, you will be better able to decide the kind of technical or specialized information you should include.

4. *What interests and concerns the receiver?* It's not necessary to play psychoanalyst here, but do use your practical understanding of human nature and of the particular reader to establish what will create interest or concern. How will the receiver likely react to your information or suggestions? Is he or she known as a stickler for details or as someone who gets impatient with particulars? As someone impressed by creativity or nervous about quick change?

Will an older employee feel threatened by the ideas of a young "upstart"? What specific objections will the receiver likely raise?

5. *What is your experience with the receiver?* If you have dealt with the receiver before, you can benefit by recalling what was positive or negative in the relationship. You can try to avoid potential areas of friction and repeat what worked. Occasionally, you might even decide to send correspondence elsewhere.

   A junior employee in an auditing firm learned this lesson early in her career. She had a manager who was repeatedly critical of her inattention to details. When she wrote a memo to him presenting an imaginative idea for saving time on a large auditing account, he dismissed the concept with the comment that she was just trying to avoid detailed work again. Some time later, she presented the idea to a different manager, who both accepted the idea and offered her high praise. The moral is that past experience can colour thinking and influence the reception of a message.

   Past experience may also be company experience. If you are trying to collect money owed, for example, you should see if the creditor has often been delinquent with payments and what the response has been to previous appeals. Similarly, if you are writing a promotional letter to customers, you should find out how they reacted to earlier promotions.

6. *What is the receiver's environment?* Diverse cultural backgrounds create different expectations. In an increasingly multicultural society, and with growing international trade, understanding the receiver's cultural environment will reduce the chance of friction in communication. Although one cannot become an instant expert on other cultures, being aware that there are cultural differences will at least help you avoid the arrogance of assuming that others will or should react as you do.

   The political and economic climate can also shape communication needs. Widespread public concern about pollution might affect a report to a manager on the purchase of new machinery. An economic downturn, or the threat of one, might shape a sales letter to a customer or an internal proposal for an expensive acquisition.

   Understanding the broader environment of the receiver can in many instances make a dramatic difference to the effectiveness of communication.

7. *Will the correspondence reach secondary readers?* In some cases, a secondary reader can assume major importance. For example, a performance evaluation may become a lawyer's weapon in a lawsuit for wrongful dismissal. An internal report on a chemical spill might somehow find its way into a press exposé of pollution. "Be prepared" is the best motto. Consider who *might* read the communication as well as who definitely will read it.

   This is also the case with electronic communication. The security of e-mail cannot be guaranteed, and we sometimes hear about messages being mistakenly forwarded or circulated to the wrong recipients. Even when you delete material, it can usually be retrieved by someone with sophisticated computer skills.

   In situations where confidentiality matters, remember that what you write down, whether in a paper document or e-mail, has a long life.

It may seem that this detailed list of questions is too elaborate to bother with. In fact, getting a precise fix on the context of the communication task is really not very time-consuming. With a routine letter or memo to a familiar associate, you will gauge your receiver quickly. Even if the task is more problematic, you will soon discover that the few minutes spent considering these questions will prevent false starts and discarded drafts—or unwanted results. Your analysis will help you create receiver-based communication that gets results.

BECOMING A GOOD LISTENER

Listening is probably the most underrated of all the communication skills, probably because it seems so easy. Yet a common complaint from subordinates about managers at all levels is that they don't listen. Research has shown that managers generally rate themselves as better listeners than their employees rate them (Brownell, 1990).

Often a manager's poor listening behaviour reflects the old notion that a manager's job is to tell others what to do and see that they do it. Although good managers do indeed have to spend time talking with others (instructing and advising them), increasingly they recognize the need to involve employees throughout the organization in making suggestions and problem solving, as a way of improving performance and productivity. Such effective upward communication depends on management's willingness to listen.

What are the guidelines for effective listening? First of all, it helps to understand Carl Rogers'(1995) distinction between passive and active listening.

Passive listening means listening without giving a response, other than the odd nod or show of comprehension. It's appropriate when the talker merely wants to let off steam or muse out loud. *Active listening*, by contrast, creates a constant interaction between speaker and listener. By directly responding to what the speaker says, through comments and questions, the listener helps direct the conversation. An active listener can, in fact, retain control of a conversation.

If you want to be an active listener, according to Rogers, you need to have *empathy*— an understanding of the speaker's perspective and feelings. Empathy is not the same as sympathy or feeling sorry for the speaker, but rather implies awareness. Four kinds of "mirroring" techniques will help you show this awareness:

1. *Paraphrasing,* in which you restate in different words the speaker's point: "You mean . . ."

2. *Clarifying,* in which you ask for a restatement or fuller explanation: "What exactly do you mean by . . . ?"

3. *Reflecting feelings,* in which you respond to the emotions behind the words: "It sounds as if you're feeling . . ."

4. *Summarizing,* in which you pull together the speaker's points: "What I hear you saying is . . ."

Beyond mirroring the speaker's remarks, here are some ways to become a good listener:

1. *Stop talking.* Sometimes this is a hard thing for busy managers to do, especially those used to giving orders. Don't be afraid of silence. Give others time to collect their thoughts. If they take time getting to the point, be patient. Don't interrupt to finish sentences for them. Wait until they pause, and then clarify or try to draw them out.

2. *For a lengthy discussion, pick a spot where neither of you will be distracted.* Telephone calls or other disruptions can interrupt the flow of a discussion. Clear your mind of other matters so that you can concentrate on the conversation.

3. *Show by your posture and expression that you are attentive.* Leaning forward, for example, can show concern for the other person, as can facing the speaker squarely rather than turning partly away. Eye contact also helps signal that the listener is attentive, although staring or glaring will certainly not encourage relaxed conversation.

4. *Be open rather than judgmental.* Try not to let preconceptions or biases about the speaker shape what you are hearing. Concentrate on the substance rather than the style. At the same time, try to get some sense of the pattern and direction of the speaker's remarks.

5. *Be alert to nonverbal cues.* The speaker may betray deeper or more conflicting feelings than the words indicate. Nonverbal cues can often alert you to areas where you should probe deeper to find a hidden message.

Sometimes we assess the speaker by the pace of the speech. A fast talker may be impatient with a slow talker, or a slow talker may be suspicious of someone who speaks at a fast clip. The typical difference in speed between "fast-talking" Northerners in the United States and the slower "drawl" of Southerners has affected attitudes in many a conversation. On the whole, a listener who matches the speed of the speaker's talk will produce a more positive atmosphere in the conversation. There are exceptions, however. For example, people who are upset or excited often talk faster than usual, sometimes at a breathless pace. We can help calm them down by responding in a slower, more moderate way—a technique doctors use with agitated patients.

Listening to Understand

Although much of this discussion about listening involves strengthening a relationship with others, there are times when the point of your listening is simply to understand some information, as when you are receiving instructions, finding out background information to a problem, or attending a speech or lecture. Often in these instances it's useful to take notes, as long as getting down details doesn't prevent you from catching the overview or "big picture." Don't try to put everything into notes unless you are skilled at shorthand or are able to review your short-form scribble immediately afterward. Instead, try to concentrate first on understanding the flow of the talk and the main argument before attending to the details.

It can be helpful to write the speaker's key points in one column on a page and the examples or justifications in another column to the right. You might also try leaving space at the right of the page to fill in your own comments after the talk. That way, at a later date you can easily review at a glance the speaker's ideas and your response to them. Personalizing the information will help you to remember it.

Listening as a Critic

Occasionally your task as listener will be to evaluate—to assess the information critically. For example, you may need to assess a marketing or sales proposal or to review other corporate plans. The danger here is that you can become so intent on finding weak spots or problems that you don't really hear what is being said. Sometimes your own biases and emotions can get in the way, so that you unwittingly "tune out" the speaker's message. In either case, the result is distortion or misunderstanding.

Instead, try to concentrate on coming to a full understanding before reaching evaluative conclusions. Brief note-taking can help. You might also jot down beforehand questions that are central to your assessment, so that after you are sure you have understood the presentation you can use them as a guide for your evaluation. If you have only a general idea of what the topic will be, here are some basic questions that can help you evaluate:

* What is the main strength of this idea?
* Are there any factual errors or distortions?
* Is the point of view balanced? Is there an underlying bias?
* What are the alternatives to the proposal, and have they been adequately considered?
* What are the short-term and long-term implications of the ideas?
* How could the ideas be implemented practically? What are the barriers to their implementation and could they be overcome?
* As a result of this speech, what needs to be changed, re-examined, or explored further?

Remember that a speaker cannot talk as fast as your brain can process the information. There's a lot of "empty time" when, as a listener, you can easily be distracted. A more useful alternative to daydreaming is to use that time to review or summarize the sequence of ideas, to consider implications, and to anticipate where the talk is heading. It's worth reiterating, however, that your first duty, even as a critic, is to listen carefully to what is being said.

WRITING TO ANALYZE, READING TO ANALYZE

Critical reading and viewing are essential skills for all kinds of writing. Analysis is a more specific aim where those critical reading and viewing skills are applied to particular subjects. Analysis involves dividing a whole into parts that can be studied both as individual entities and as parts of the whole.

Rhetorical analysis is a kind of analysis that divides a whole into parts to understand how an act of speaking or writing conveys meaning. Thus the goal of a rhetorical analysis is to understand how a particular act of writing or speaking influenced particular people at a particular time.

Visual analysis is closely related to rhetorical analysis. The tools of rhetorical analysis have been applied to understanding how other human creations make meaning, including art, buildings, photographs, dance, memorials, advertisements—any kind of symbolic communication.

Literary analysis takes into account elements of literature such as plot, character, and setting, paying particular attention to language and metaphor. The goal of literary analysis is to interpret a literary text and support that interpretation with evidence or, more simply, to make a discovery about a text that you share with your readers.

Text and Context

A rhetorical, visual, or literary analysis may be concerned with either text or context, but often it examines both. Textual analysis focuses on the features of a text—the words and evidence in a speech, the images and patterns in a picture, and so on. For a textual analysis, ask

- What is the subject?
- What is the author's claim or what are the main ideas?
- What is the medium of the text? a newspaper? Web site? scholarly journal? a photograph? a short story?
- What appeals are used? What are the author's credentials, and how does he represent himself? What facts or evidence does he present? What values does he share with you and the rest of his audience? What emotions does he try to evoke?
- How is the text organized?
- What kind of style does the author use? Formal or informal, satirical or humorous? Are any metaphors used?

Contextual analysis reconstructs the cultural environment, or context, that existed when a particular rhetorical event took place, and then depends on that recreation to produce clues about persuasive tactics and appeals. For a contextual analysis, ask

* Who is the author? What else has she written or said on this subject? Who does she borrow from or quote? What motivated her to address this issue?
* Who is the audience? What are the occasion and forum for writing? Would the argument have been constructed differently if it had been presented in a different medium? What motivated the newspaper, magazine, or other venue to publish it?
* What is the larger conversation? When did the text appear? Why did it appear at that particular moment? Who or what might this text be responding to?

WRITING A RHETORICAL ANALYSIS

People often use the term *rhetoric* to describe empty language. "The Governor's speech was just a bunch of rhetoric," you might say, meaning that the Governor offered noble-sounding words but no real ideas. But rhetoric originated with a much more positive meaning. According to Aristotle, rhetoric is "the art of finding in any given case the available means of persuasion." Rhetoric is concerned with producing effective pieces of communication.

Rhetoric can also be used to interpret or analyze. Students of rhetoric know not only how to produce effective communication, but also how to understand communication. The two skills complement each other: Becoming a better writer makes you a better analyst, and becoming a better analyst makes you a better writer.

Components of a Rhetorical Analysis

What is the author's purpose?	**Identify the purpose** Some texts have an obvious purpose; for example, an ad wants you to buy something. But texts can have more than one purpose. A politician who accuses an opponent of being corrupt may also be making a case for her own honesty.
Who is the audience?	**Examine the audience** The most effective texts are ones that are tailored specifically for an audience. What can you determine about the actual audience's values, attitudes, and beliefs? How does the author create an audience in the text by making assumptions about what the audience believes?
Who is the author of my text?	**Examine the author** How did the author come to this subject? Is the author an expert or an outsider?
What is the background of my text?	**Examine the context** What else has been said or written on this topic? What was going on at the time that influenced this text?
Which rhetorical appeals are used in my text?	**Analyze rhetorical appeals** Aristotle set out three primary tactics of argument: appeals to the emotions and deepest held values of the audience (pathos), appeals based on the trustworthiness of the speaker (ethos), and appeals to good reasons (logos).
How does the language and style contribute to the purpose?	**Examine the language and style** Is the style formal? informal? academic? Does the writer or speaker use humor or satire? What metaphors are used?

Keys to Rhetorical Analysis

Choose a text that you care about
Your paper will require close multiple readings of the text. Your interest (or lack of interest) in your text will come through in your paper.

Write a descriptive title
The title of your essay should indicate the focus of your analysis.

Check your thesis
Make sure your thesis is sensible and realistic as well as being supported by evidence and examples in the text.

Interrogate evidence
Look closely at the evidence supporting the writer's claims. Is it convincing? Are there gaps? Can it be interpreted in a different way? Is counterevidence acknowledged?

Examine underlying values, attitudes, and beliefs
When a writer or speaker neglects the audience's values, attitudes, and beliefs, the text is rarely persuasive.

Identify fallacies
Be aware when only one side of the story is being presented, when claims and accusations are grossly exaggerated, and when complex issues are oversimplified.

Identify relationships
An effective rhetorical analysis makes connections, showing how strategies in the text are responses to other texts and the larger context.

Recognize complexity
Many texts cannot be reduced to a sound bite. Successful rhetorical analyses often read between the lines to explain why a statement may be ironic or what is not being said. Readers appreciate being shown something they may not otherwise have noticed.

WRITING A VISUAL ANALYSIS

We are bombarded by images on a daily basis. They compete for our attention, urge us to buy things, and guide us on our way home from work. These visual texts frequently attempt to persuade us; to make us think, feel, or act a certain way. Yet we rarely stop to consider how they do their work.

Visual texts leave room for the audience to interpret to a greater degree than many verbal texts, which make them particularly rich subjects for analysis.

Components of a Visual Analysis

What kind of visual is it?	**Describe what you see** Is it a single image, part of a series, a sign, a building, or something else? What are the conventions for this kind of visual?
What is the image about?	**Consider the subject** What does the image depict? What is the setting? What is the purpose? Are words connected with the image?
How is the image arranged?	**Analyze the composition** What elements are most prominent? Which are repeated? Which are balanced or in contrast to each other? Which details are important?
What is the context?	**Examine the context** Who created the image? When and where did it first appear? Can you determine why it was created?
What visuals are like it?	**Look for connections** What is the genre? What kind of visual is it? What elements have you seen before? Which remind you of other visuals?

Keys to Visual Analysis

	Choose a visual text that you care about If an image or other visual text means something to you, you will find it easier to analyze.
	Pay close attention to details Identify the key details that keep the viewer's attention and convey meaning. Also, examine the point of view—the viewer's perspective of the subject.

Provide a frame for understanding
You will need to provide a context for understanding
a visual text, giving a sense of how it is a response to
events and trends going on at the time and how it was
initially understood.

Go beyond the obvious
A successful visual analysis gets readers to make
connections and see aspects that they otherwise would
not have noticed.

HOW TO READ ANALYSES

Make notes as you read, either in the margins, if it is your own copy, or on paper or a
computer file. Circle any words or references that you don't know and look them up.

What kind of analysis is it?	▓ Is it a rhetorical analysis? a literary analysis? an analysis of a visual? an analysis of an object?
Where did it come from?	▓ Who wrote the analysis?
	▓ What do you know about the writer's background that might have influenced the analysis?
Who is the intended audience?	▓ What clues do you find about whom the writer had in mind as the readers?
	▓ What does the writer assume that the readers already know about the subject?
	▓ What new knowledge is the writer providing?
What is the focus of the analysis?	▓ What does the writer have to say about the context or background?
	▓ What does the writer have to say about how the text or object is composed?
What is the significance of the analysis?	▓ Does the writer make specific claims?
	▓ What did you learn or come to understand differently by reading the analysis?
How is it composed?	▓ How does the writer represent herself or himself?
	▓ How would you characterize the style?
	▓ If there are any photographs or other graphics, what information do they contribute?

SELECT A TEXT TO ANALYZE

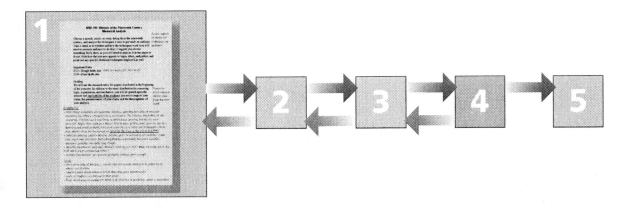

Examine the assignment	▓ Read your assignment slowly and carefully. Look for the key words *analyze* or *critique*. These key words tell you that you are writing an analysis.
	▓ Make a note of any information about the length specified, date due, formatting, and other requirements. You can attend to this information later. At this point you want to zero in on the subject and your analytical claim.
Find a text to analyze	▓ Look for a text or image that offers an argument or opinion—one that tries to influence the thoughts, feelings, or actions of its audience.
	▓ Newspaper editorials, activist Web sites, speeches, art, and advertisements are all good sources of texts for analysis.
Make an analytical claim	▓ Ask: What will my analysis reveal for readers that they might not otherwise have realized about the text?

▨ Think about the evidence you will need to support your claim. It may come from the text itself, or from your research into the piece's context.

Research the context	▨ What else was being written and said about this subject at the time the text was written?
Research the author and audience	▨ What events were taking place that might have influenced the author?
	▨ Who is the author? What else has he or she said on this subject? What motivated him or her to produce this text?
	▨ Who is the audience? Where did the text first appear (or, why was this image made or created)? Why did it appear at that particular moment?

WRITING A POSITION ARGUMENT, READING A POSITION ARGUMENT

Many people think of the term argument as a synonym for debate. College courses and professional careers, however, require a different kind of argument—one that, most of the time, is cooler in emotion and more elaborate in detail than oral debate. At first glance an argument in writing doesn't seem to have much in common with debate. But the basic elements and ways of reasoning used in written arguments are similar to those we use in everyday conversations. Let's look at an example of an informal debate.

Sean: I think students should not pay tuition to go to state colleges and universities.

Carmen: Cool idea, but why should students not pay?

Sean: Because you don't have pay to go to high school.

Carmen:	Yeah, but that's different. The law says that everyone has to go to high school, at least to age 16. Everyone doesn't have to go to college.
Sean:	Well, in some other countries like the United Kingdom, students don't have to pay tuition.
Carmen:	Their system of education is different. Plus you're wrong. Students started paying tuition at British universities in fall 1998.
Sean:	OK, maybe the United Kingdom isn't a good example. But students should have a right to go to college, just like they have the right to drive on the highway.
Carmen:	Why? What evidence do you have that things would be better if everyone went to college? It would put an enormous drain on the economy. People would have to pay a lot more in taxes.

In this discussion Sean starts out by making a claim that students should not have to pay tuition. Carmen immediately asks him why students should not have to pay tuition. She wants a reason to accept his claim. Scholars who study argument maintain that *an argument must have a claim and one or more reasons to support that claim.* Something less might be persuasive, but it isn't an argument.

If Sean's assertion were a bumper sticker, it might read "MAKE COLLEGE FREE FOR ALL." The assertion is a claim but it is not an argument, because it lacks a reason. Many reasons are possible for arguing for free tuition:

* College should be free for all because everyone is entitled to a good education.
* College should be free for all because the economy will benefit.
* College should be free for all because a democracy requires educated citizens.

When a claim has a reason attached, then it becomes an argument.

A reason is typically offered in a **because-clause,** a statement that begins with the word *because* and that provides a supporting reason for the claim. Sean's first attempt is to argue that students shouldn't have to pay to go to college because they don't have to pay to go to high school.

The word *because* signals a **link** between the reason and the claim. Just having a reason for a claim, however, doesn't mean that the audience will be convinced. When Sean tells Carmen that students don't have to pay to go to public high schools, Carmen does not accept the link. Carmen asks **"So what?"** every time Sean presents a new reason. Carmen will accept Sean's claim only if she accepts that his reason supports his claim. Carmen challenges Sean's links and keeps asking "So what?" For her, Sean's reasons are not good reasons.

Benjamin Franklin observed, "so convenient a thing it is to be a rational creature, since it enables us to find or make a reason for every thing one has a mind to do." It is not hard to think of reasons. What is difficult is to convince your audience that your reasons are *good reasons*. In a conversation, you get immediate feedback that tells you whether your listener agrees or disagrees. When you are writing, there usually is not someone who can give you immediate feedback. Consequently, if you are going to convince someone who doesn't agree with you or know what you know already, you have to be more specific about what you are claiming, you have to connect with the values you hold in common with your readers, and you have to anticipate what questions and objections your readers might have.

Components of Position Arguments

What exactly is my issue?	**Define the issue** Your subject should be clear to your readers. If readers are unfamiliar with the issue, you should give enough examples so they understand the issue in concrete terms.
What exactly is my stand on the issue?	**State your position** You may want to state your thesis in the opening paragraph to let readers know your position immediately. If your issue is unfamiliar, you may want to find out more before you state your position. In any case, you should take a definite position on the issue.
What are the reasons for my position?	**Find one or more reasons** You need to give one or more reasons for your position. Write as many because-clauses as you can think of. Use the ones that are most convincing.

Where can I find evidence?

Provide evidence

In support of your reasons, provide evidence—in the form of examples, statistics, and testimony of experts—that the reasons are valid. When the issue is unfamiliar, more evidence than usual is required.

Who disagrees with my position?

Acknowledge opposing views and limitations of the claim

If everybody thinks the same way, then there is no need to write a position argument. Anticipate what objections might be made to your position. You can answer possible objections in two ways: that the objections are not valid or that the objections have some validity but your argument is stronger

Keys to Position Arguments

Understand your goal

A well-written and well-reasoned position argument may not change minds entirely, but it can convince readers that a reasonable person can hold this point of view. Position arguments do not necessarily have winners and losers. Your goal is to invite a response that creates a dialog.

Be sensitive to the context

Even position arguments that have become classics and in a sense "timeless" frequently were written in response to a historical event; for example, Martin Luther King Jr. wrote his powerful argument for civil disobedience, "Letter from Birmingham Jail," in response to a published statement by eight Birmingham clergymen. A careful analysis of a recent or historical event often provides your argument with a sense of immediacy.

Rely on careful definitions	What exactly does *freedom of speech* mean? What exactly does *privacy* mean? What exactly does *animal rights* mean? Getting readers to accept a definition is often the key to a position argument. For example, torturing animals is against the law. Animal rights activists argue that raising and slaughtering animals for food is torture and thus would extend the definition. If you can get readers to accept your definition, then they will agree with your position.
Use quality sources	Find the highest-quality sources for citing evidence. Recent sources are critical for current topics, such as the relationship of certain diets to disease.
Create credibility	You have probably noticed that many times in the course of reading, you get a strong sense of the writer's character, even if you know nothing about the person. Be honest about strengths and weaknesses and about what you don't know, and avoid easy labels. If readers trust you are sincere, they will take you seriously.
Cultivate a sense of humor and a distinctive voice	A reasonable voice doesn't have to be a dull one. Humor is a legitimate tool of argument, especially when the stakes are high and tempers are flaring.
Argue responsibly	When you begin an argument by stating "in my opinion," you are not arguing responsibly. Readers assume that if you make a claim in writing, you believe that claim. More important, it is rarely just your opinion. Most beliefs and assumptions are shared by many people. When other members of your community share your opinion, your readers should consider your position seriously.

HOW TO READ POSITION ARGUMENTS

Make notes as you read, either in the margins or on paper or a computer file. Circle any words or references that you don't know and look them up.

What is it?	■ What kind of a text is it? An article? an essay? a chart? a scientific report? a Web site? an executive summary? What are your expectations for this kind of text? ■ What media are used? (Web sites, for example, often combine images, words, and sounds.)
Where did it come from?	■ Who wrote the analysis? ■ Where did it first appear? In a book, newspaper, magazine, online, in a company, or in an organization?
What is the writer's thesis or main idea?	■ What is the writer's topic? What effect is he or she trying to determine the cause of? ■ Why is this topic important? ■ What are the key ideas or concepts that the writer considers? ■ What are the key terms? How does the writer define those terms?
Who is the intended audience?	■ What clues do you find about whom the writer had in mind as readers? ■ What does the writer assume that the readers already know about the subject? ■ What new knowledge is the writer providing?
What are the reasons that support the claim?	■ Is there one primary reason? ■ Are multiple reasons given? ■ Do you find any fallacies in the reasons (see pages 18–19)?
What kinds of evidence are given?	■ Is the evidence from books, newspapers, periodicals, the Web, or field research? ■ Is the evidence convincing that the causes given are the actual causes?
How is it composed?	■ How does the writer represent himself or herself? ■ How would you characterize the style? ■ How effective is the design? Is it easy to read? ■ If there are any photographs, charts, or other graphics, what information do they contribute?

HOW TO WRITE A POSITION ARGUMENT

These steps for the process of writing a position argument may not progress as neatly as this chart might suggest. Writing is not an assembly-line process.

As you write and revise you may think of additional reasons to support your position. Your instructor and fellow students may give you comments that help you to rethink your argument. Use their comments to work through your paper or project again, strengthening your content and making your writing better organized and more readable.

1 FIND AN ISSUE

- Make a list of possible issues.
- Select a possible issue.
- Read about your issue.

2 DEVELOP REASONS AND WRITE A WORKING THESIS

- Take a definite position.
- Develop reasons by considering whether you can argue from a definition, compare or contrast, consider good and bad effects, or refute objections.
- Support your reasons by making observations and finding facts, statistics, and statements from authorities.
- Write a working thesis.

Analyze your potential readers

What do your readers likely know about the issue?

What views do your readers likely have about the issue?

Do your readers likely agree or disagree with your position? If they disagree, why exactly do they disagree?

3 WRITE A DRAFT

- Introduce the issue and give the necessary background.
- Think about how readers will view you, the writer.
- If you argue from a definition, set out the criteria.
- Avoid fallacies.
- Address opposing views.
- Make counterarguments if necessary.
- Conclude with strength.
- Choose a title that will interest readers.

4 REVISE, REVISE, REVISE

- Check that your position argument fulfills the assignment.
- Make sure that your claim is arguable and focused.
- Check your reasons and add more if you can.
- Add additional evidence where reasons need more support.
- Examine the organization.
- Review the visual presentation.
- Proofread carefully.

5 SUBMITTED VERSION

- Make sure your finished writing meets all formatting requirements.

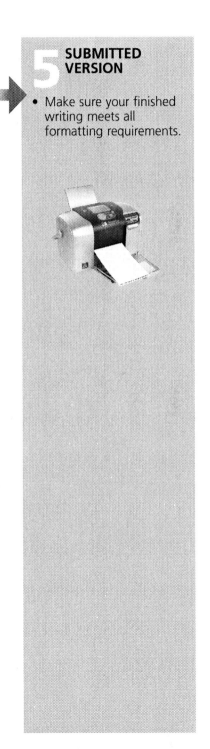

REPORT WRITING

"Effective communication is the foundation of great leadership. Without it, plans, strategies, and dreams remain handcuffed to the boardroom table."

Fred Jaques (former President and CEO, Dare Foods)

"Clear and direct communication has never been more important. Today's business executives have less time to analyze the information they receive and yet there is more risk inherent in the decisions they are making with it."

Bev Park (Chief Financial Officer, TimberWest)

Whether they are formal or informal, good business reports have a common quality: objectivity. The very word *report* suggests a vehicle not for opinion but for cool-headed reflection based on facts. In writing a report, you will be providing material on which other project participants will rely to make decisions. They will want information and advice they can trust.

They will also want a report that is easy to understand. Since managers have many demands on their time, they don't want to waste it sifting through an unnecessary clutter of details. Your job is to select and present the material in such a way that they can quickly grasp the essential features.

Informal reports are more common than formal ones. They are usually shorter than formal reports, often only two or three pages, and they are more conversational, using frequent personal pronouns and contractions.

An informal report also has a less "ornate" physical structure than a longer formal report. It is often written as a letter or memo, with the content divided into sections and subsections with headings.

DETERMINING THE PURPOSE

There are two main kinds of informal reporting, and the one you use will depend on your purpose in writing:

1. *The Informational Report.* This simply gives the facts of a situation, often on a regular schedule, for example, a monthly sales report. Some companies have printed forms for regularly scheduled reports, and the writer has only to complete the necessary information in specified categories. The details recorded on forms like these tend to be routine. As a consequence, the reader or readers may not really pay attention to the report, even though they are interested in having the information on record. Such a report may be filed rather than read.

    A way to prevent regular informational reports from becoming mere bureaucratic busywork is to change the emphasis from the routine to the exceptional. Exception reporting is a way of highlighting the information readers ought to pay attention to. It reports on the significant changes from the routine—the achievements and the trouble spots.

2. *The Analytical Report.* In both large and small businesses, this is the more common kind of report and the more challenging to write. It is a problem-solving report, analyzing a situation and recommending a certain course of action. The primary reason for such a report is to help others make a decision; the writer wants to convince the reader of the appropriateness of the analysis and the resulting recommendations or conclusions. Moreover, since presenting ideas or solutions is a harder task than presenting facts, the writer of an analytical report needs to take greater stock of the anticipated reader response in deciding how to organize the report.

PLANNING THE REPORT

To make sure that a report is effective, you need to set aside a block of time for planning. Then when you sit down to write, you will have a firm idea of where you are heading and how you are going to get there.

Earlier in this chapter, we discussed the kind of assessment you should always make of the reader and the reason for writing. Remember that it's important to determine at the outset exactly what type of person you are addressing: consider the reader's position, knowledge, concerns, and possible objections or biases. In the same way, you should decide the precise reason or reasons for writing the report, including the results you hope to obtain from it. If you spend some time on this assessment, you will find it easier to organize and focus your material. In turn, you will find the report easier to write.

The next step is to work out in exact terms the subject of your study. In defining your subject, think of building a fence around a topic. What exactly are the boundaries of your discussion? What will be included and what will be left out? By being as exact as possible, you will create from the start a clear picture of the territory you are covering and make it easier to organize your analysis. For example, "A Study of Cars" is too vague, whereas "A Cost-Benefit Analysis of Three Options for Company Cars" is more precise. The subject might not be the eventual title of the report; the title might in the end be "A Recommendation to Buy X as a Company Car." Nevertheless, defining the subject clearly will help keep the proportions of the study manageable and identify for potential readers the exact nature of the report.

You don't want to spend time on areas of marginal importance or on details that the reader won't care about. For example, if you are asked to write a report on the kind of car the company should lease for its sales force, you will be wasting time—yours and the reader's—if you examine every kind of car available, from sports cars to luxury sedans. It is better to establish in advance the kind or price of vehicle worth considering seriously and then to analyze in detail the two or three most suitable options. You might also determine beforehand whether buying should be considered as well as leasing.

Ordinarily a short report does not require a great deal of research. It is usually written by a person with expertise on the subject. Although the writer may have to gather some facts beyond his or her immediate knowledge, generally the information is the kind that can be collected with two or three telephone calls or a quick Web search. If you do have to do extensive research for an informal report, the next chapter offers some advice.

CHOOSING THE BEST ORDER

Two considerations will determine the best order for a report:

1. *What is the most important information?* For an analytical report, the most important information is likely to be the conclusions drawn from the investigation or the recommendations for solving a problem. For an informational report, it may merely be a summative statement that generalizes from the facts or draws attention to the most important ones. In any case, construct a hierarchy of information or ideas; decide what matters most and what matters least. The information or ideas you select as being most important will become your key points.

2. *What is the reader's likely reaction?* You can assume that readers of informational reports want to receive the information, even if it is routine. Similarly, most analytical reports are written at the request of a reader who will be interested in the conclusions or recommendations. In rare cases, however, the reader may be predisposed to reject your conclusions because of a personal bias or conflicting interests. A manager who dislikes change or easily feels threatened can be negative by habit. Predicting reader response is an important step in deciding how to organize your report.

DIRECT AND INDIRECT ORGANIZATION

1. *Direct Order.* When the reader will be pleased or interested, put the key points before your explanation of how you reached them. This is the best order for most business reports. For a short report, try following this sequence:

Purpose

$\downarrow$

Key Points (conclusions or recommendations)

$\downarrow$

Discussion of Findings

Unlike an essay, a report needs no final, summary paragraph. As with a newspaper report, the vital information is at the beginning and the least important details are at the end. (Make an exception if you are sending a short report to an outsider in letter form, in which case you can end with a goodwill close.)

2. *Indirect Order.* For those occasions when the reader of an analytical report will be displeased or skeptical, follow the path of least resistance. Build gradually toward the conclusions or recommendations by following this sequence:

Purpose

$\downarrow$

Discussion of Findings

$\downarrow$

Key Points (conclusions or recommendations)

Now let's discuss what goes into each section.

ELEMENTS OF THE REPORT

Purpose

Open with a short statement of purpose. At its simplest this may be a sentence that says, "This report examines paper use in our office and recommends ways to reduce it." Or it can link purpose with recommendations: " This report on paper waste in our office recommends a smart-card system to control printing costs." This statement can be worded differently if the subject line or title clearly reveals the aim of the report. If the method of obtaining information is important—if the recommendations are based on a survey, for example—you can include the method in the introductory statement.

Key Points

Most short reports have either conclusions or recommendations, depending on whether they are informational or analytical. In a short direct-order report, you can usually introduce these points in a concise paragraph linking them to the statement of purpose. If there are a number of recommendations or conclusions, list them with the most important first. You may also want to summarize the main findings that support the conclusions or recommendations. Sometimes you can indicate the main recommendation of a short report in the title, for example, "Recommendation to Install Skylight in Reception Area." In this case, merely summarize the findings leading to the recommendation.

You may find it easiest to write this section last, after you have completed the detailed discussion. It will then be obvious which points should be inserted after the statement of purpose.

Discussion of Findings

Here you show how the facts lead to the conclusions or recommendations. This is the most extensive part of the report and may have several headings. It can be organized in various ways, depending on the subject. The most common methods of organizing the body of the report are as follows:

Order of Importance

Here you simply follow the direct approach again. For example, if you have determined the different causes or effects of a problem, start with the most important one and give the details. For each point or finding, make a new section and heading. If the focus of your report is a list of recommendations, you can make each one the subject of a section.

Classification or Division

This method of organizing divides a topic into classes or component parts. Here are some examples:

- A report on the environmental damage to fish in a certain body of water could classify findings according to the different types of fish.
- A study of the recreational habits of people in an area might classify the target population according to age groups, income groups, or types of occupation. Alternatively it could be organized according to types of recreation.
- A marketing study for a new invention might be divided according to the traditional four Ps: product, promotion, price, and place.

    When classifying or dividing the subject

- *Do incorporate all relevant information* within the categories you have devised.
- *Don't let information overlap categories.* For example, a classification of stores shouldn't have small stores and department stores as two of the categories, since it's possible to be a small department store.
- *Don't put vastly different amounts of information in each of the categories.* If one category has most of the information and the remainder have little, you should try to create different categories or to merge some of the small ones.

Chronological Order

This arrangement groups information according to time periods. It can be an effective way to report on trends, for example, the health problems of babies over the last 50 years or house construction needs for the next 20 years. It can also be the obvious choice for reporting a sequence of events or actions.

    Take care that you don't choose this order just because it's easiest to arrange. Save it for situations where the sequence itself matters or a time frame makes the information easier to understand.

Spatial Order

Here the division is according to geography or location. This would be an appropriate order for reporting on individual branch offices or for analyzing buying trends in various regions.

Comparison

The best way to compare the merits of two or more options is to create an alternating arrangement. Use the criteria for judging them as the basis for division; then compare the alternatives within each section. For example, suppose you are investigating cars for a company fleet and comparing the two most likely cars on the basis of purchase price, maintenance record, and gas consumption. You can organize your findings this way:

Point-by-point comparison:
1. Purchase price
   a) Car X
   b) Car Y
2. Maintenance record
   a) Car X
   b) Car Y
3. Gas consumption
   a) Car X
   b) Car Y

Another way to organize comparisons is by parallel arrangement in which the various options are examined fully one by one.

Block comparison:
1. Car X
   - purchase price
   - maintenance record
   - gas consumption
2. Car Y
   - purchase price
   - maintenance record
   - gas consumption

This arrangement is not as effective, however, since the reader has to skip back and forth to determine relative merits. Use it only when the things being compared are so diverse that it is impossible to establish common criteria.

WRITING THE REPORT

Overcoming Writer's Block

Some reluctant writers will do anything rather than put pen to paper. They put off the fateful moment with inventive delaying tactics. One such ploy is to do yet another round of research and to build up such an array of facts that more study is needed. Of course such unnecessary analysis only leads to further writing paralysis.

If you recognize yourself in this description, take note that there's a better way. The cause of your reluctance to write is probably not laziness so much as fear that you won't do a good enough job. If this is the case, remember that few successful writers get their results by just sitting down and producing polished copy. Rather, they know how to rewrite, revise, and edit. You can follow their example by not aiming for perfection in the first draft; as soon as you have decided how to organize the material in the report, try to get it all down on the page as quickly as possible.

Here are three methods experienced writers have found useful in preventing or overcoming writer's block:

1. *Dictating.* Some people find that they can overcome writing paralysis by dictating the first draft. Speaking doesn't seem as formidable as writing. This method works best if you have already devised an outline for your report and have mostly to fill in the details of sections. You should be prepared to do some heavy editing of the transcribed draft.

2. *Composing Onscreen.* This method is helpful even if you are not a good typist. Since it's easy to change what you have written—to add, delete, or move whole sections around—you will feel less constrained by your wish to write a perfect first draft.

3. *Free Writing.* Start with the part of the report you understand best or find easiest to explain and put your thoughts down as they come, regardless of order. Keep writing continuously without hesitating and correcting as you go. You might even begin simply by saying "The point I want to make is . . ." and continue from there. The aim is to get the writing juices flowing. If you don't stop until your thoughts run out, you may be surprised at the amount of material you've written. This method requires more revision than most, but at least you have something on the page to work from.

Whatever method you use, don't worry about your grammar or spelling as you write; simply keep working until you've got all the ideas and information down. When you have a draft in front of you, you will be over the major hurdle.

Writing Objectively

The opening sentence of this chapter states that reports should be objective. A report that is free of personal prejudice and subjective opinion will surely have more influence than one that is not. Yet it's not easy to be objective, particularly if you have a special interest in your proposals or recommendations. Here are some guidelines that will help keep your reports as unbiased as possible:

1. *Identify your assumptions.* If you have assumed that some aspects of a given topic are not worth discussing in the report, say so. If you have chosen to limit the topic, give the reason. For example, you may have decided to limit your study of possible company cars to two-door models, based on the assumption that the drivers would rarely have more than one passenger.

    By identifying your assumption, you demonstrate your thoroughness—you have considered all possibilities and have fixed upon the most appropriate ones.

2. *Substantiate your opinions.* Your conclusions and recommendations should follow from the facts. Personal opinion can have weight if the person expressing it is an authority on the subject, but in most cases opinion needs the support of evidence or explanation. Don't imply what you cannot prove. In using statistics, show the level of uncertainty for any calculated values if you can. If your findings aren't foolproof, show where the uncertainty lies.

3. *Avoid subjective language.* Words such as *awesome* or *terrible* have an overcharged, emotional tone. Instead of saying, "Ergon Products experienced fantastic growth in sales last quarter," let the facts speak for themselves: "Ergon Products had a 30 per cent sales increase during the fourth quarter."

4. *Be specific.* Concrete language is livelier than abstract language. It can also be clearer. Although you needn't give specific details for every idea or fact you include in a report, you should try to be exact when referring to people, places, times, and amounts—especially when you think the information might be disputed:

    X After the press contacted plant personnel, it was reported that some of the storage equipment was faulty.

    ✓ After *Globe* reporter June Fisher called Harry Brown last Friday, she reported that two storage tanks had cracks.

    X Plant management was involved in the safety discussion process.

    ✓ Jim Peters, the plant manager, and Helen Falt, the assistant manager, came to three meetings of the Employee Safety Committee.

Be especially careful with ambiguous phrases or words that can have more than one meaning. Terms such as *windfall profit* or *downsizing* can have various interpretations, depending on the reader.

EDITING THE REPORT

When you have finished the first draft, it's time to take a break and forget about it for a while. Go to a movie or to the gym for a workout. Not only do you deserve a reward, but you will edit more effectively if you come back to the job refreshed. When you leave enough time before editing to forget what you've said, you'll be better able to assess the draft. You'll quickly spot the weaknesses and confusing parts in your report when you go through it as a relatively detached reader rather than as a harried writer.

The crucial guideline for editing is to put yourself in the reader's shoes. Just as you anticipate the reader's attitudes and expectations when you plan the report, so in editing you should check to see if you've adequately responded to them.

Experienced writers are sometimes able to edit different aspects of their writing at the same time, but if you are not experienced, your revisions will be more effective if you work through your report several times. The best place to begin is with the organization of your material. First ask yourself these questions:

1. *Is the report properly focused?* Will the reader be able to state the central message in a sentence or two? Does the choice and arrangement of detail point to this message?

2. *Is the report complete?* Has it addressed the reader's concerns? Will the reader have unanswered questions? Have I presented all the evidence and put it in a form that is easy to follow? If I have not been able to provide some important details, have I explained why?

3. *Do the conclusions and recommendations fit logically with the findings?* Are the links between them explicit? Have I considered all the evidence fairly? Would the reader be able to reach a different conclusion from the same evidence? In other words, do my conclusions seem objective or do they reflect a personal bias?

4. *Are there any inconsistencies, contradictions, or ambiguities in what I have said?* Could the reader misinterpret any part?

Once you've addressed these higher-order issues, you can turn to the surface structure of your report—to the grammar, punctuation, spelling, and style.

Most people find that editing onscreen is more difficult than editing on paper. The risk of missing errors seems to increase when you scroll through text on a monitor. For this reason, it's usually a good idea to print a hard copy for your final proofread, as this will increase the likelihood that you'll catch all errors and typos.

Consider the kinds of mistakes you have made in past writing and do a special check for these. If your special weakness is joining sentences with commas, for example, run through the report looking only for these faulty splices.

Underlying all your stylistic editing should be the three basic precepts of effective writing: be clear, be concise, be forceful.

Headings

Make Headings Descriptive

Each section and subsection of a report should have a heading. Try to make headings "high information"—as descriptive and specific as possible—especially in your discussion of findings. They should tell the story of the report so that a reader glancing through it will recognize the important points. In fact, descriptive headings often reflect key points. Notice the difference between the following sets of headings for a short report comparing brands of office carpeting:

Low-information headings:

a) Durability

b) Cost

c) Colour choice

High-information descriptive headings:

a) Brand X is most durable

b) Brand Z is least expensive

c) Brands X and Y have preferred colours

It's not always possible to make every heading reflect a key point. Occasionally a heading that simply tells the nature of the content will serve well. For example, if you must have a separate section explaining how you conducted your research, it may be appropriate to call it simply "Method." On the whole, though, the more descriptive the headings, the easier the report will be to read and remember. Descriptive headings are a decided advantage.

Keep Headings Short

Although complete sentences are often useful for headings, keep them short.

X In the future, laptops will show a substantial decrease in price

✓ Laptop prices will drop

Make Headings Parallel

Since headings act as signposts, they should all be written in the same grammatical form. The following headings are not parallel because they switch from one type of grammatical structure to another:

X • Location
  • Ordering supplies
  • Hiring staff

The correct parallel structure is

✓ • Location
  • Supplies
  • Staff

or, if more information is required

✓ • Five-year lease has been signed
  • Supplies for first quarter have arrived
  • Staffing has been finalized

Vertical Lists

As well as having visual impact, lists allow for quick comprehension. They emphasize that you are making a number of points and help distinguish one point from another. Whenever you can simplify material by using a list, do so. As a rule of thumb, try listing three or more consecutive items or ideas. Conversely, if a list becomes too long—say, beyond six or seven items—try grouping some of the items to make a smaller list. If you will be referring to any items in a list later in the report, number the items. If not, you can simply introduce each item with a dash (–) or a bullet (•).

Here are a few tips to consider when you are creating headings:

- Capitals have more impact than lowercase letters, but text in all caps is hard to read because there are no ascenders (for example, "d" or "h") or descenders ("j" or "y").
- Boldface is more emphatic than italics.
- Underlining is no longer used for two reasons: it's difficult to read because it cuts through descenders; and it implies a hyperlink.
- Text in italics is harder to read than conventional typescript. Reserve italics for short headings rather than large blocks of print.
- Frequent changes of typeface create a cluttered look. Keep to two at most.
- Sans serif fonts such as Arial (with no extensions on the letters) are recommended for titles and headings.

Use **parallel phrasing** for all items in a list. Notice the difference in readability between the first list describing problems with some machinery and the two revised versions, which have parallel phrasing:

✕ Non-parallel:
  - breakdowns frequent
  - you will find service is slow
  - costly spare parts

✓ Parallel (point form):
  - frequent breakdowns
  - slow service
  - costly spare parts

✓ Parallel (sentence form):
  - Breakdowns are frequent.
  - Service is slow.
  - Spare parts are costly.

START WITH YOUR READERS

Imagine yourself in the shoes of your reader. Pretend for a moment that someone else has written about your subject. What do you, the reader, want from the writer?

Tell Your Reader What You Are Writing About

An accurate and informative title is critical for readers to decide if they want to read what you have written. Furthermore, the title is critical to allow the reader to return to something read earlier.

Some genres require **abstracts**, which are short summaries of a document. Abstracts are required for scholarly articles in the sciences and social sciences as well as dissertations. Business reports and other reports often have executive summaries, which are similar to abstracts but often briefer.

Make Your Organization Visible to Readers

Most longer texts and many shorter ones include headings, which give readers an at-a-glance overview and make the text easier to follow and remember. Headings visually indicate the major and subordinate sections of a text.

Some genres have specific formats for organization, such as the APA-style report of research that is divided into four parts: introduction, method, results, and discussion. If you are writing in a genre that requires a specific format, follow it. Readers will be irritated if you don't.

Help Your Reader to Navigate Your Text

Do the little things that help readers. Remember to include page numbers, which word processing software can insert for you. Make cross references to other parts of your document when a subject is covered elsewhere. If you are citing sources, make sure they are all in your list of works cited.

Help Your Reader to Understand the Purposes for Different Parts of Your Text

A traditional way to add information that you don't want to interrupt your running text is with footnotes. Today writers often use boxes or sidebars to supply extra information. If you use boxes or sidebars, indicate them with a different design or a different color. The key is to make what is different look different.

You do research every day. If you compare prices online before you buy an airline ticket, or if you look up a detailed course description before registering for a class, you are doing research. If you want to settle an argument about the first African American to win an Olympic gold medal, you need to do research. In college, research means both investigating existing knowledge that is stored on computers and in libraries, and creating new knowledge through original analysis, surveys, experiments, and theorizing. When you start a research task in a college course, you need to understand the different kinds of possible research and to plan your strategy in advance.

If you have an assignment that requires research, look closely at what you are being asked to do.

The assignment may ask you to review, compare, survey, analyze, evaluate, or prove that something is true or untrue. You may be writing for experts, for students like yourself, or for the general public. The purpose of your research and your potential audience will help guide your strategies for research.

Pull quotes are often set off from the body text with a larger font and a different color.

THE FOUR Rs OF PLANNING

As emphasized earlier, the first step in planning any piece of correspondence is to think about the reason for writing and about the receiver. For a long, formal report you need to add two more Rs to your planning sheet: restrictions and research.

Assessing the Reason for Writing and the Receiver

Formal reports are usually less personal than informal ones. They omit the contractions of personal conversation and tend to name fewer individuals. Traditionally, formal reports tried to give a sense of objectivity by omitting the personal *I* or *we*. As a result, passages were often convoluted and difficult to read. While pronoun-free reports are still the practice in some circles, business writers are increasingly using *I* or *we* in formal reports to produce clearer and more forceful writing. (In informal reports, personal pronouns are not only tolerated but recommended.) However, avoid "I think" or "in my opinion" phrases when you can complete the thought without them:

   ✗   I found that the fittings were defective.

   ✓   The fittings were defective.

   ✗   In my view, the market value will rise in the spring.

   ✓   Market value will probably rise in the spring.

If you are part of a group, using *we* lends the collective weight of a group and seems more objective than the singular *I*. Regardless, it's better to use *I* or *we* than to resort to something impersonal like *the writer(s)* or *the author(s)*.

Deciding on Research

Before beginning your research, explore the subject itself to avoid taking too narrow a path and overlooking important alternatives. Good questions are an effective stimulus for seeing different perspectives on an issue. Here are some ways to start:

1. *Brainstorming.* By yourself or with a colleague, blitz the subject. Jot down all the questions you can think of that relate to the topic, in whatever order they occur. Don't be negative or rule anything out at this point.

2. *Tree Diagramming.* Assume that the subject is the trunk and add as many large and small branches as you can to represent the different aspects of the subject (see Figure 1.1). Again, think of the branches as questions. Tree diagramming can be useful by itself or as a second stage of random brainstorming.

3. *The Five Ws Approach.* In researching a story, journalists consider the Ws of reporting: Who? What? When? Where? Why? For your research planning, try asking the same five questions and add another: How? Use the basic questions to formulate other subquestions.

FIGURE 1.1 *Tree Diagram.*

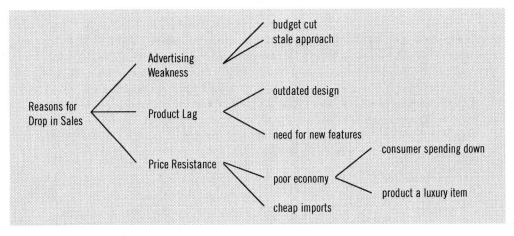

4. *The Three Cs Approach.* A more thorough way to explore a topic is to ask questions about three areas:

   ▧ *Components.* How can the subject be divided? How many different ways are there to partition it?

   ▧ *Change.* What are the changed or changing elements of the subject? What are the causes or effects of certain actions? What trends are there?

   ▧ *Context.* What is the larger issue or field into which this subject fits? How have others dealt with the problems associated with the subject?

Once you have stretched your mind exploring the possibilities of a subject, move in the other direction. Think of limiting the subject and defining the precise focus of your study. Weigh the time and expense of the research against its importance to the report. Remember that it's better to explore a limited topic well than a broad one superficially.

TEAMWORK AND COLLABORATIVE COMMUNICATION

The days of sitting alone at a desk crafting a report or gathering information for a presentation are over. Today's high-tech business environment has created new expectations for quick results and a rapid exchange of information, requiring the ability to collaborate on tasks and work as part of a communications team.

A recent trend, especially in business courses, is to ask students to work together on a written report. This approach mimics the increased emphasis on teams in the working world. Collaboration can make the task easier for all, but in some ways it can also be more difficult. Differing personalities and ways of working, as well as differing skill sets in the team, may cause tensions and result in an inferior piece of work that pleases no one. On the other hand, when collaboration creates a well-organized and conscientious team effort, the result is often a better report than any single member of the team could produce in the same amount of time.

Without realizing it, you probably engage in collaborative communication activities every day. In its most basic form, it might involve interactive situations such as asking a colleague how to express an idea or getting an associate to proofread your writing. Collaboration also takes the form of cooperative writing, where a task is divided into sections or parts that are individually written and then integrated into the final product. Perhaps the most complex type of collaboration is co-authoring, where participants actually create a piece of writing together.

When you are involved in situations that involve collaboration, there are a number of principles you need to observe to keep the process running smoothly:

1. *Build an effective team.* You may have been involved in group presentations where one or two individuals did all the work and others benefited without making any significant contribution. Teamwork can be frustrating when participants don't work well together, but it can be very productive when proper protocols are established and observed. If possible, limit the size of the team to three or four members. Assign and assume responsibilities so that leadership roles and group interaction are clearly defined and understood. How can one avoid the traps and receive the benefits of collaboration? Plan early to weigh the differing skills and knowledge each member of the group can contribute:

   * Who should take overall charge of the schedule and logistics? You need a strong but fair leader for this task.

   * Who should complete the particular parts of the first draft? Establish from the outset the intended length of each part and the format to be used. Who should do the final edit? To keep the style uniform, one person is best for this task. To avoid disputes, the editor needs the authority to override any individual contributor who might be possessive about an idea or how to express it.

   Sometimes members are assigned to a group by the instructor, which makes it all the more important to work out from the start what each can contribute to the project. If the choice is yours, the temptation is to work only with like-minded individuals. The danger here is groupthink, with nobody challenging the prevailing view—which the instructor will likely do later, with penalties for gaps or simplistic thinking.

2. *Create schedules and meet deadlines.* Although flexibility is always a good idea, make sure everyone on the team is aware of the final date for completing the project and then schedule each of the steps you will need to take in order to get there on time.

3. *Develop strategies for conflict management.* A frequent complaint about collaborative writing is that the contributions among members of the group are uneven, even though the marks for the writing are equal. One member of the group may in the end produce the lion's share of the work while another is a weak performer or may even seem a freeloader. There is no perfect solution to this problem except to realize that in collaborative writing, as with any sports team, it's better to focus on getting the job done well than on who does most.

If it's clear early on that someone is weak in the conceptual or drafting aspect of the assignment, give that person all the logistical tasks, such as arranging the meetings, assembling the drafts, and producing final copies of the report on time. Checking specific data or doing other research may also be a valuable contribution.

Feedback and evaluation are essential, but they should be constructive. If conflict becomes negative, it's important to divert it. Teach yourself to be a good listener and an active participant. Accept constructive criticism and use it to make corrections and improvements, and make sure that any criticism you express is positive and diplomatic. Occasionally, to avoid gross unfairness, an instructor may ask each team member to rate the contribution of the others, but this approach can also undermine group harmony and the lessons in teamwork that collaborative writing is intended to foster.

If you feel unfairly treated in any particular piece of collaborative writing, see if you can learn from the experience and handle matters differently next time. In any case, remember that group assignments are a common feature of many organizations you may ultimately work for, so treat your collaborative project as essential training for the workplace, where your job may depend on your ability to be an effective team member.

4. *Observe gender and cultural differences.* As in any communication, members of collaborative teams need to be sensitive to differences in style and approach among members. Some men might have learned to adopt a fairly assertive style, for example, while some women might have been taught to be deferential and tentative in their approach. Be aware of these differences in yourself and others, and try to make allowances for them.

   Intercultural collaboration also requires an awareness of different perspectives and attitudes. If you're assigned to an international or intercultural writing team, remember that your way isn't the only way. Earlier in this chapter, we discussed some strategies for effective intercultural communication.

5. *Explore online collaboration.* Collaboration is a form of networking, and electronic networking has become the norm in today's business environment. Commonplace examples are conference calls and e-mail. Intranets allow people in different locations to work together on an ongoing basis. Networked computers make it possible to share files among a number of participants, so that everyone has simultaneous access to the same project-specific information. Computer-mediated environments make it possible to collaborate through teleconferences, Webconferences, and Webcasts. Take the time to explore the technology available to you, and make full use of the systems and facilities at your disposal. Learning to use your electronic environment will increase efficiency, avoid duplication, and save valuable time.

FINDING INFORMATION

1. *Ask your librarian.* The best research sources will vary according to your subject. Staff at your college library are well-trained and knowledgeable and can often save

you time by directing you to the sources which are the most appropriate for your topic.

2. *Use the library catalogue.* Most libraries today have computerized catalogues which are available from a remote location such as your home computer. Searchable by author, title, and subject, the catalogue will give you a list of relevant holdings and their location. If a particular source is unavailable at your library, you can probably obtain it through interlibrary loan.

3. *Search library databases.* Most libraries now have access to extensive databases that allow you to quickly find needed information online. A librarian can help you determine which databases are the most relevant for your topic. CD-ROM indexes enable you to search by author, title, or key word, giving you a list of all articles on your subject with an abstract or summary and sometimes the full text.

4. *Access information online.* A Web search will usually provide you with a broad range of sites dealing with your subject. Be judicious in selecting online sources, however. Remember that anyone can publish on the Web, so check the site to determine if it is hosted by a credible organization or institution, and make sure the information is frequently updated.

   Newsgroups, discussion lists, and forums may also be useful, but the information in these posts is difficult to verify. Be especially wary of blogs, which are often personal journals or newsletters and may not have much validity as a research tool.

5. *Consult internal sources.* If you are doing a report on a particular company or organization, don't overlook the most accessible source of information—internal records and the employees themselves. Many an unsuspecting report writer has spent days searching for facts that are readily available in internal files. If the topic is one of continuing concern to the company, chances are that someone has looked at it, or an aspect of it, before. Some of the facts from an earlier investigation may be out of date, but it's likely that other information is timely and relevant.

   Even when an earlier report doesn't exist, it is still sensible to find out if other people have worked on the topic. They are usually glad to discuss the issues. A short telephone inquiry or memo may save you valuable research time or give you helpful suggestions for your exploration. Reinventing the wheel does nobody any good.

6. *Check the reliability of information.* Establish whether any of the second-hand facts you get from your research will need verifying. Remember that a source with a special interest may exaggerate or gloss over certain information, often unconsciously. Even statistical data should undergo scrutiny. Any observer of election polls and campaigns knows that while statistics may not lie, they can certainly distort. If you have to get fresh data through a questionnaire or survey, make sure the results are as reliable and valid as possible. If you are not familiar with proper sampling techniques and have no knowledge of statistical reliability, consult someone who is competent in those areas. The cost of obtaining outside help may be less than the cost of losing your credibility through faulty data.

DESIGN PAGES

Word processing programs design pages for you with their default settings for margins, paragraph indentations, and justification. Even if you use the default settings, you still have a range of options. Thinking about design will lead to better decisions.

Choose the orientation, size of your page, and columns

You can usually use the defaults on your word processing program for academic essays (remember to select double-spacing for line spacing if the default is single-spaced). For other kinds of texts you may want a horizontal rather than a vertical orientation, a size other than a standard sheet of paper, and two columns or more rather than one.

Divide your text into units.

The paragraph is the basic unit of extended writing, but think also about when to use lists. This list is a bulleted list. You can also us a numbered list.

Use left aligned text with a ragged right margin.

Fully and justified text aligns the right margin, which gives a more formal look but can also leave unsightly rivers of extra white space running through the middle of your text.

Be conscious of white space.

White space can make your text more readable and set off more important elements. Headings stand our more with white space surrounding them. Leave room around graphics. You don't want words to crowd too close to graphics because both the words and the visuals will become hard to read.

Giddens 3

stay in the military after their commitment ends. Congress first gave the military the authority to retain soldiers after the Vietnam War when new volunteers were too few to replace departing soldiers. In November 2002 the Pentagon gave stop-loss orders for Reserve and National Guard units activated to fight terrorism (Robertson).

- This policy is neither forthcoming, safe, nor compassionate toward those most directly impacted–the soldiers and their families.
- As the United States became more and more entrenched in the conflict in Iraq, the military was stretched thinner and thinner.
- By 2004, approximately 40% of those serving in Iraq and Afghanistan came from the ranks of the part-time soldiers: the Reserves and the National Guard (Gerard).

While these individuals did know that their countries could call if they enlisted, they continue to bear an inordinate burden of actual combat time, and this new policy continues to create situations further removed from the job for which they had enlisted. Recruiters often pitch the military–including the Reserves and the Guard–to young, impressionable, and often underprivileged kids.

The Pitch

I have experienced this pitch firsthand and seen the eyes of my class-mates as the recruiter promised them a better and richer tomorrow. Seeing a golden opportunity for self-respect and achievement, young men and women sign on the dotted line. Today, other young men and women are

Be aware of MLA and APA design specifications.

MLA and APA styles have specifications for margins, indentations, reference lists, and other things.

Checklist for Evaluating Document Design

1. **Audience**   Who is the intended audience? Will the design be appealing to them? How does the design serve their needs?

2. **Genre**   What is the genre? Does the design meet the requirements of the genre? For example, a brochure should fit in your pocket.

3. **Organization** Is the organization clear to readers? If headings are used, are they in the right places? If headings are used for more than one level, are these levels indicated consistently?

4. **Readability**   Is the typeface attractive and readable? Are the margins sufficient? Is any contrasting text, such as boldface, italics, or all caps, brief enough to be legible? If color is used, does it direct emphasis to the right places?

5. **Layout**   Can the basic layout be made more effective? Is there adequate white space around headings, images, and graphics?

Documentation: Accurately Citing Your Sources

When you incorporate ideas from other sources into your work, you are using other writers' *intellectual property*. Using another writer's words, content, unique approach, or illustrations without crediting the author is called **plagiarism** and is illegal and unethical. The following techniques will help you properly credit sources and avoid plagiarism:

plagiarism—
the act of using someone else's exact words, figures, unique approach, or specific reasoning without giving appropriate credit.

- *Make source notes as you go.* Plagiarism often begins accidentally during research. You may forget to include quotation marks around a quotation, or you may intend to cite or paraphrase a source but never do. To avoid forgetting, write detailed source and content notes as you research. Try writing something like "Quotation from original, rewrite later" next to quoted material you copy into notes, and add bibliographic information (title, author, source, page number, etc.) so you don't spend hours trying to locate it later.

- *Learn the difference between a quotation and a paraphrase.* A *quotation* repeats a source's exact words, which are set off from the rest of the text by quotation marks. A *paraphrase* is a restatement of the quotation in your own words. A restatement requires that you completely rewrite the idea, not just remove or replace a few words. As Figure 1.2 illustrates, a paraphrase may not be acceptable if it is too close to the original.

FIGURE 1.2 *Avoid plagiarism by learning how to paraphrase.*

QUOTATION

From Searle, John R. "I Married a Computer." Rev. of *The Age of Spiritual Machines*, by Ray Kurzweil. *New York Review of Books* 8 Apr. 1999: 34+.

"We are now in the midst of a technological revolution that is full of surprises. No one thirty years ago was aware that one day household computers would become as common as dishwashers. And those of us who used the old Arpanet of twenty years ago had no idea that it would evolve into the Internet."

UNACCEPTABLE PARAPHRASE

The current <u>technological revolution</u> is <u>surprising</u>. <u>Thirty years ago, no one</u> expected computers to be <u>as common</u> today as air conditioners. What once was the Arpanet has <u>evolved into the Internet</u>, and no one expected that.

ACCEPTABLE PARAPHRASE

John Searle states that we live in a technologically amazing time of change in which computers have "become as common as dishwashers" (37). Twenty years ago, no one could have predicted the Arpanet would become the Internet (37).

Source: Lynn Quitman Troyka and Douglas Hesse, *Simon & Schuster Handbook for Writers*, Fourth Canadian Edition (Toronto, ON: Pearson Education Canada, 2006) 519–520.

- *Use a citation even for an acceptable paraphrase.* Take care to credit any source that you quote, paraphrase, or use as evidence. To credit a source, write a footnote or endnote that describes it, using the format preferred by your instructor. Writing handbooks, such as the *Simon & Schuster Handbook for Writers, Fourth Canadian Edition* by Lynn Quitman Troyka, explain the two standard documentation styles from the American Psychological Association (APA) and the Modern Language Association (MLA). A good writing handbook tells you how to cite various types of sources in the body of a paper and compile a list of works cited at the end of your paper.
- *Understand that lifting material off the Internet is plagiarism.* Words in electronic form belong to the writer just as words in print form do. If you cut and paste sections from a source document onto your draft, you are committing plagiarism.

Instructors consider work to be plagiarized when a student

- submits a paper from a Web site that sells or gives away research papers.
- buys a paper from a non-Internet service.

* hands in a paper written by a fellow student or a family member.
* copies material in a paper directly from a source without proper quotation marks or source citation.
* paraphrases material in a paper from a source without proper source citation.

Students who choose to plagiarize are placing their academic careers at risk because of instructors' increasing use of anti-plagiarism computer software. These programs find strings of words that are identical to those in a database and alert the instructor to suspicious patterns. When a physics professor at the University of Virginia in the United States suspected that his students were copying term papers, he ran their papers through a program that looked for similarities of six or more consecutive words. He found 122 cases of abuse. These students are facing possible expulsion.

GET ANALYTICAL!

AVOID PLAGIARISM

Think about plagiarism and explore your views on this growing problem.

Complete the following:

* Why is plagiarism considered an offence that involves both stealing and lying? Describe how you look at it.

  _____

  _____

* Citing sources indicates that you respect the ideas of others. List two additional ways that accurate source citation strengthens your writing and makes you a better student.

  1. _____

  2. _____

* What specific penalties for plagiarism are described in your college handbook? Explain whether you feel that these penalties are reasonable or excessive and whether they will keep students from plagiarizing.

  _____

  _____

* Many experts believe that researching on the Internet is behind many acts of plagiarism. Do you agree? Why or why not?

  _____

  _____

TEAMWORK

Much writing in the workplace and in organizations—especially important writing tasks like reports, analyses, and proposals—is done by teams of people. The better you understand how to write effectively with others, the more enjoyable and more productive the process will be for you.

ORGANIZE A TEAM

Unlike sports teams where a coach is in charge, writing team members often have to organize themselves.

Analyze the assignment	▒ Identify what exactly you are being asked to do.
	▒ Write down the goals as specifically as you can and discuss them as a team.
	▒ Determine which tasks are required to meet those goals. Be as detailed as you can. Write down the tasks and arrange them in the order they need to be completed.
Make a work plan	▒ Make a time line. List the dates when specific tasks need to be completed and distribute it to all team members. Charts are useful tools for keeping track of progress.
	▒ Assign tasks to all team members. Find out if anyone possesses additional skills that could be helpful to the team.
Keep goals in mind	▒ Revisit the team's goals often. To succeed, each team member must keep in mind what the team aims to accomplish.
	▒ Communicate often. Most writing teams will not have an assigned leader. Each team member shares responsibility.

Successful teams work well together. All the members share responsibility and commitment to the team's goals.

What Makes a Good Team?

In sports, in the workplace, and in everyday life, successful teams have well-defined goals and work together to achieve these goals. Successful teams communicate well, make good decisions together, act quickly on their decisions, and continuously evaluate their progress. Successful teams achieve the right balance so that each team member can contribute.

WORK AS A TEAM

Work closely together in creating and revising content. You'll enjoy writing more and you'll have the benefit of more ideas.

Carry out the plan

- Decide on a process for monitoring progress. Set up specific dates for review and assign team members to be responsible for reviewing work that has been done.

- When you have a complete draft, each team member should evaluate it by providing written comments.

Understand the Team Process

Analyze
Take time to analyze the writing assignment with your team members. Discuss the goals of the assignment as a group.

Question
Ask as many questions as you can think of about the assignment and about how the team will work together.

Listen
Listen carefully to each team member's ideas and how they can contribute to achieving the goals.

Decide
Write down the team's goals. Make a work plan that lists dates when each task needs to be completed. Assign tasks to team members.

Create
Work closely together in creating content. It's more fun to work with other people, and you'll have help when you get stuck.

Evaluate
Evaluate often if you are meeting the goals on your time line. If something isn't getting done, find out why. When you complete a draft, each member of the team should evaluate it.

Revise
Compare your evaluations and decide as a group what revisions and additions need to be made. Decide who will revise each section.

Review
Arrange for one or more people outside your group to review your work. Meet to decide what additional changes need to be made in light of the external review.

- Meet to compare evaluations and decide on a plan for revising and adding content.

- After revising, arrange for one or more people to review the project. Meet again to determine if additional changes are needed.

Be aware of team dynamics

Teamwork requires some flexibility. Different people have different styles and contribute in different ways. Keep talking to each other along the way.

- Deal with problems when they come up.

- If a team member is not participating, find out why.

- If team members have different ideas about what needs to be done, find time to meet so that the team can reach an agreement.

- Get the team together if you are not meeting the deadlines you established in the work plan and, if necessary, devise a new plan.

WORKING TOGETHER

WHAT TO DO WHEN PROBLEMS ARISE IN TEAMS

Working together in a team is most often a rewarding experience, but you need to know how to deal with problems when they arise. Generally it is better to make an effort to resolve problems within the team before asking your instructor to intervene. In a group of four or five students, discuss how you might respond as a group to a team member who

1. is "missing in action,"
2. doesn't come prepared,
3. doesn't answer email,
4. is disrespectful to others,
5. refuses to allow any to critique or revise his or her work.

PRESENTATIONS

"Being able to communicate ideas in a way that gets right to the heart of an issue is an art everyone should learn. It's so fundamental to good leadership. Throughout their careers, leaders need to hone their writing and speaking crafts, reworking and polishing them until they glow."

Helen Handfield-Jones (President, Handfield Jones Inc.)

"Communicating well means more than being correct, although that matters. It means understanding your readers or listeners and their needs and then being able to adapt your message to suit the person and the occasion."

Rob Dexter (Chairman and CEO, Maritime Travel)

ORAL PRESENTATIONS

Although in our daily work we speak more often than we write, many of us have not overcome the fear of having to address a group. Yet the oral presentation is an important part of business communications, whether it is a speech or proposal to some external business organization or, as is more common, an outline of plans to a group of colleagues. The term *oral presentation* covers a variety of formal and informal speaking activities. For convenience, in this chapter the term *talk* will refer to informal presentations and the term *speech* will refer to formal addresses. Whatever the specific demands of your job, if you hope to climb up the managerial ladder it's important to master the skill of speaking in front of others.

The advantage of speaking rather than writing is that it permits immediate feedback. Listeners can comment or ask questions, and the speaker can respond to their nonverbal reactions and clarify any confusing points. On the other hand, the audience cannot go back over material. Speaking is therefore not a good channel for conveying a lot of detailed information. The message in an oral presentation has to be relatively simple if it is to have an impact on the audience. Since simple does not mean simple-minded, planning for an oral presentation is just as important as it is for a written document.

Assessing the Reason and Receivers

Are You Informing or Persuading?

While humour can add spice to any business presentation, the main aim is usually to inform or persuade. Although professional speakers may also aim to entertain in their speeches, professionals rarely have the comedian's gift—or the need to be funny. If your purpose is to inform, you should emphasize facts. If it is to persuade, you may consider an appeal to emotion as well as to reason. Even if you are selling a straightforward business proposition, you may have to overcome resistance. As a first step in planning, consider the results you want to achieve with the audience. What exactly do you want listeners to do, to think, or to feel?

What Kind of Audience Will You Have?

For most internal business presentations, it is fairly easy to assess the listeners. Most will be aware of your experience and why you are talking to them; you won't have to establish credibility. They will be interested in your subject, since it will presumably have a bearing on the organization as a whole. And as associates they will be fairly homogeneous in their backgrounds or experience. Still, it's worthwhile considering answers to the following questions:

* Who are the key decision makers or opinion makers, and what are their needs and concerns?
* What will the audience already know and what should you explain?
* Where might resistance to your ideas come from and how can you counter it?

With a formal speech to outsiders, the task of assessing the audience is more difficult:

* The listeners are more likely to come from diverse backgrounds or occupations. The only common bond you can assume is the one that draws them to the organization that has invited you to speak. It's a good idea, therefore, to try to pinpoint some shared concern they will probably have, whether it is economic, political, or cultural.
* Your speech may not be the attraction. The audience may be assembled for reasons other than to hear you—for example, they may be coming for some organizational business that follows the speech or simply for the fellowship of the group. You can't assume they will be interested in the topic. A light or anecdotal approach may be more appropriate than a speech heavy on specialized facts or subtleties.
* You may have to establish your own credibility. Although as a guest speaker you will no doubt be introduced by someone who will outline your background, it might be wise to include in your speech a few indicators of your relevant experience—without blowing your own horn.

Assessing the Conditions

How Much Time Do You Have?

Whatever the length of time allocated to your presentation, stick to it. If listeners expect a half-hour talk and you speak for only 15 minutes, they may feel cheated, especially if they have given up valuable time—or paid money—to attend.

Far worse than being too brief, however, is being long-winded. Even 10 minutes beyond the expected length can seem like an eternity to an audience. Psychologists have suggested that most people's attention span is not longer than 20 minutes, and many people's thoughts begin to wander before that. If your presentation is scheduled right before a meal, the audience may be even more restless. (Can food for thought compete with lunch?) On the other hand, if it is scheduled right after a heavy meal, the audience may be sleepy. According to a survey by New Jersey–based Motivational Systems, 4 out of 10 top executives admitted to having dozed off—or "fallen dead asleep"— while listening to a business presentation, and others might have as well but were too embarrassed to admit it ("Street Talk," 1989). If you anticipate these problems, you can plan to counteract them by building more changes of pace into the presentation and accentuating possible dramatic elements.

Of course, it's difficult to tell in advance exactly how long you will take, but timing yourself in rehearsal will provide a guide. When preparing your presentation, mark off a rough timing guide and include in the plan some "nice to know" but not necessary detail. Then when you are speaking, you can choose to omit or keep the detail, depending on how close you are to your guide. If it looks as if you are going to be way behind, summarize the remaining material and end on time rather than push on relentlessly through the whole speech.

What Is the Physical Layout and Technical Setup?

* Find out how large the room is and whether you will have a microphone.

* If a door into the room is placed so that anyone coming in late will distract the audience, try to arrange for an alternative entrance during the presentation or see if latecomers can be kept out. Although these solutions are not always possible, it's annoying to see a good speech disrupted when all eyes turn to observe latecomers.

* Check to see that any audiovisual aids you need will be on hand and in good working order.

* Find out if you will be speaking in front of a lectern or a table. A portable lectern is usually available in facilities where people give presentations. If you prefer to use one, ask for it.

Using a lectern can be both an advantage and a disadvantage. It allows a speaker to look at notes unobtrusively—to move just the eyes up and down rather than the head. It can also hide nervous hands. On the negative side, it presents a physical barrier between speaker and audience, increasing the sense of formality and distance. If you are giving a short, informal talk or presentation, you are probably better to do without a lectern.

Organizing the Material

A common prescription for speakers is, "Tell them what you are going to say, say it, and then tell them what you have said." If this sequence seems repetitive, remember that listeners, unlike readers, cannot review what has gone before. As an aid to memory, therefore, it's a good idea to build in some repetition. Think of a presentation as having

- an introduction that previews
- a body that develops
- a close that reviews

Since the body takes up most of the presentation, it should be developed first.

Planning the Body

1. *Identify the theme.* Just as it's sensible to work out a thesis before writing an essay or to clarify your subject before writing a report, so in a speech you should begin with the theme of your presentation. In an informative talk, it will be factual ("How we plan to market Softee soap" or "Discoveries from our European sales trip"); in a persuasive talk or speech, it will have an argumentative edge ("Why we should move toward computer-integrated manufacturing" or "The need to improve internal communications"). The theme needn't be your eventual title; rather, it's a planning device, a linchpin to hold together the various facts or ideas you want to discuss.

2. *Choose the basic method of organization.* Your options are similar to those for a written report. Select whichever method makes your material most manageable for you as the planner and most interesting and dynamic for the listener. There are several possibilities:

- order of importance
- chronological order
- geographic or spatial order
- classification or division
- comparison

Another simple way to organize is to consider the message as a solution to a problem. It's the common "get 'em on the hook, get 'em off the hook" approach. The introduction points out the problem and the rest of the speech explains how to solve it. The explanation, however, will still need organizing in one of the preceding ways.

How direct or indirect you should be depends on your analysis of the audience. In most instances, the direct approach works best. When the receiver's mind has a sense of order, it can more easily assimilate the details. For example, with a problem/solution approach, if you not only point out the problem in the introduction but also indicate the solution, the audience will be prepared for the explanation that follows. The direct approach is especially useful for a business presentation when you and the audience are in general agreement about objectives and goals.

If the audience is likely to be opposed to your ideas, however, you might want to be more indirect, building gradually to your solution and keeping the most effective argument until the end. Another option is to direct the audience by pointing out in the introduction that you will be proposing a solution but not disclosing the specifics until you have laid the groundwork.

3. *Create three main sections.* Keith Spicer (1984), an accomplished speaker, maintains that three is the magic number for an effective presentation. Certainly students have long been accustomed to a three-part exam answer, and a three-part structure underlies much of our literature, music, religion, and art. Although two, four, or five parts can also work, the three-part body is a good rule of thumb. You can organize around categories ("the three stages in our marketing campaign") or points ("three ways to improve productivity").

4. *Help the audience remember your points.* Use frequent numerical reminders such as "My second discovery in reviewing costs," or "The third reason we need to enlarge the sales force."

5. *Support your points with specifics.* In an informative presentation you will naturally be presenting facts. In a persuasive one, anecdotes, quotations, and dramatic examples may be as effective as evidence or statistics. You may appeal to reason or emotion, but keep in mind that your aim is to gain support rather than simply to state the facts.

    You may wonder: "Should I give evidence or arguments contrary to my position?" If you are talking to the converted, to people who share your view, you can simply keep to the points that reinforce it. On the other hand, if you are talking to a group that is skeptical, you will add to your credibility by being balanced in your presentation. Discuss alternative points of view and give contrary evidence while pressing your own case. Even if the audience is on your side, a two-sided argument will strengthen your case over the long term.

6. *Draw word pictures for the audience.* Your points will have more effect if you put them in visual terms. Let the listeners see the implications of your findings or the consequences of following or not following your suggestions. Images have impact.

Planning the Beginning and Ending

Once you have planned the body, you will more easily be able to work out the opening and closing.

1. *Spark the audience's interest.* The more captive the listeners and the less they know about your topic, the more you will have to work to capture their attention. If you are not well known to them, personally or by reputation, the opening lines are doubly important. Here are some common attention-grabbers:

    ※ *A joke.* This approach is only for those who have a good sense of timing. If you can't tell a joke well, don't try. Few moments are more embarrassing than the long pause after a joke that doesn't work. A joke is not a mandatory opening; nor will any old joke do. While a good joke will warm a crowd, it must be related to the topic or the occasion for it to be effective.

- *A topical anecdote.* If you do not feel comfortable telling a joke, a short description of an incident related to your topic or the context can build rapport with the audience. The incident might have something to do with the organization the audience belongs to, with your own preparation for the speech, or even with an occurrence earlier in the day—anything that is lighthearted and will bring you and your listeners together. Naturally, the more topical it is the more the audience will appreciate it and the more it will remove the impression of a "canned" presentation—one prepared well in advance for an unspecified audience.

- *A startling fact or statistic.* This can be a dramatic opener, if relevant, and can help make the topic itself seem more important. For example, an opening statistic on the number of working hours lost because of alcoholism could raise interest in a speech on ways to combat alcoholism in the workplace.

- *A quotation.* This approach works well only if the quotation itself is startling or dramatic. Quoting the trite words of a well-known person will not do— unless your main purpose is to refute them.

These are not the only ways to begin a speech or talk, but whatever tactic you use, think of your listeners and what will draw them into your address.

2. *Reveal your plan.* Tell how you are going to proceed and what the main sections of your presentation will be. This will help listeners to remember main points and also reassures them that you have a plan and don't intend simply to ramble on.

3. *At the end, close quickly.* Summarize the main points of your presentation and then finish in a forceful way. The ending can be uplifting or funny, dramatic or moralistic, a quotation or a colourful phrase. But at least try to end with a flourish rather than a fizzle.

Using Audiovisual Aids

Visuals help not only to clarify material and give it impact but also to keep an audience alert. Visual aids are especially useful for internal business presentations, which are often held in stark, single-coloured seminar rooms lit with fluorescent lighting. The problem with these "classroom" surroundings is that sameness makes people drowsy; hypnotists know that a person who has a fixed focus over a period of time will begin to feel sleepy. Along with their other merits, visual aids force a shift in focus from the speaker to the medium and thus combat sleepiness.

Visual aids can have a negative side, however. If you are a dynamic speaker, they may lessen the momentum by shifting the focus away from what you are saying. They can also be overused. A constant stream of transparencies or slides can annoy an intellectual audience, especially if the message is readily understood without them. Despite these potential drawbacks, however, you should get used to handling visuals as a supplement to talking.

Today's presentation graphics programs have revolutionized the use of visuals, making it easy to create presentations on a computer and display them with a multimedia projector. Presentation programs offer a wide range of features:

* Graphics features make it easy to incorporate charts, diagrams, drawn objects, and artwork into your presentations.
* Multimedia capabilities allow you to include sound, music, and videos.
* Animation features allow you to "build" the presentation, adding text or graphics as you speak.
* An annotation feature allows you to draw or write on a slide during your presentation to call attention to a specific point or recapture your audience's attention.
* You can print speaker notes to use as a prompt during your delivery or handouts to give to your listeners as "take-home" items for further reference.
* You can publish your presentation on the Internet or an intranet or send it as an attachment to an e-mail message.

Here are some pointers for designing effective visuals:

* Be sure to limit any screen to six lines of print. Any more and the reader will be distracted and lose focus.
* Use a large font that is easy to read from the back of the room. A useful rule of thumb is 36 points for titles and 24 points for body text.
* Use a horizontal (landscape) rather than a vertical (portrait) layout so that heads in the audience don't block the view.
* In a bland and monochrome room, design slides with colours to add life. However, use no more than three in a single illustration. Avoid a combination of green and red, since colourblind people can't distinguish them.

A note of caution: In preparing your multimedia materials, be careful to avoid common pitfalls:

* Don't use audiovisual effects simply to repeat the obvious. Audiovisuals work best when they supplement your speech and lose impact if they merely duplicate what you are saying.
* Avoid overkill. Don't overload your slides with special effects that might appear gimmicky.
* Don't just read from the visuals. Remember that your listeners can read faster than you can talk. They will become impatient if they are waiting for you to get through what they have already read.

Delivering the Presentation

There are four ways of speaking to a group:

1. *Reading from a Prepared Text.* Choose this approach when the exact words are important—when any confusion, ambiguity, or mistakes could have serious consequences. Academics usually read papers to other academics, who may query the particular points or even the phrasing. Business and government leaders will usually read from a text when the issues are major ones and they want to avoid misinterpretation by the audience—and any reporters. People introducing guest speakers often read biographical information to make sure they have the correct details.

   Unfortunately, unless the speaker is trained, a reading voice tends to lull the audience. The presentation also lacks spontaneity, the sense of a speaker grappling to express ideas and creating a subtle suspense. Unless you have no other practical recourse, therefore, do not read. If you must read a prepared script, try these techniques:

   * Type the speech on every third line in large print so that it is easy to read at a glance.
   * Fill only the top two-thirds of a vertical page with print, so that you don't have to bob your head up and down noticeably as you glance from page to audience and back.
   * Underline the key words in each sentence, and practise emphasizing them.
   * Mark on the script places where you can change your pace or tone to give variety and drama.
   * Look up from the page as often as you can. Try to begin and end sentences while looking at the audience so that you can accentuate your message. In other words, look down between sentences to recall your points and then look up to deliver them.
   * Practise reading the speech aloud beforehand so that you know the material well enough to maintain visual contact with the audience.

2. *Memorizing.* Although an actor can memorize speeches and deliver them flawlessly, very few others can. The danger is that in a rush of nerves a speaker may forget the text and become more hopelessly lost than if the speech had never been committed to memory. If you have ever been in an audience when a memorized speech came unstuck, you will recall squirming at the speaker's silent agony. For most presentations, you would be wise not to put your memory to the test by relying totally on it. It's better to memorize only the order of ideas and perhaps some colourful phrases or opening and closing sentences.

3. *Impromptu Speaking.* Few things are more nerve-racking than being asked to address a group on the spot without any advance preparation. If you have the gift of the gab, you might rise to the challenge brilliantly; however, for most inexperienced speakers it's a matter of instant sweaty palms. Luckily, in business

you will rarely have to give an impromptu presentation unless it's a very informal occasion (such as a birthday party or other celebration); for business meetings most organizers have the courtesy to give advance notice.

If you are asked to give an impromptu talk, remember that the audience will not expect much. Be short and to the point, making a few specific remarks that relate to the occasion. If you treat the task with good humour and pleasantness, the audience will likely respond to you in the same way. You can also try to anticipate those occasions when you might be asked to say a few words, planning your approach just in case. (As Will Rogers reportedly said, "A good impromptu speech takes two weeks to prepare.")

4. *Extemporaneous Speaking.* This kind of presentation is prepared in advance but delivered fresh—that is, the exact wording is figured out as the speaker goes along. It combines the benefits of prior organization and spontaneity. Whether the business occasion calls for an informal talk or a formal speech, extemporaneous speaking is usually the best method.

Sometimes, if you know the material well, you can speak without any notes, relying on your memory of a prepared outline. If you feel uncomfortable without some memory aids, try putting the outline on small cue cards. Don't try to squeeze the entire speech onto cards; use only the key points and any quotations. If it will give you more confidence, write the opening and closing sentences out in full. Then, if you have prepared well, you will probably find that you don't have to use the notes. The mere fact of having them there will relieve you of any anxiety about forgetting.

Delivery Techniques

Look confident. Don't worry about being nervous before a speech. Most speakers are, even seasoned public speakers. The trick is not to appear nervous, since speaker nervousness is somehow contagious. Conversely, a seemingly confident, relaxed speaker will make an audience relax. How do you appear confident? Here is a guide:

1. *Have good posture.* A speaker who walks purposefully and stands erect conveys a sense of command. Try not to slouch or to drape yourself over the lectern.

2. *Wear clothing that is appropriate and comfortable.* There's no point in allowing what you are wearing to distract an audience from what you are saying. Unless special clothing is a deliberate part of the drama you are creating—a kind of costume—it's better to be on the conservative side. In any case, if you wear jewellery, avoid any that jangles; if you tend to put your hands in your pockets and can't break the habit, remove loose change.

3. *Establish eye contact.* As you speak, think of the audience not as a group but as a number of individuals. (Some speakers say it creates confidence to think of the audience as individuals without clothes.) In any case, look for someone who is especially attentive and establish eye contact. Later, switch to other parts of the room and do the same with different individuals. Try to hold your eye contact

for a few seconds with one person before moving to another. Eyes that flit about a room give an impression of nervousness.

This technique will help you feel comfortable with the audience and establish rapport. It will also help you adapt to audience response if necessary— to explain in more detail if you notice quizzical looks or even to leave out some details if you notice fidgeting.

4. *Slow down.* It's natural, when you are nervous, to speak quickly—to try to get it over with in a hurry. Unless you are normally a slow speaker, take the opposite tack. Before you start to speak, pause for a minute to get your bearings and look over the audience. Take a few deep breaths to relax. Smile. Then begin slowly and deliberately. At appropriate spots, when you are changing your emphasis, pause again. Silence can speak: an occasional deliberate pause will generate suspense over what is to follow—and wake up the audience.

5. *Speak clearly and with varied tones.* Don't mumble. Articulate your words. When you don't have a microphone, project your voice to the back of the room. When you do have a microphone, stay about 15 cm away from it. If you are not in the habit of public speaking, you will likely have to concentrate on articulating the words and pronouncing word endings.

Nervousness tends to flatten the voice. To counter this effect, deliberately widen your range. Exaggerate the tones and stress key words in each sentence. In general, give a downward emphasis to the ends of sentences. Tentative speakers often let their voices rise at the end of sentences, suggesting that they are not confident. When you are rehearsing make sure that you have a downward thrust when emphasizing your points.

Although you don't want to push beyond your natural range, remember to use the lower end of your natural register. Low-pitched voices are generally the most pleasing. Breathing from the stomach rather than the upper chest will help increase both the resonance and the depth of your voice.

6. *Be natural with gestures and movement.* Some people talk with their hands; others don't. While gestures can be an effective way of reinforcing points or expressing moods, there's no point trying to change your style to something you are not comfortable with. Artificial gestures can distract from your presentation. So can repetitive or fidgety movements. However, if you like to use your hands, be assured that they will make you seem less stiff and constrained. In any case, keep from gluing your hands together throughout your talk or from planting them in your pockets. If you leave them free, you will probably use them naturally for emphasis.

A tip: if your hands feel awkward hanging at your sides—like five-kilogram hams rather than helpers—try a tension-release exercise. Just before you walk up to speak, press your wrists hard against your sides for 30 seconds. Release. Notice how light your hands feel. They will seem to float up, ready for use.

Is it helpful to move around while talking? Although constant walking about can be distracting, taking the odd step here and there, if you feel natural doing so, can be useful. It makes the listeners shift focus and helps them stay alert.

Don't feel you have to move during a presentation, however; many good speakers prefer to stand still the whole time.

7. *Practise.* Go through your presentation as often as you can, not only to check the timing but also to strengthen your delivery. If possible, rehearse in front of a video camera; playing the tape back will allow you to see and hear nervous mannerisms and other weaknesses. If you don't have access to a video camera, try standing in front of a mirror with a tape recorder. The more you repeat the exercise and the more familiar you are with the material, the more confident you will feel about delivering it.

A practice tip: if you stumble, don't start again. Make yourself carry on to the end, however badly you do it. The point is to get used to expressing your ideas in different ways, so that you relax with the wording of your thoughts. If instead you go back and keep repeating material until it is "word perfect," you will likely end up with a memorized tone to your presentation. Rest assured that if you have to struggle for a word during your actual delivery you will add to the sense of spontaneity.

Coping with Nerves

It's natural to feel somewhat nervous. It's even desirable. Top speakers and actors know that nervousness releases adrenalin, giving a burst of energy that will help them perform well. Trouble comes with an excess of nervousness. It can produce not only mental stress but also physical discomfort. Chest and voice muscles can tighten, making talking and even breathing difficult.

The strategy is to relax those muscles deliberately. Before you speak, practise breathing deeply from the stomach. Put your hand on your stomach to make sure it is expanding and contracting. Try to loosen the throat muscles by humming a song. When not in view of the audience, make exaggerated faces so that your mouth and jaw are loosened.

When you do get up to speak, stand and survey the audience for a few seconds before beginning. Take a couple of deep breaths, and establish eye contact with a friendly-looking face. Above all, don't apologize or say that you are nervous. If you look confident, the audience may never think otherwise.

By far the best strategy for stage fright, however, is to practise. You will find that the adrenalin rush is a little less each time you repeat a performance. You won't lose all nervousness, but you will feel in control of it.

Handling Questions

With many business presentations, getting feedback through questions will increase the likelihood of achieving the desired results with the audience. When you are giving a speech or presentation, consider whether you should encourage questions and whether they should be raised during the speech or afterward. If you want questions, let the audience know at the start how you will handle the process.

The advantage of taking questions throughout a talk is that the audience becomes more involved rather than sitting back as passive listeners. The disadvantage is that constant interruptions can diminish momentum and allow focus to be lost. Probably a good guideline is to assess the formality of the occasion; save spontaneous questioning for the most informal talks and provide a question period for more formal presentations. For some highly formal speeches, you may choose to have no questions.

When you invite questions, it's important to control the process. Anticipate the kinds of questions you may be asked and figure out how you will answer them. You may decide to have some extra backup information on hand. Remember also what the purpose and focus of your presentation are and don't let yourself get sidetracked. Here are the main problems that can arise with questions along with some suggestions on how to handle them:

- *A Confused Question.* Reformulate or paraphrase the question in simple terms before you answer it. This practice can be useful for all questions, since it gives both you and the audience time to think.

- *A Hostile Question.* The trick is not to be defensive or hostile yourself. See first if you can rephrase the question so that it is not emotionally loaded. Then try to use facts to answer it. If you appear unruffled and try to address the matter, the audience will appreciate your poise.

  When answering, address the audience as a whole rather than looking at the questioner. This will divert attention from the source of hostility and reduce the chance of the questioner persisting.

- *A Two-part or Complex Question.* Separate the parts and answer one part at a time. If this sequence might take too long, answer one part and suggest that you would be pleased to discuss the other issues informally later.

- *An Off-topic Question.* Mention that you think topic X is an interesting one you would like to discuss if you had the time but that your focus at this presentation is Y. If you can, suggest that you would be prepared to handle topic X at another time.

- *A Question You Cannot Answer.* If you haven't got the answer, admit it. If possible, say that you will get a response to the questioner later.

- *A Scene Stealer.* Occasionally members of the audience will use a question-and-answer period as a platform for their own opinions rather than to ask a question. If someone starts to launch into a speech, try to take advantage of a pause and politely interrupt. Ask the speaker to state the question briefly so that others have time to raise their questions. Then in your answer steer the audience's attention back to the points you want to stress—to the focus of your presentation.

- *An Underground Questioner.* This person can be disruptive. Instead of asking an open question, this individual makes critical comments or asks snide questions in an undertone loud enough for others to hear. The best approach if this behaviour persists is to single out the offender. You can say, "Do you want to ask something?" or "Can you speak out so that everyone can hear?" or "Can the person giving a talk in the back row share the question with other members of the audience?" Such a direct approach will usually silence disrupters.

* *A Reticent Audience.* Sometimes a question period needs help getting started, particularly with a large crowd. If you anticipate that this will be the case, arrange for someone you know in the audience to ask the first question. Keep eye contact with all parts of the audience when you respond, encouraging people sitting in different locations to speak up. Another option is to ask the first question yourself. For example, you can say, "You may be wondering . . ." and then address the issue.

When a lengthy or contentious question-and-answer period finishes, it's a good idea to bring the audience's attention back to the main point of your talk. A brief closing statement will place the final emphasis where you want it to be.

EXAMINING YOUR PERSONAL VALUES

Things which matter most must never be at the mercy of things which matter least.

Goethe

Objectives

After studying this chapter, you should be able to:

* Formulate a mission statement after identifying your values
* Identify external and internal motivational factors
* Translate values and motivation into goals
* Identify the types of goals
* Set attainable goals
* Identify areas of civic interest
* Identify your problem-solving preferences, skills, and styles
* Apply your style and values to goals and actions

The need to make a difference in the world motivates doctors and researchers to spend hours looking for cures for diseases; it drives inventors and business owners to stay up nights trying to find a better idea; it causes artists and novelists to create art; and it leads people to engage as citizens in the hopes of creating a better world. How we choose to use our lives to make a difference, through the process of understanding who we are, is the subject of this chapter.

In his book *Soul of a Citizen*, Paul Loeb states, "Public participation is the soul of democratic citizenship." What leaves many of us on the sidelines, he suggests, is not "an absence of desire to connect with worthy groups that take on wise causes. We need to believe that our individual involvement is worthwhile, that what we might do in the public sphere will not be in vain." In other words, we want to feel like what we do matters.

In practice, participating in our communities almost always gives us a sense of purpose we're not likely to find anywhere else. We also gain a deeper understanding of ourselves and develop new skills. We learn how to work together with others and to act on our deepest values and convictions. Civic service, in essence, often strengthens who we are as individuals.

To make a difference in the world by engaging in civic action, we begin by coming to know our underlying values—our core selves. "Citizenship means more than voting, paying taxes, or obeying laws. It is a powerful expression of self," according to Marianne Williamson, author of *The Healing of America.* If citizenship is an expression of self, self must first be identified. As we become more self-aware and develop more self-mastery, we become more powerful citizens. We become more effective in creating, re-creating, and sustaining our vision for our democracy. We become better prepared to create change for the greater well-being of ourselves, our communities, and our world.

As we grow and transform our own abilities as citizens and leaders, we will more positively influence the growth and transformation of society. When Gandhi said, "We must be the change we wish to see in the world," he gave us profound guidance in our development as citizens. He professed that as we devote ourselves to our personal development, we embody and model the vision we have for our communities. Joseph Jaworski, founder of the American Leadership Forum, has also discovered through his research and experience that personal transformation is the key to societal transformation. In his book with Betty Sue Flowers, *Synchronicity: The Inner Path of Leadership,* Jaworski concludes that attention to our inner lives is integral to effectively shaping our collective future.

The personal journey toward effective citizenship can begin with identifying values, goals, and motivations, and developing a strategy for dealing with challenges. The purpose of this chapter is to help you gain awareness, develop practices, and make choices that will lay the foundation for a lifetime of effective citizenship.

DETERMINING VALUES

Values—
central beliefs and attitudes that guide our choices, either consciously or unconsciously

Values are our central beliefs and attitudes that guide our choices, either consciously or unconsciously. We all have values, though we may not be aware of what they are. As children, we learn to value the things our parents and communities teach us to value. As we mature, we gain the ability to choose our values based on our own internal guidance and expression of self.

Values can be those things that we are fundamentally committed to, our highest principles; they are the things in life that we consider worthy for their own sake. As you consciously become aware of, and choose, your values, they become an internal guidance system. To make good decisions, set appropriate goals, and manage priorities, it is important to identify the values that are central to who you are today and to who you want to become.

MAKING IT HAPPEN: ADAM WERBACH, SIERRA CLUB

Adam Werbach became president of the Sierra Club shortly after graduating from college. A self-proclaimed mediocre student, who was sent home from grade school for fighting, Werbach channeled his passion into environmental activism in high school.

During one high school summer, he decided to volunteer for the Big Green campaign, a grassroots effort to build voter support for a sweeping state ballot initiative on environmental policy. Within minutes of walking into campaign headquarters, Werbach was appointed to organize high school volunteers for the project. He remembers saying, "Me? I've never done anything like this before. I'm just a high school student!" The organizer in charge replied, "This is your chance. Now is the time to start. There's the phone. Read these papers. Get to work."

Werbach organized more than 300 California high school students that summer to canvass door-to-door and staff phone banks. After failing in their attempt to sway enough votes to pass Big Green, Werbach was extremely disappointed. However, his peers would not allow him to wallow in defeat and pressured him to move on to another project. After calling organizations he had worked with on Big Green, he accepted an invitation from the Sierra Club to come to one of their executive committee meetings to share with them his ideas for student involvement.

Werbach's first project was organizing a summer camp to train student leaders. He then organized the Sierra Student Coalition (SSC), which supported high school and college students in direct lobbying for national environmental policy, and he registered tens of thousands of 18- to 24-year-olds to vote. When Werbach encountered resistance from the Sierra Club board of directors toward the SSC, he decided to run for membership on the board. Any member of the Sierra Club could run for the board, and the national membership of the Sierra Club elected Werbach.

After two years as a member of the board, Werbach proved to be a valuable asset to the organization and was elected president of the Sierra Club by his fellow board members. He was 23 years old. When people ask Werbach if he is too young for his job, he replies, "No, I'm too old. A 15-year-old would get more done." Werbach observes: "As we get older, we begin to accept the unacceptable. We accept that bad things happen. We rationalize. We follow too much advice. . . . We need to rekindle the youth within us. . . . The older we get, the less encouragement we find to experiment and wander beyond the boundaries of a constructed world."

Adapted from *Act Now, Apologize Later* by Adam Werbach. New York: HarperCollins Publishers, 1997.

Our values are our guides as to when and how we act to elicit social change. More so than reasoned arguments or gathering the right information, we rely on what we know at the core of who we are. If we trust our convictions, we can take stands whether we have formal credentials or expert knowledge on an issue. Taking the time to define your values and then align your actions with them can significantly impact your ability to achieve what you most desire for your life, community, and world.

FIGURE 2.1 *Wheel of Life*

Identifying Life Areas

Identifying and defining values is usually a work-in-progress. Since our identities are constantly open to change and redefinition, the values that we hold are also open to change. By practicing self-reflection, you can learn how to be more intentional in your decisions and actions. You can learn to assess how your actions are expressing the things that are important to you.

The first step in assessing values is to examine how important the various aspects of work and life are to you. Look at the Wheel of Life shown in Figure 2.1, and consider what areas of life might have a particular significance. We may find that some areas are more important than others at varying times in our lives; however, the wheel symbolizes our lives as a whole. Keeping the wheel segments balanced, as demonstrated in our lives, will help us proceed smoothly. Start to identify values in each of the areas. For each category, identify the importance by ranking it from 1 to 10, with 10 being the most important.

He who has a why to live can bear with almost any how.

Nietzsche

Identifying Values

The following box lists some sample character traits and values that can be used as a starting point in developing a list of personal values. Consider how much you value the following traits, and use these traits to help you distinguish values. For instance, you may value being reliable to your family or being committed to your education. What are traits and values that you would add to your list?

Creating a Mission Statement

One way to clarify the values that guide our lives is to develop a personal mission statement. This statement can help us make choices with clarity and integrity. As we become more and more aligned with our values and purpose, our choices become instant and natural expressions of ourselves. A personal mission statement can help us develop a vision of self, of what we see as our purpose in life, how we want to contribute to life, and where we find meaning and joy.

> If you don't know what your passion is, realize that one reason for your existence on earth is to find it. Real success means creating a life of meaning through service that fulfills your reason for being here.
>
> Oprah Winfrey

CHARACTER TRAITS AND VALUES

ACCOUNTABLE

Accountability may include being:

Reliable	Trustworthy
Dependable	Responsible
Loyal	Secure

COMMITTED

Committed may mean being:

Participative	Focused
Enthusiastic	Persistent
Energetic	Productive
Faithful	

OPEN

Openness may include being:

Fair	Unbiased
Patient	Open-minded
Tolerant	Joyful

HONEST

Honesty may include being:

Authentic	Genuine
Outspoken	Sincere
Truthful	Frank
Balanced	

RESPONSIBLE

Responsibility entails taking control of our own lives without blame or victimization.

GIVING

Giving may include being:

Dedicated	Compassionate
Accepting	Nurturing
Contributing	Helpful
Cooperative	Generous
Appreciative	Considerate
Forgiving	Respectful
Friendly	

ACTION!: CREATING A MISSION STATEMENT

1. By answering the following questions, you can gather information to help you define what is most important to you. Let your emotions guide you. Be aware of when you feel happy, satisfied, and free of personal judgment.

   * Describe a time in your life when you were doing something that felt very satisfying. What are the things that caused you to feel this way? Who were you with? What were you doing?

   * Who has been an influential person in your life? What are the traits of this person that you admire? What qualities of this person would you like to emulate?

   * What do you want to be like in your life? What are the traits and qualities that are most important to you?

   * What do you want to have in life (happiness, friendship, great food, and so forth)?

   * What do you want others to have?

   * What are some of the roles you play in life (for example, family member, community member, student, employee)? Choose a person with whom you interact in a particular role. What would you like that person to say about the contribution you make?

2. Develop a draft of your mission statement. Your statement can be a few words or a few paragraphs. You should be able to use it as a guide to who you want to be as well as how you want to be. Examples of some mission statements include:

   * I have a wonderful life and dramatically contribute to the quality of life on earth.

   * I am a force for loving relationships in my family, and I support my loved ones in being their best selves.

   * I promote beneficial change, and I am a catalyst for sustainability and harmony on earth.

3. Next, reflect on and assess your mission statement. Answer the following questions:

   * Does this mission statement bring out the best in me?

   * Am I excited and happy about the person I am when I use this statement for guidance?

   * Do I feel challenged by, uplifted by, and purposeful about this statement?

   * Does this statement empower me to be of service to others in any way?

   * How do others and/or the greater community or world benefit when I embody this statement?

Acting with Integrity

Webster's New Collegiate Dictionary defines **integrity** as *"the state of being whole or complete; acting with moral soundness."* When our actions are an honest expression of ourselves, we have personal integrity. As we become more intentional about using our values to guide our actions, we develop greater personal integrity.

Integrity–
the state of being
whole or complete

Each of us must consider our own definition of moral soundness in order to assess the integrity of our actions. Among the widely accepted qualities of morality in our culture are fairness, honesty, service, excellence, patience, and treatment of others with dignity. The U.S. Declaration of Independence speaks to the self-evident value of human dignity: "We hold these truths to be self-evident: that all men are created equal and endowed by their Creator with certain inalienable rights, that among these are life, liberty and the pursuit of happiness."

Acting with integrity is integral to the concept of democracy. It gives direction to our appropriate engagement as citizens.

Congruence

Becoming more self-aware allows you to become more intentional about your choices and how they affect the quality of your life and the lives of others. **Congruence,** which means "to be in agreement or alignment," is another aspect of acting with integrity. To achieve true congruence in your life, what you think, say, and do must be in alignment.

Congruence–
to be in agreement
or alignment

As philosopher Parker Palmer describes the lives of people who have acted on their deepest beliefs: "These people have understood that no punishment could be worse than the one we inflict on ourselves by living a divided life." And nothing could help them heal that rift like making the decision "to stop acting differently on the outside from what they knew to be true inside."

Congruence is about looking at what you think, say, and do in relation to all the choices you make—from how you dress, what you buy, and how and with whom you spend your time to what kind of lifestyle you have. The actions we take have the power to transform our values into positive, lasting impacts. We may hold generosity as a value, but the act of behaving generously is what creates congruence. When our actions do not align with our values, we experience internal conflict, as well as conflict within our relationships and external world. The consequences of this conflict may include stress, depression, fatigue, anger, or anxiety. These negative feelings can further separate us from our integrity and, in a self-perpetuating manner, create more blocks to self-awareness. Rachel Naomi Remen suggests that "the loss of emotional or spiritual integrity may be at the source of our suffering conscience. . . . Stress may be as much a question of a compromise of values as it is a matter of time pressure and fear of failure."

Conversely, when we act in accordance with what is true for us, we experience positive feelings. These may include happiness, satisfaction, passion, certainty, and abundance. Our feelings give us immediate feedback and are important guides for acting with integrity.

Stephen Covey, in his book *Seven Habits of Highly Effective People,* refers to the concept of congruence as the "inside-out" approach. Covey relates that if you want to create change in some area of your life, focus on what you think and say, and how you act, in that area. For instance, if you want to have better friendships, think about and practice being a more concerned and giving friend. If you want to be a force for peace in the world, notice whether you have aggressive or negative thoughts and how these thoughts might color your actions. Consider how you might change your thinking and, in turn, how you can contribute to peace in your relationships and community. The inside-out approach can support congruence by reminding you to first turn your awareness inside in order to create the alignment of your thoughts, words, and actions.

Congruence is apt to be a lifelong work-in-progress. By continually evaluating our beliefs, choices, and lifestyle patterns for congruence, we can become more powerful agents of change.

Understanding Motivation

Motivation—
the intensity of desire to engage in an activity

Identifying how we are **motivated** can help us determine whether we are acting in accordance with our values or the values of others. Being an effective citizen requires that we develop the ability to think for ourselves, to listen to and be motivated by our own guidance. When we act from our own values and experience self-worth from within, we are internally motivated. When we act to please others or act in alignment with the values of others, we are externally motivated.

External Motivation

External motivation—
the desire to perform an activity to gain the approval of others

Part of human nature is self-protection and the drive to sustain oneself. Many of us have learned to protect and nurture ourselves through gaining the approval of others. We may have learned as children that we gain love by pleasing others or that we can only feel valuable when others approve of us. If we make decisions based on the desire for acceptance from others, we are said to be externally motivated. The danger in **external motivation** is that we may compromise our values and priorities in the pursuit of approval from others. This inevitably produces internal conflict—and the negative feelings that accompany it.

Internal Motivation

Internal motivation—
the desire to perform an activity simply for the pleasure and satisfaction that accompany the activity

An internally motivated person consults his own guidance in decision making. For this person, well-being and self-worth come from within and are not dependent on the validation of others.

Social change usually involves upsetting or challenging an existing system or belief. This necessarily includes attracting the disapproval of others. Developing strong **internal motivation** helps us to engage as potential change agents. When we act on personal values that satisfy and uplift us, we are less likely to be defeated by the disapproval of others. As Eleanor Roosevelt said, "No one can hurt you without your consent."

As citizens trying to effect change, we may encounter the apathy of others. When others don't find passion or meaning in the things that we do, it can cause us to question the validity of our own passion and meaning. However, if we are motivated by a strong internal alignment to our own values and empowerment, we will be less likely to be discouraged by the inaction or lack of enthusiasm of others.

Sam Daley-Harris, founder of a nonprofit group dedicated to ending hunger, describes how a strong identification with the things he valued helped him to become motivated no matter what others did:

> It turned out that I wasn't hopeless about the technical feasibility of ending hunger, I was hopeless about human nature. I feared *people* would never get it together. That night, however, I realized there was a particular part of human nature I had some influence over—my own. Up to that point, for me, commitment had a certain "I will if you will" quality to it. "I'll recycle if you will," I might have thought. "Oh, you won't? Then I won't either." In that darkened hotel banquet hall, I experienced commitment in a new way, a kind of "I will whether you will or not."

When your self-worth comes from within, things may change in the world, but they cannot compromise your sense of value and empowerment. A study conducted by the University of Rochester's Human Motivation Research Group found, for example, that people whose motivation was internal exhibited more interest, confidence, excitement, persistence, creativity, and performance than those who were motivated by external rewards.

> It is essential that the student acquire an understanding of, and a lively feeling for, values. He must acquire a vivid sense of the beautiful and of the morally good.
>
> Albert Einstein

Reflecting

Self-awareness takes time—and intention. Jill Ker Conway, former president of Smith College, reasons that when lives are overscheduled and overstimulated there is no space for people to sit and reflect. This kind of reflective space is what allows us to build the skills of self-awareness and self-determination. Self-determination comes about by knowing ourselves and choosing our experience based on our own preferences and creative impulses rather than on those of others. Conway suggests that we can encourage greater reflectiveness through such activities as journal writing, letter writing, and spending time in quiet and reflection.

In a more effective society, citizens, according to Paul Loeb, "would have time to think and reflect, to be with their families and friends, and to engage themselves in their communities. This would foster a culture that allows us to slow down the pace of global change, challenge mindless consumption."

TRANSLATING VALUES AND MOTIVATION INTO GOALS

No formula exists for determining our optimum lifestyle and appropriate civic engagement; we must each find our own path. We will all likely direct our efforts toward different results. *Webster's New Collegiate Dictionary* defines a **goal** as "the end toward

Goal—
the end toward which effort is directed

which effort is directed." A goal is a statement of something we want to be, do, or have—for instance, "I want to be a research scientist," or "I want to travel around the world." You already began distinguishing some of your goals during the process of creating your personal mission statement. Goals are our intentions. They provide clarity and focus for our thoughts, words, and actions and guide us to specific outcomes about which we are passionate. Our own unique set of values and motivating factors determines our goals.

> The shift from incoherence to coherence can bring dramatic effects: a 60-watt light bulb whose light waves could be made coherent as a laser, would have the power to bore a hole through the sun—from 90 million miles away.
>
> William A. Tiller

Having energy and enthusiasm is crucial, but if that energy and effort are scattered, they are far less likely to create a specific intended result. Concentrated effort is an extremely powerful force. Consider the ability of concentrated light to cut metal. The light energy propelled from a normal 60-watt bulb is traveling very quickly (at the speed of light), but the energy is scattered, or diffused. It is sent out in every direction. If the light from the same 60-watt bulb were concentrated, as in a laser beam, it could penetrate metal. Likewise, if we focus our efforts toward a specific goal, we concentrate our energy on achieving it.

Goals can greatly increase our effectiveness. Our thoughts, words, and actions are energy forces; by focusing them toward specific, intentional points, we intensify their strength. With awareness of our passions and strengths, we can choose meaningful goals. When we choose goals that are in alignment with our values and personal integrity, we access energy that supports our process. If we choose a goal that conflicts in some way with our integrity or personal mission, the conflict dissipates our energies and compromises our strength.

Types of Goals

When determining goals, it is important to set ones that extend beyond your own needs. Subordinating our personal achievements to something beyond our own immediate self-interests in order to be of service to others or a cause allows us to experience a deeper sense of meaning and self-worth. The commitment to live according to our deepest values not only creates a more stable center in our lives but also helps us to better navigate the challenges we face along the way.

Individual Goals

Individual goals are goals that you set by yourself and for which you alone develop and implement a strategy for achieving. They can be goals that you have for your own development and achievement as well as goals that affect society What makes them individual goals is that you alone are responsible for achieving them.

Collective Goals

Collective goals are set, collectively, by members of a group. Necessarily, each member of the group has a role to play in achieving the goal. In addition, all members will gain something in common by achieving the goal. Collective goals can be initiated by an individual, but if they are intended to benefit a group, they should be formulated and agreed upon by the group.

Short-Term and Long-Term Goals

Having both short-term and long-term goals can be rewarding. Short-term goals are usually less complex and easier to achieve than long-term goals. We build momentum with each goal we complete, so setting short-term goals helps ensure that we'll have frequent victories.

Long-term goals (which take one year or longer to reach) keep us headed in the right direction and can provide a sense of greater purpose. These goals may require longer to achieve their

A collective goal inspires the commitment of all those working toward it.

result, so it helps to break down the overarching, or long-term, goal into smaller goals that may be reached in shorter periods of time. Goals that involve a civic interest or challenge are usually longer term. These goals usually involve a collective strategy, and institutions or social systems are generally slow to change. Breaking a long-term goal into smaller, "short-term" goals can provide a sense of accomplishment—and thus motivation—if our ultimate goal requires patience and perseverance over a long period of time.

Prioritizing

Most of us have several goals in different life areas that we would like to achieve. Prioritizing goals can be confusing if you think in terms of which goal is more important. Over the long term, all of your goals are probably important, or they wouldn't be goals. When prioritizing, think in terms of *timing:* "Which goal will I focus on more right now?"

When deciding which goals to focus on first, consider the following:

- Will achieving certain goals first make others easier to achieve?
- Do any of your goals express values that are more important to you than others?
- Which goals will create the greatest impact toward your solution with the fewest resources?
- Which goals will create long-term results?
- Which goals have the greatest chance of success?

Dealing with Conflicting Goals

Because the resources we have to spend on our goals—money, time, and energy— are limited, goals can often seem at odds with one another. Working on one goal can mean slipping on another one. Managing your goals effectively as a group helps avoid frustration.

Some suggestions for dealing with several goals at once include the following:

- **Stay focused.** Don't set too many goals at the same time, and make sure that your goals are in alignment with your most important values.
- **Have at least one simple goal and one difficult goal at any given time.** The simple goals motivate you as you accomplish them rapidly. The difficult goals keep you challenged and growing.
- **Have at least one short-term and one long-term goal at any given time.** As with simple goals, short-term goals help ensure that you'll have frequent victories. Long-term goals keep you headed in the right direction.
- **Be flexible.** Decide which of your goals (and tasks) are most important, but be willing to change a goal or even put it on hold for a while, if necessary.
- **Look for ways to combine goals and tasks.** If you can work on two or more goals at once, you can consolidate your resources.

Goal Setting

Once you have determined your values, set a mission statement, and become aware of the types of goals, you can more easily begin setting goals. The Wheel of Life discussed earlier in this chapter contains various areas of focus in our lives. While these areas appear to be separate, our behavior and choices in any given area affect other areas. Because we are part of society as citizens, our choices and behaviors affect others as well. By using your personal mission statement, and by using self-reflection when setting goals in the different areas of your life, you can ensure that your goals reflect the person that you most want to be. Using the Wheel of Life, begin the goal-setting process by asking yourself what you would like to do, be, or have in each of the categories. For example, if you value financial independence, then you might set a goal of finding a well-paying job or making and sticking to a budget. If you value helping others, you might set a goal of spending several hours a week doing volunteer work. Your goals can also be concrete, such as saving enough money to buy a car, or they can be abstract, such as working to control your temper.

You can set many goals at this point without worrying about spreading yourself too thin because we make a distinction between setting a goal and managing a goal or project. At this stage, think of many goals you would like to shoot for even if you are focused on other things right now. However, also remember the importance of balance. Make sure to set goals across different areas of your life: health, finance, family, relationships, personal growth, career, and so forth. The number of categories in which you should set goals depends on your particular situation. How well-balanced is your life right now? What are your priorities? Are you already strong in some areas but weak in others? Answers to questions like these will give you a sense of where to focus your efforts. In general, expect to focus on a few goals in more than one category at a time. It's okay to set a lot of goals in multiple categories.

Guidelines for Attainable Goals

Most goal-setting theorists suggest that goals should have certain characteristics to make them more easily attainable. In general, goals should be as follows:

Written. Research has shown that by simply writing down your goals, you increase your odds of achieving them, on average, by 300 percent.

A study conducted by Yale University in 1953 has—despite its age—some telling results about the importance of goals. A survey given to the Yale senior class asked the students several questions, including three that addressed goals. The goal-related questions were as follows:

- Have you set goals?
- Have you written them down?
- Do you have a plan to accomplish these goals?

Only 3 percent of the class answered "yes" to these questions. Twenty years later, the members of this class were surveyed again. The research showed that the 3 percent of the class who had set goals were happier and more successful than those who did not have goals. In addition, the 3 percent who had set goals had 97 percent of the wealth of the entire class. In other words, these 3 percent were wealthier than the entire rest of the class combined. This study illustrates that setting goals can lead to accomplishment and fulfillment.

Realistic. Believing that your goals are at least possible for you to achieve will more likely motivate you. More important, you—not anyone else—must believe in these goals. However, just because you should believe that a goal is possible does not mean that you must expect it to be easy or even probable.

A goal is realistic if you stand reasonably good odds of accomplishing it, given enough time and effort on your part. You must have some control over the effort in order for goals to be realistic. The majority of the goals you set should be very realistic, or you risk becoming frustrated if you do not accomplish any of them.

Challenging. Although you will also want to have some easier goals, some of your goals should be challenging. Challenging goals force you to grow. However, limit the number of challenging goals or tasks you set to avoid becoming overwhelmed or frustrated. When our goals are so challenging that we wonder whether they are realistic, it might make sense to break the goals down into smaller, incremental goals.

Measurable and specific. Your goals should be measurable and specific enough for you to know definitively whether they have been completed. Although some goals are ongoing or will likely be works in progress throughout your life and thus may not in themselves be measurable, the individual tasks that you will later assign to these goals should be very specific and measurable. For instance, one of your overall goals may be to end AIDS in Africa. Specific tasks associated with that may be to effect a policy whereby the United States gives $5 billion per year to Africa for AIDS prevention, or to institute a training program that educates 500,000 people per month.

Adaptable. The goals you set now may not be perfect; even if they are, situations can change over time, making them imperfect. The reality is that most people's goals do change over time. In fact, goals usually should change, at least slightly, in response to things that change around you or to new life events.

Although it's important to set goals and to have something for which to strive, once you have set the goals you need to detach from the outcome. "You're not guaranteed specific results as you have defined them, but you gain the satisfaction of living your life for a higher purpose."

Time-sensitive. When considering your group of goals as a whole, many of them should have a concrete deadline. However, some may be ongoing, such as attaining excellent health or creating world peace. Such goals will have no end date, though they should be tracked and monitored; the individual tasks that compose the goals should have deadlines.

Congruous. To be effective, your goals should conform to your value system and be internally motivated. If you set goals to meet someone else's expectations or that do not fit within your values, you will find it more difficult to reach them. Your goals should fit into what you want to do, be, or have in your life. If you find it difficult to develop the motivation to achieve a goal, first look at where the goal fits into your value system and do some self-evaluation. Honest evaluation of why you want to achieve a goal can lead to insights and personal discovery.

For example, your friend may have the goal "to buy a bigger house than my brother's." Asking the question "Why a bigger house?" could reveal that your friend wants to compete with his brother. Maybe there also are other issues to be addressed, such as the need for self-esteem and respect, which owning a larger house will not solve. Perhaps a more congruous goal would be "to earn my brother's respect." Identifying the root goal could have a profound impact on this person's life that could not be achieved with a house of any size.

Positive. Goals are more likely to motivate us subconsciously when stated positively and proactively. You may notice this in advertising messages. Nike says "Just Do It" instead of "Stop Sitting There." If your goal is to stop procrastinating, how can you state your ultimate goal, or what you really want, in a positive way? For example, saying, "I want to move with speed and direction in all my tasks and responsibilities" is more proactive. Negatively framed goals require not doing something and thus focus our attention on what we don't want instead of on a positive vision. Positive goals keep us clear and focused on the images of what we want.

ACTION!: DETERMINING THE VALUES BEHIND THE GOAL

For each of the goals you set, see if you can determine its underlying values. For example:

GOAL

Graduating in May

CORRESPONDING VALUE(S)

Being committed, perseverance, responsibility, patience, valuing education

---

CHOOSING WHERE AND HOW TO ENGAGE AS CITIZENS

Choosing where to start engaging as citizens involves observing ourselves and where we experience curiosity and passion for the world around us. "We all have passions if we choose to see them," says Po Bronson, author of *What Should I Do with My Life*? Bronson states: "Most of us don't get epiphanies. We don't get clarity. Our purpose doesn't arrive neatly packaged as destiny. We only get a whisper. A blank, nonspecific urge. That's how it starts."

> Where the needs of the world and your talents cross, there lies your vocation.
>
> Aristotle

As a citizen, you may see many areas that need attention in your community and beyond. You have already begun the process of narrowing down areas and issues that interest you. To be as effective as possible in addressing areas of need, it helps to narrow your focus of engagement.

By looking at the life areas that you value most, you can identify how some of these areas are affected by the policies of our government and other influential entities, such as major corporations. For instance, if health is important to you and you find it a challenge to afford health insurance, you may consider how government policies or the policies of insurance companies affect your ability to care for your health. By distinguishing such connections, you may see areas of civic engagement that call to you personally.

Effective Engagement

As we look at all of the things that interest us, it becomes clear that there are some things we have influence over and some that we don't. Where do we spend most of our time? What do we think about most often? We find an overall landscape of things that concern us. This **landscape of interests** may be filled with such things as classes, jobs, children, peace, concern for the environment, or finances. Within our landscape of interests, those items that we have control over are our **frame of action.**

Landscape of interests— those items we are concerned about

Frame of action— those items within our landscape over which we have control

By looking at our landscape of interests and our frame of action and determining where we spend most of our time and energy, we can discover quite a bit about our level of efficiency. Effective citizens focus their energy in the frame of action. They work on things they can do something about, and they exhibit energetic, positive qualities.

On the other hand, citizens often become discouraged and blocked if they spend most of their energy focusing on items in the landscape of interests over which they have no control. They may focus on others' faults and the fault of "the system," and thus spend much of their time blaming others and feeling victimized.

Some social problems can seem overwhelming. When we focus on the things we can do, however, we find that we are often empowered to do even more. For instance, providing proper nutrition to every child around the world may seem like a colossal undertaking. However, by looking at what we can actually do, we empower ourselves. For example, we can influence government policy by communicating with our elected officials, we can organize food drives, and we can research the problems and causes and talk to others who share our concerns.

When we proactively look for where we can engage, we become most effective. As we experience success through our efforts, our beliefs about our ability to effect change strengthen. In this way, our frame of action expands to include a larger area within which we can have an influence.

Understanding Our Problem-Solving Preferences

People differ in the ways they prefer to engage as citizens. This is important to understand when determining where you will experience the greatest fulfillment through your involvement. The ability to learn and solve problems is one of the most important skills you can acquire to be effective in your life, and especially as citizens, but we all have a different problem-solving process and unique skills. You will probably recognize that you are better at some of the following skills than others, and that you rely on some more than others when solving problems. As a result, you have developed a unique problem-solving style. The following skills are organized in general categories rather than a comprehensive list of all of the possible skills and styles. Although the categories are not intended to define or limit you or your style, most people find that they have a predominant style. This guide may help you understand strengths you can use to learn new things or to solve problems. You may also increase your effectiveness as a learner and problem solver by improving on the skills presented here that don't come as naturally.

Problem-Solving Skills

The skills most of us use for learning or solving problems are as follows:

Intuition. This skill involves dealing with people and emotions. People using this skill would tend to rely more on "gut feeling" than on a systematic approach

FIGURE 2.2 *Frame of Action*

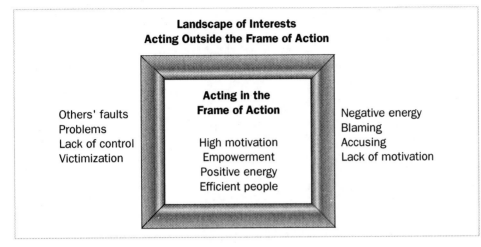

Landscape of Interests
Acting Outside the Frame of Action

Others' faults
Problems
Lack of control
Victimization

Acting in the
Frame of Action

High motivation
Empowerment
Positive energy
Efficient people

Negative energy
Blaming
Accusing
Lack of motivation

to problems. In new situations, someone with strong intuition skills would be open-minded, sensitive to the needs of others, and adaptable to change.

Observation. This skill entails understanding ideas and situations from different points of view. In a learning situation, people using this skill would rely on patience, objectivity, and listening but would not necessarily take any action. In new situations, observers would rely on thoughts, feelings, and interpretations in forming opinions.

Conceptualization. People with developed conceptualization skills use logic and ideas, rather than feelings, to understand problems or situations. Typically, using this skill would involve relying on systematic planning and development of theories and ideas to solve problems.

Experimentation. Solving problems using this skill incorporates active involvement. Experimenting with approaches to influence or change situations takes place, as opposed to simply watching a situation. People who use this skill value getting things done and seeing the results of their influence and ingenuity.

A person's problem-solving style is a combination of these four basic skills. Because of this, you often may be pulled in several different directions when addressing a problem. Complete the Problem-Solving Inventory in the accompanying box to evaluate the way you solve problems and how you deal with day-to-day situations in your life. We all have a sense that people attack problems, and learn, differently. Combining your scores for each skill can indicate which of the four problem-solving styles best describes you. This inventory may help you better understand yourself and others.

Problem-Solving Styles

Understanding problem-solving styles—and their strengths and weaknesses—can increase your learning power, your ability to get along with others and work in teams, and your adaptability for solving problems. The problem-solving styles are combinations of the four basic problem-solving skills. To get your overall style score for the inventory, add the following columns together:

Column 3 + Column 4:   Technician

Column 1 + Column 2:   Diplomat

Column 3 + Column 2:   Strategist

Column 1 + Column 4:   Activist

Following are descriptions of the four basic styles:

Technician. This style combines the skills of conceptualization and experimentation. People with this style are best at finding practical uses for ideas and theories. If this is your preferred style, you have the ability to solve problems and make decisions based on finding solutions to questions or problems. You would rather deal with technical tasks and problems than with social and interpersonal issues.

Diplomat. This style combines the skills of intuition and observation. People with this style are best at viewing concrete situations from many points of view. Their approach to situations is to observe rather than to take action. If this is your style, you may enjoy situations that call for generating a wide range of ideas, such as brainstorming sessions. You have an imaginative ability and sensitivity to feelings.

Strategist. This style combines the skills of conceptualization and observation. People with this style are best at understanding a wide range of information and putting it into concise, logical forms. If this is your style, you probably are less focused on people and more interested in abstract ideas and concepts. Generally, people with this style find it more important that a theory have logical soundness than practical value.

Activist. This style combines the skills of intuition and experimentation. People with this style enjoy carrying out plans and involving themselves in new and challenging experiences. Your tendency may be to act on "gut" feelings rather than on logical analysis. In solving problems, you may rely more heavily on people for information than on your own technical analysis.

A C T I O N !

Problem-Solving Inventory

Instructions. You will be asked to complete 12 sentences. Each has four endings. Rank the endings for each sentence according to how well you think each one fits with how you would go about solving a problem or learning something. Recall some recent situations where you had to solve a problem or learn something new. Then, using the spaces provided, rank a "4" for the sentence ending that describes what is most like you, down to a "1" for least like you. Be sure to rank all of the endings for each sentence.

Example:

1. When I am in
   a group:

   [2] I am happy   [3] I am careful   [1] I am energetic   [4] I am quiet

The Inventory

1. When I solve problems:
   - [ ] I like to deal with my feelings
   - [ ] I like to watch and listen
   - [ ] I like to think about ideas
   - [ ] I like to be doing things

2. I make the best decisions when:
   - [ ] I trust my hunches and feelings
   - [ ] I listen and watch carefully
   - [ ] I rely on logical thinking
   - [ ] I work hard to get things done

3. When I am solving problems:
   - [ ] I have strong feelings and reactions
   - [ ] I am quiet and reserved
   - [ ] I tend to reason things out
   - [ ] I am responsible about things

4. I learn best by:
   - [ ] feeling
   - [ ] watching
   - [ ] thinking
   - [ ] doing

5. When I solve problems:
   - [ ] I am open to new experiences
   - [ ] I look to all sides of issues
   - [ ] I like to analyze things and break them down into their parts
   - [ ] I like to try things out

6. When I am solving problems:
   - [ ] I am an intuitive person
   - [ ] I am an observing person
   - [ ] I am a logical person
   - [ ] I am an active person

7. I learn best from:
   - [ ] personal relationships
   - [ ] observation
   - [ ] rational theories
   - [ ] a chance to practice things

8. When I solve a problem:
   - [ ] I feel personally involved
   - [ ] I take my time before acting
   - [ ] I like ideas and theories
   - [ ] I like to see results from my work

9. When I make decisions:
   - [ ] I rely on my feelings
   - [ ] I rely on my observations
   - [ ] I rely on my ideas
   - [ ] I like to try things out

10. When I am solving problems:
    - [ ] I am an accepting person
    - [ ] I am a reserved person
    - [ ] I am a rational person
    - [ ] I am a responsible person

(continued)

ACTION!

11. In a new situation: ☐ I get involved   ☐ I like to observe   ☐ I like to evaluate things   ☐ I like to be active

12. I learn best when: ☐ I am receptive and open-minded   ☐ I am careful   ☐ I analyze ideas   ☐ I am practical

TOTAL the scores from each column   ☐ Column 1   ☐ Column 2   ☐ Column 3   ☐ Column 4

Each of the totals corresponds to one of the four basic problem-solving skills.

Column One: Intuition

Column Two: Observation

Column Three: Conceptualization

Column Four: Experimentation

Plot your scores on the grid below to get a visual representation of your preferred skills.

Intuition

```
                              45
                              40
                              35
                              30
                              25
                              20
                              15
                              10
                               5
                               0
Experimentation  45 40 35 30 25 20 15 10 5 0 |                              Observation
                                              0 5 10 15 20 25 30 35 40 45
                               0
                               5
                              10
                              15
                              20
                              25
                              30
                              35
                              40
                              45
```

Conceptualization

Adapted from "The Learning Style Inventory" by David Kolb, © 1985, McBer & Company.

>>>>> **A C T I O N !** <<<<<

Problem-Solving Exercise

In which category of problem-solving style did you score highest? ....

Based on your result, answer the following questions.

1. What do you really like about your problem-solving style? What are your strong points?

   ....

   ....

2. What do others say you could do better in working with them?

   ....

   ....

3. What really stresses you out?

   ....

   ....

4. What kind of activities match your style in terms of creating social change?

   ....

   ....

How can the knowledge gained from the questions above be applied to work situations? Discuss what kind of work situations might best fit each problem-solving style. What are some of the challenges that coworkers who belong to different personality groupings might encounter with one another?

Myers-Briggs Type Indicator® Instrument

In 1921 Swiss psychologist Carl Jung (1875–1961) published the book *Psychological Types,* in which he argued that behavior follows patterns, and that these patterns are determined by the different ways people use their minds. In 1942 Isabel Briggs-Myers and her mother, Katharine Briggs, began to put Jung's theory into practice. They developed the Myers-Briggs Type Indicator instrument®, which after more than 50 years of research and refinement has become the most widely used instrument for identifying and studying personality. Following is an overview of the four temperaments put together by

David Keirsey and Marilyn Bates based on Myers-Briggs. They may help you determine your preferences for engaging as a citizen.

Extroversion versus introversion (E/I). This category deals with the way we interact with others and the world around us. *Extroverts* prefer to live in the outside world, drawing their strength from other people. They are outgoing and love interaction. They usually make decisions with others in mind. They enjoy being the center of attention.

Introverts draw their strength from the inner world. They need to spend time alone to think and ponder. They are usually quiet and reflective. They prefer to make decisions by themselves and do not like being the center of attention.

Sensing versus intuition (S/N). This category deals with the way we learn and deal with information. *Sensing* types gather information through their five senses. They have a hard time believing something if it cannot be seen, touched, smelled, tasted, or heard. They like concrete facts and details. They do not rely on intuition or gut feelings. They usually have a great deal of common sense.

Intuitive types are not very detail oriented. They can see possibilities, and they rely on their gut feelings. Usually, they are very innovative. They tend to live in the future and often get bored once they have mastered a task.

Thinking versus feeling (T/F). This category deals with the way we make decisions. *Thinkers* are very logical people. They do not make decisions based on feelings or emotions. They are analytical and sometimes do not take others' values into consideration when making decisions. They can easily identify the flaws of others. They can be seen as insensitive and lacking compassion.

Feelers make decisions based on what they feel is right and just. They like to have harmony, and they value others' opinions and feelings. They are usually very tactful people who like to please others.

Judging versus perceiving (J/P). This category deals with the way we live. *Judgers* are very orderly people. They must have a great deal of structure in their lives. They're good at setting goals and sticking to them. They seldom, if ever, play before their work is completed.

Perceivers are less structured and more spontaneous. They do not like timelines. Unlike judgers they will play before their work is done. They will take every chance to delay a decision or judgment. Sometimes, they can become involved with too many things at one time.

Matching Styles and Values to Action

Choosing activities and causes that are an appropriate match for your personal values and skills helps you engage positively as a citizen. Choosing how and where you engage using the tools and skills outlined in this chapter will help you practice democracy with integrity and efficacy.

Using the guidance of your own personal mission statement, you may have already distinguished causes or areas of interest that you want to explore. Once you choose an issue or organization, you must decide *how* you can best be of service.

You are now familiar with different styles of engagement and your preferences for engaging. If your style is that of the activist, you may find that you have a flair for participating in marches, public protests, or public education. If, however, you have more of a technician's style, you may find that you excel in helping favorite nonprofit organizations set up computer databases or Web sites. If you are more of an introvert, you may not choose to engage in fund-raising. You are more likely to be empowered as a citizen if you use your unique talents and are guided by your unique values.

Be creative. If no obvious fit exists between an issue or organization that interests you and what you feel you have to offer, consider inventing a way to engage. As you remain true to your personal gifts and interests and resolute in your desire to make a difference, you will find a way to serve your community and the world.

You can't wait for inspiration. You have to go after it with a club.

Jack London

CONSIDERING DIVERSITY

RELATING TO OTHERS

Among your most meaningful, life-changing experiences at college will be those that take you out of your "comfort zone" and force you to question your thinking and even your basic beliefs. Encountering the diversity of the people around you can inspire this kind of questioning. As you read this chapter, you will explore how accepting differences and rejecting prejudice can lead to respect for others and strong teamwork skills, both of which are key ingredients for success in school and beyond.

In this chapter, you will investigate how analytical, creative, and practical abilities can help you build the cultural competence that will allow you to relate successfully to others. You will explore how to communicate effectively, investigating different communication styles and methods for handling conflict. Finally, you will look at how your personal relationships can inspire you and enhance your college and life experience.

Being able to "recognize and respect people's diversity, individual experiences and perspectives" is highlighted by the Conference Board of Canada's Employability Skills 2000+ report. Furthermore, the Canadian Charter of Rights and Freedoms offers everyone in Canada "freedom of thought, belief and expression." Diversity isn't just part of your academic experience, it's part of every Canadian's life.

HOW DO YOU EXPERIENCE DIVERSITY?

Whether you grew up in a small town, a suburb, or a large city, inevitably you will encounter people who are nothing like anyone you've ever met. They may be of a different race or mix of races, have different religious beliefs, or express their sexuality in non-traditional ways. With society becoming more diverse, the likelihood of these encounters is increasing.

Canada has always been a nation of immigrants, and immigration levels are on the rise again. As Monica Boyd and Michael Vickers point out in their article "100 Years of Immigration in Canada," "Record numbers of immigrants came to Canada in the early

1900s. During World War I and the Depression years, numbers declined, but by the close of the 20th Century, they had again approached those recorded almost 100 years earlier."[1] According to Statistics Canada's *The Daily,* immigrants make up roughly 18 percent of Canada's population. While early immigrants to Canada tended to come from Europe, recent immigrants tend to come from Asia and the Middle East. Seventy-three per cent of new immigrants to Canada live in three general areas: Vancouver, Montreal, and Toronto.[2]

The Diversity Within You

To think about the concept of diversity, look first within yourself. You are a complex jumble of internal and external characteristics that makes you markedly different than everyone else. Just as no two snowflakes are alike, no two people are alike—not even identical twins.

Everything about you—your gender, race, ethnicity, sexual orientation, age, unique personality, talents, and skills—adds up to who you are. Accepting your strengths and weaknesses, your background and group identity is a sign of psychological health. You have every reason to feel proud and to make no apologies for your choices, as long as they do not intentionally hurt anyone.

Diversity on Campus

College and university campuses reflect society, so diversity on campus is on the upswing. You are likely to meet classmates or instructors who reflect Canada's growing diversity, including:

- bi- or multiracial individuals or individuals who come from families with more than one religious tradition.
- non-native people who speak English as a second language and who may be immigrants.
- people who are older than "traditional" 18- to 22-year-old students.
- classmates and instructors in wheelchairs or who have other disabilities.
- people practising different lifestyles—often expressed in the way they dress, their interests, their sexual orientation, and leisure activities.

Every time you meet someone new, you have a *choice* about how to relate—or whether to relate at all. No one can force you to interact or to adopt a particular attitude because it is "right." Considering two important responsibilities may help you analyze your options:

Your responsibility to yourself is to carefully consider your feelings. Observe your reactions to others. Then, use critical thinking to make decisions that are fair to others and right for you.

Your responsibility to others lies in treating people with tolerance and respect. You won't like everyone, but acknowledging that others have a right to their

FIGURE 3.1 *The value of an open-minded approach to diversity in Canada.*

Your Role	Situation	Closed-Minded Actions	Open-Minded Actions
Fellow student	For an assignment, you are paired with a student old enough to be your mother.	You assume the student will be clueless about the modern world. You think she might preach to you about how to do the assignment.	You get to know the student as an individual. You stay what open to you can learn from her experiences and knowledge.
Friend	You are invited to dinner at a friend's house. When he introduces you to his partner, you realize that he is gay.	You are turned off by the idea of two men in a relationship. You make an excuse to leave early. You avoid your friend after that.	You have dinner with the two men and make an effort to get to know more about them, individually and as a couple.
Employee	Your new boss is of a different racial and cultural background than yours.	You assume that you and your new boss don't have much in common. You think he will be distant and uninterested in you.	You rein in your stereotypes. You pay close attention to how your new boss communicates and leads. You adapt to his style and make an effort to get to know him better.

opinions builds understanding. Being open-minded rather than closed-minded about others is necessary for relationships to thrive.

Figure 3.1 demonstrates the dramatic difference between an open-minded and a closed-minded approach to diversity.

Accepting others depends on being able to answer the following question with a firm yes: *Do I always give people a chance no matter who they are?* Prejudice, stereotyping, and discrimination often get in the way of fairness to others. Your problem-solving skills will help you overcome these barriers.

> Minds are like parachutes. They only function when they are open.
>
> Sir James Dewar

HOW CAN YOU DEVELOP CULTURAL COMPETENCE?

Cultural competence refers to the ability to understand and appreciate differences among people and change your behaviour in a way that enhances, rather than detracts from, relationships and communication. According to the National Center for Cultural Competence, to develop cultural competence you must act upon the following five steps:[3]

1. Value diversity.
2. Identify and evaluate personal perceptions and attitudes.
3. Be aware of what happens when different cultures interact.

4. Build knowledge about other cultures.

5. Use what you learn to adapt to diverse cultures as you encounter them.

As you develop cultural competence, you heighten your ability to analyze how people relate to one another. Most important, you develop practical skills that enable you to connect to others by bridging the gap between who you are and who they are.[4]

Identify and Evaluate Personal Perceptions and Attitudes

Whereas people may value the *concept* of diversity, attitudes and emotional responses may influence how they act when they confront the *reality* of diversity in their own lives. As a result, many people have prejudices that lead to damaging stereotypes.

Prejudice

prejudice—
a preconceived judgment or opinion, formed without just grounds or sufficient knowledge.

Almost everyone has some level of **prejudice**, meaning that they prejudge others, usually on the basis of characteristics such as gender, race, sexual orientation, and religion. People judge others without knowing anything about them because of

- *influence of family and culture.* Children learn attitudes, including intolerance, superiority, and hate, from their parents, peers, and community.
- *fear of differences.* It is human to fear, and to make assumptions about, the unfamiliar.
- *experience.* One bad experience with a person of a particular race or religion may lead someone to condemn all people with the same background.

Stereotypes

stereotype—
a standardized mental picture that represents an oversimplified opinion or uncritical judgment.

Prejudice is usually based on **stereotypes**—assumptions made without proof or critical thinking about the characteristics of a person or group of people. Stereotyping emerges from

- *a desire for patterns and logic.* People often try to make sense of the world by using the labels, categories, and generalizations that stereotypes provide.
- *media influences.* The more people see stereotypical images—the airhead beautiful blonde, the jolly fat man—the easier it is to believe that stereotypes are universal.
- *laziness.* Labelling group members according to a characteristic they seem to have in common takes less energy than exploring the qualities of individuals.

Stereotypes stall the growth of relationships because pasting a label on a person makes it hard for you to see the real person underneath. Even stereotypes that seem "positive" may not be true and may get in the way of perceiving people as individuals. Figure 3.2 shows some "positive" and "negative" stereotypes.

FIGURE 3.2 *Stereotypes involve generalizations that may not be accurate.*

Positive Stereotype	Negative Stereotype
Women are nurturing.	Women are too emotional for business.
White people are successful in business.	White people are cold and power hungry.
Gay men have a great sense of style.	Gay men are sissies.
People with disabilities have strength of will.	People with disabilities are bitter.
Older people are wise.	Older people are set in their ways.
Asians are good at math and science.	Asians are poor leaders.

Use your analytical abilities to question your own ideas and beliefs and to weed out the narrowing influence of prejudice and stereotyping. Giving honest answers to questions like the following is an essential step in the development of cultural competence:

- How do I react to differences?
- What prejudices or stereotypes come to mind when I see people in real life or the media who are a different colour than I am? From a different culture? Making different choices?
- Where did my prejudices and stereotypes come from?
- Are these prejudices fair? Are these stereotypes accurate?
- What harm can having these prejudices and believing these stereotypes cause?

With the knowledge you build as you answer these questions, move on to the next stage: Looking carefully at what happens when people from different cultures interact.

Be Aware of What Happens When Cultures Interact

As history has shown, when people from different cultures interact, they often experience problems caused by lack of understanding, by prejudice, and by stereotypic thinking. At their mildest, these problems create roadblocks that obstruct relationships and communication. At their worst, they set the stage for acts of discrimination and hate crimes.

Discrimination

Discrimination refers to actions that deny people equal employment, education, and housing opportunities, or that treat people as second-class citizens. If you are the victim of discrimination, it is important to know that the Canadian Charter of Rights and Freedoms is on your side: You cannot be denied basic opportunities and rights because of your race, creed, colour, age, gender, national or ethnic origin, religion, marital status, potential or actual pregnancy, or potential or actual illness or disability (unless the

GET CREATIVE!

EXPAND YOUR PERCEPTION OF DIVERSITY

Heighten your awareness of diversity by examining your own uniqueness.

Being able to respond to people as individuals requires that you become more aware of the diversity that is not always on the surface. Brainstorm ten words or phrases that describe you. The challenge: Keep references to your ethnicity or appearance (brunette, gay, Aboriginal, wheelchair dependent, and so on) to a minimum, and fill the rest of the list with characteristics others can't see at a glance (laid-back, only child, 24 years old, drummer, marathoner, interpersonal learner, and so on).

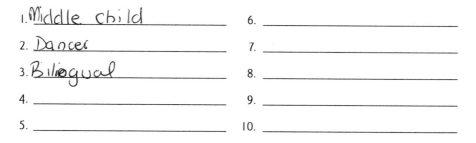

1. Middle child
2. Dancer
3. Bilingual
4. _____
5. _____
6. _____
7. _____
8. _____
9. _____
10. _____

Use a separate piece of paper to make a similar list for someone you know well—a friend or family member. Again, stay away from the most obvious visible characteristics. See if anything surprises you about the different image you create of this familiar person.

---

illness or disability prevents you from performing required tasks and unless accommodations are not possible).

Despite these legal protections, discrimination is common and often appears on campuses. Students may not want to work with students of other races. Members of campus clubs may reject prospective members because of religious differences. Outsiders may harass students attending gay and lesbian alliance meetings. Instructors may judge students according to their weight, accent, or body piercings.

Hate Crimes

hate crime—
a crime motivated by a hatred of a specific characteristic thought to be possessed by the victim.

When prejudice turns violent, it often manifests itself in **hate crimes** directed at racial, ethnic, and religious minorities, and at homosexuals. The Canadian Criminal Code defines hate crimes as crimes "motivated by bias, prejudice or hate based on race, national or ethnic origin, language, colour, religion, sex, age, mental or physical disability, sexual orientation, or any other similar factor." According to Statistics Canada's 2004 Pilot Survey of Hate Crime:[5]

- 57% of hate crimes are motivated by the victim's race or ethnicity.
- The most likely targets of hate crimes in Canada are Jews, Blacks, and Muslims.

▓ The most common incidents categorized as hate crimes include vandalism (the most common hate crime in Canada), assault, uttering threats, arson and hate propaganda. These statistics include only reported incidents, so they tell only a part of the story—many more crimes likely go unreported by victims fearful of what might happen if they contact authorities.

Build Cultural Knowledge

The successfully intelligent response to discrimination and hate, and the next step in your path toward cultural competence, is to gather knowledge. You have a personal responsibility to learn about people who are different from you, including those you are likely to meet on campus.

What are some practical ways to begin?

▓ *Read* newspapers, books, magazines, and Web sites.

▓ *Ask questions* of all kinds of people, about themselves and their traditions.

▓ *Observe* how people behave, what they eat and wear, how they interact with others.

▓ *Travel internationally* to unfamiliar places where you can experience firsthand different ways of living.

▓ *Travel locally* to equally unfamiliar places where you will encounter a variety of people.

▓ *Build friendships* with fellow students or co-workers you would not ordinarily approach.

Building knowledge also means exploring yourself. Talk with family, read, seek experiences that educate you about your own cultural heritage. Then share what you know with others.

Adapt to Diverse Cultures

Here's where you take everything you have gathered—your value of diversity, your self-knowledge, your understanding of how cultures interact, your information about different cultures—and put it to work with practical actions. With these actions you can improve how you relate to others and perhaps even change how people relate to one another on a larger scale. Think carefully and creatively about what kinds of actions feel right to you. Make choices that you feel comfortable with, that cause no harm, and that may make a difference, however small.

Dr. Martin Luther King Jr. believed that careful thinking could change attitudes. He said:

> The tough-minded person always examines the facts before he reaches conclusions: in short, he postjudges. The tender-minded person reaches conclusions before he has examined the first fact; in short, he prejudges and is prejudiced.... There is little hope for us until we become tough minded enough to break loose from the shackles of prejudice, half-truths, and down-right ignorance.[6]

When you meet different people, you discover many ways of being and learning. After having a stroke, this student learned how to write with her feet using a special device.

Try the following suggestions. In addition, let them inspire your own creative ideas about what else you can do in your daily life to improve how you relate to others.

Look Past External Characteristics

If you meet a woman with a disability, get to know her. She may be an accounting major, a daughter, and a mother. She may love baseball, politics, and science fiction novels. These characteristics—not just her physical person—describe who she is.

Put Yourself in Other People's Shoes

Shift your perspective and try to understand what other people feel, especially if there's a conflict. If you make a comment that someone interprets as offensive, for example, think about why what you said was hurtful. If you can talk about it with the person, you may learn even more about how he or she heard what you said and why.

Adjust to Cultural Differences

When you understand someone's way of being and put it into practice, you show respect and encourage communication. If a friend's family is formal at home, dress appropriately and behave formally when you visit. If an instructor maintains a lot of personal space, keep a respectful distance when you visit during office hours. If a study group member takes offence at a particular kind of language, avoid it when you meet.

Help Others in Need

Newspaper columnist Sheryl McCarthy wrote about an African American who, in the midst of the 1992 Los Angeles riots, saw an Asian American man being beaten and helped him to safety: "When asked why he risked grievous harm to save an Asian man he didn't even know, the African-American man said, 'Because if I'm not there to help someone else, when the mob comes for me, will there be someone there to save me?'"[7]

Stand Up Against Prejudice, Discrimination, and Hate

When you hear a prejudiced remark or notice discrimination taking place, think about what you can do to encourage a move in the right direction. You may choose to make a comment, or to get help by approaching an authority such as an instructor or dean.

Sound the alarm on hate crimes—let authorities know if you suspect that a crime is about to occur, join campus protests, support organizations that encourage tolerance.

Recognize that People Everywhere Have the Same Basic Needs

Everyone loves, thinks, hurts, hopes, fears, and plans. When you are trying to find common ground with diverse people, remember that you are united first through your essential humanity.

KENTE

The African word *kente* means "that which will not tear under any condition." *Kente* cloth is worn by men and women in African countries such as Ghana, Ivory Coast, and Togo. There are many brightly coloured patterns of *kente,* each beautiful, unique, and special.

Think of how this concept applies to people. Like the cloth, all people are unique, with brilliant and subdued aspects. Despite mistreatment or misunderstanding by others, you need to remain strong so that you don't tear, allowing the weaker fibres of your character to show through. The *kente* of your character can help you endure, stand up against injustice, and fight peacefully but relentlessly for the rights of all people.

Endnotes

1. Monica Boyd and Michael Vickers, "100 Years of Immigration in Canada," *Canadian Social Trends.* Autumn 2000, p. 2.
2. Statistics Canada, *The Daily.* Tuesday, January 21, 2003.
3. "Conceptual Frameworks/Models, Guiding Values and Principles," National Center for Cultural Competence, 2002 [on-line]. Available at: http://gucchd.georgetown.edu/nccc/framework.html (May 2004).
4. Information in the sections on the five stages of building competency is based on Mark A. King, Anthony Sims, and David Osher, "How Is Cultural Competence Integrated in Education?" Cultural Competence [on-line]. Available at: www.air.org/cecp/cultural/Q_integrated.htm#def (May 2004).
5. Statistics Canada, *The Daily.* June 1, 2004.
6. Martin Luther King, Jr., from his sermon, "A Tough Mind and a Tender Heart," *Strength in Love.* Philadelphia: Fortress Press. 1986, p. 14.
7. Sheryl McCarthy, *Why Are the Heroes Always White?* p. 137.

DEFINING THE COMMON GOOD

Tens of thousands of protesters demonstrated in Quebec City in April 2001 as government leaders and officials from thirty-four countries met to discuss the establishment of a free-trade area that would include almost all of North and South America. Generally, the protesters were peaceful. However, some of the youthful protesters hurled teddy bears, rocks, and other objects across the 3.8-kilometre-long chain-link fence that had been erected to keep protesters out of the centre of Quebec City, where the Summit of the Americas was being held. Police responded with tear gas, pepper spray, rubber bullets, and stun guns. About four hundred protesters were arrested. Fifty-seven protesters and forty-five police officers were hurt.

The protest was part of the anti-globalization movement that had shut down meetings of the World Trade Organization in Seattle in 1999 and continues to demonstrate at the meetings of various international organizations committed to developing a global free-market capitalist economy. The Quebec City protesters—including students, environmentalists, trade unionists, social activists, and nationalists from many countries, but especially from across Canada—argued that the proposed Free Trade Area of the Americas (FTAA) agreement would give private, profit-oriented corporations the right to provide such public services as education and health care and reduce governments' power to protect the environment and workers.

The events at Quebec City illustrate some important features of the nature of politics. For example, exaggeration is commonplace as interested parties struggle to affect public opinion. Members of the general public who tried to make sense of the Quebec City events received very different interpretations from government, protesters, and the media. The Canadian government claimed that the summit was a major step toward ensuring democracy throughout the Americas. Protesters asserted that the terms of a free-trade agreement would subvert democracy in the interests of big corporations. The mass media highlighted the clashes between protesters and police, but generally devoted little attention to the arguments for and against the proposed free-trade agreement.

Politics involves not only governments, legislatures, and politicians, but also a wide range of groups and individuals. Different interests, values, opinions, and perspectives are responsible for many of the conflicts that occur in politics and make achieving the common good of the political community a difficult challenge, as we discuss in this chapter.

POLITICS AND CONFLICT

Conflict and disagreement are important basic features of politics for four major reasons:

- people have different interests
- people embrace different values
- people have different identities
- people struggle for power in the political arena

Different Interests

The policies that are adopted for a political community often benefit (or harm) some members of the political community more than others. For example, the business community generally supports free trade because it expects to benefit by having better access to larger markets for its goods and services. Business executives like the fact that free-trade agreements can limit governments' ability to pass laws and regulations that restrict trade and investment. In general, the business community sees free-trade agreements as desirable because they reduce the ability of government to "interfere" in business decision making.

Unions, on the other hand, worry that free-trade agreements will make it easier for business to relocate to low-wage countries. The workers that unions represent may face the loss of their jobs or pressure to accept lower wages and poorer working conditions. And student organizations are concerned when they see proposals for free trade in services because they fear that this will lead to the erosion of publicly funded education by making it easier for profit-seeking corporations to provide educational services.

Different Values

The values that people seek to achieve through political action are undoubtedly affected by their interests. We are not surprised when we hear business people praise the free-enterprise economic system and seek to reduce government regulation of business. Nor are we surprised when students demand lower tuition fees and criticize policies that might undermine publicly funded education. Of course, people will refer to general values that have widespread support to try to justify political actions designed to advance their own personal interests. For example, business people asking for a government subsidy argue that it will be good for job creation, regional development, or Canada's technological advancement—not that it will make them richer.

Nevertheless, the values that people seek to obtain through politics are not only a product of their own interests and circumstances. Consider students who are active in the non-governmental organization Oxfam because of a concern about poverty in Africa, or who participate in the letter-writing campaigns of Amnesty International because they want to promote human rights around the world. They are not seeking benefits for themselves, but rather are acting to pursue their values. These values reflect their view of what is good for humanity.

The pursuit of values, like the pursuit of one's own interests, can be a source of political conflict. For example, the disputes between pro-life and pro-choice activists over the issue of abortion reflect differences in deeply held values. Although differences concerning interests can often be settled by compromise, it can sometimes be difficult or impossible to find an acceptable compromise when opposing values are at stake. Neither pro-life nor pro-choice groups would likely be satisfied with a compromise in which abortion was legal in certain but limited circumstances.

Fortunately, there are often a variety of general values that are widely shared within a political community. For example, most Canadians would agree that freedom, equality, justice, order, prosperity, and peace are desirable values. This does not mean that we all think about these values in the same way. For example, some people think of equality as existing when all persons have the same rights and are treated in the same way by the law. Others argue that equality exists only if each individual has the same opportunity to get ahead in life. Still others define equality in terms of an equal sharing of the wealth of the country. Thus, we may agree that equality is desirable, but disagree about its meaning and consequently what policies are desirable to achieve greater equality.

Furthermore, different people often place a different priority on the values that they share with others. For example, even though many people value both freedom and order, these values sometimes conflict. For those who place a higher value on freedom, police attempts to limit protest activity in the name of maintaining order may be viewed as unjustified. Those who place a higher value on order may expect the police to curtail protest demonstrations because of the risk of unruly behaviour.

The existence of shared values, therefore, does not eliminate disagreement over the policies that a political community should adopt. However, it can be the basis for discussion about how best to achieve the shared values and for co-operation in achieving goals based on those values.

Different Identities

People within a political community will often identify with one or more particular groups. One may, for example, think of oneself primarily as Canadian, Québécois, or Albertan; Italian-Canadian, Aboriginal, or black; gay, working class, or Muslim; female, student, or Catholic; or various combinations of such identities. Those identifying with particular groups will often evaluate the actions of government or the platforms of political parties in light of those identities. This may involve seeking redress for perceived injustices, equitable representation for their group in Parliament, assistance in preserving or developing their identity, some ability for the group to govern itself, or simply some form of recognition of the worthiness of the group.

Different identities can lead to conflict and disagreement because of the different interests or values of groups. However, the desire for recognition can also lead to disagreement. For example, the idea that the distinctive identity of Quebec society should be recognized in the Canadian constitution has resulted in serious political disagreements.

The Competitive Struggle for Power

When we think about politics, our attention is often drawn to the struggle for political power. High-profile political events such as election campaigns, the selection of the leader of a political party, and Question Period in the House of Commons can be easily understood as part of an ongoing struggle for power.

Most politicians enjoy being in positions of political power and vigorously compete to gain and maintain their positions. The desire to have power to affect or control decision making for the community and the longing for the status of high political office can be strong motivating factors for political competition. As well, some people engage in political activity because they enjoy the competition that it often involves. To work hard for a candidate or party and see them win an election can be as exciting as being on a winning hockey team.

"Don't they understand that politics is about power?"

Most political activity, however, is motivated primarily by a desire to affect the direction and policies of the political community. Power is usually a means to an end rather than a goal in itself (Easton, 1953). Even on the international level where the pursuit of power is often most evident, power is often sought to achieve particular objectives, such as protecting the security of a country, rather than for its own sake.

The extent to which the interests and values of a particular group are taken into account in decision making is strongly affected by the power that a group is able to bring to bear in affecting that decision. The demonstrators protesting in Quebec City were trying to show that they were not simply powerless individuals who could be ignored: rather, they were a group that needed to be reckoned with. By mobilizing a substantial number of determined supporters and attracting media attention, they were able to raise concerns that might otherwise have gone unnoticed. The general public was largely unaware of the Summit of the Americas and the issues involved in negotiating the FTAA until the public spectacle of the demonstrations brought it to their attention.

Raising public awareness is one way in which a group can try to affect government politics, particularly in the long run. In the short run, however, the Quebec City demonstration had little effect on the free-trade negotiations, other than encouraging government spokespersons to emphasize the democratic principles agreed to at the Summit of the Americas.[1] Other powerful forces, such as the business representatives who were directly involved in consultations about free-trade negotiations and had good access to top government officials, likely have had a greater impact on the positions taken by the Canadian government. Power is often exercised behind closed doors and is thus not visible to the casual observer.

Politics and Conflict Resolution

Although war and violent forms of conflict are a significant part of the reality of politics, most conflicts and disagreements are settled in a more peaceful fashion. Indeed, much political activity is directed at the resolution of conflicts. Governments and political parties often attempt to find compromises to try to keep different groups reasonably satisfied. In the view of British political scientist Bernard Crick (1963), politics in democratic countries involves listening to discordant interests, conciliating them, and bringing them together so that each contributes positively to the process of governing. When decisions are made after considerable discussion, consultation with groups that have differing interests and values, and efforts to find acceptable compromises, a consensus about a particular course of action may develop. The use of fair and widely accepted procedures for making decisions can assist in resolving conflicts and gaining acceptance for the decisions that are made.

Because human beings are not only competitive individuals concerned with their own interests, but also social beings concerned with the well-being of the communities with which they identify, political conflicts can be resolved, particularly where shared values are present within the community. Thus although disagreement and conflict is an important feature of politics, the attention given to political conflict by the media can lead us to overlook the extent of co-operation and consensus that exists in well-functioning political communities.

BASIC CONCEPTS

Politics

Politics can be viewed as a feature of all organized human activity (Leftwich, 1983). In all groups, disagreements arise as to what should be done, and different people try to get the group to adopt the course of action they prefer. Relationships of power and authority (discussed below) are important in any group, whether a family, a business, a religious organization, or the government (Dahl, 1984). However, political science generally focuses on such characteristics as they relate to the making of governing decisions.

David Easton's definition of politics as the "authoritative allocation of values for a society" (1953, p. 129) is widely used by political scientists. The "allocation of values" refers to how the limited resources of a society (more generally, those things that are desired or valued) are allocated (distributed). By referring to the *authoritative* allocation of values, Easton suggests that what is distinctive about the allocation of values through governmental institutions is that this allocation is generally accepted as binding on all persons in the community. People feel that they should accept or obey the policies of government that affect them (Easton, 1953). Politics, in this view, "concerns all those varieties of activity that influence significantly the kind of authoritative policy adopted for a society and the way it is put into practice" (Easton, 1953, p. 128). However, while many government decisions are authoritative, governments also take actions that are not considered binding on the members of the political community. For example, governments try to persuade us to adopt healthier lifestyles and often enter into voluntary agreements with industries to reduce pollution.

Politics— activity related to influencing, making, or implementing collective decisions for a political community.

For the purposes of this book, we define **politics** as activity related to influencing, making, or implementing collective decisions for a political community. Political activity includes trying to influence government decisions and policies, mobilizing support for political parties seeking to gain or maintain control of the government, and trying to change or maintain the basic characteristics of the political community. Raising awareness of problems affecting the political community and efforts to change political values, attitudes, and opinions can also be viewed as political. As well (as discussed in Box 4.1, A Broader View of Politics), taking action concerning problems that some believe should be the subject of collective decisions might also be considered political.

Power

Discussion and analysis of politics often focuses on power. Statements such as "the prime minister is very powerful," "big business is more powerful than ordinary citizens," and "the United States is the most powerful country in the world" are very frequently made. Determining the validity of such statements, however, can be difficult and controversial. Nevertheless, power is important in affecting what gets done in political life.

We often think of political activity as involving the struggle for political power and the attempts to influence the decisions of government. But this may be too limited a focus. Consider the following example.

Various environmental groups have sought to end the clear-cutting practices of forest companies in British Columbia. Having had limited success in persuading the B.C. government to pass stricter logging regulations, they turned to other methods to achieve their objective. Europeans were encouraged to participate in a boycott of products made with B.C. lumber, and pressure was put on retail businesses such as Home Depot only to sell lumber produced in an environmentally friendly manner. These activities had considerable success, and a number of B.C. forest companies began to change their logging practices.

In many ways, these activities by environmental groups are similar to what we normally consider as political. People were mobilized to try to achieve an objective that was viewed as being in the public interest. Rather than influencing government to adopt a policy that might change the actions of logging companies, environmental groups were able to directly pressure some of the companies to change their actions to deal with a public problem. The activities of environmental groups might therefore be considered political, even though the groups decided to try to affect the decisions of private businesses rather than the decisions of government.

Power can be defined as the ability to achieve an objective by influencing the behaviour of others (Nye, 2004), particularly to get them to do what they would not have otherwise done.[2] Power, in this definition, is a relationship among different individuals and groups. As such, it is not easily quantifiable and changes depending on the objective being pursued and the circumstances involved. For example, the president of the United States may be very powerful in decisions concerning the deployment of armed forces, but less powerful when trying to change American agricultural policies.

Power does not necessarily mean that one actor controls or dominates others, although the term is generally used to refer to situations where one actor is in a stronger position than other actors. Politics typically involves considerable bargaining and negotiating among different actors. Although bargaining sometimes involves exchange among equals (as when two legislators agree to support each other's proposals), the type of bargain achieved often reflects differences in power among the parties to the bargain. For example, rich countries may be in a better position than poor countries to negotiate an international trade agreement favourable to their interests because of their greater power, even if some concessions are made to poorer countries to gain their agreement or to legitimate the agreement.

Political power can be exerted in several different ways.[3] *Coercion* involves using fear or threats of harmful consequences to achieve an outcome. For example, Nazi

Power–
the ability to achieve an objective by influencing the behaviour of others, particularly to get them to do what they would not have otherwise done.

Germany's threat to invade Czechoslovakia in 1938 was successful in convincing the Czech government to allow Germany to annex part of its territory. If your employer threatens to fire you unless you work on behalf of a certain candidate in an election, coercive power has been used to intimidate you. *Inducements* involve achieving an outcome by offering a reward or bribe. For example, if your employer promises to give you a promotion should you decide to support a particular candidate, power has been exercised in the form of an inducement. *Persuasion* is a very important aspect of political life, as people are often involved in trying to persuade other people to think and act in particular ways. Persuasion may involve the use of truthful information to encourage people to act in accordance with their own interests or values, or the use of misleading information to manipulate people. In practice, it is often difficult to distinguish between persuasion based on truthful information and persuasion involving manipulation, as exaggeration and selective presentation of the facts are often used to make a persuasive argument. Power can also be exercised through *leadership*. For example, a country that is successful in providing wealth and harmony to its population may be better able to convince other countries to follow its example (Nye, 2004).

Power is often viewed negatively because of its association with domination. Those in governing positions have used the power they wield to establish, promote, or defend systems of economic, social, military, and ideological power involving domination and exploitation. As well, there are always tendencies for those with political power to use their power for their own benefit rather than for the good of the political community. In addition, those in powerful positions may become arrogant and unresponsive to the needs and desires of the population. As American Senator William Fulbright put it, "power has a way of undermining judgment, of planting delusions of grandeur in the minds of otherwise sensible people and otherwise sensible nations" (cited in Lobe, 2002, p. 3).

Power is often thought of in terms of some people, groups, or countries having *power over* others. However, we can also think about the *power to* achieve collective goals. Power is often necessary to induce people to co-operate in order to achieve objectives that benefit themselves and the political community as a whole, such as developing the economy, providing security, or protecting the environment. Such objectives may not be easily achieved by individuals, but might be achievable by using the collective power of the community organized by government. This can

Free rider problem— a problem with voluntary collective action that results because an individual can enjoy the benefits of group action without contributing.

be illustrated by what is known as the **free rider problem**. Imagine that all persons in a community agreed they would each contribute to building a road that would benefit everyone. One miserly individual might decide not to contribute to the cost of building the road, knowing that the road would still be built with the contributions of others. However, if enough people followed this self-interested logic, the road might never be built and everyone would suffer. The use of the coercive power of government (for example, to enforce the payment of taxes) is often useful or necessary to achieve the common good. However, as Box 4.2, The Tragedy of the Commons, illustrates, there are sometimes alternatives to the use of coercive action by government to achieve the common good.

The Distribution of Power

In any society, the resources that give individuals and groups the potential to exert political power are unequally distributed. Wealth, control of important aspects of the economy, social status and prestige, official position, control of information and expertise, the ability to mobilize supporters, control of the means of force, and the ability to influence people are some of the resources that can be used for advantage in politics. Although all citizens in a democracy have some potential power through their ability to vote, other resources are less equally distributed.

Understanding the distribution of power involves more than adding up the resources available to different groups. Groups differ in how effectively they use their power resources. Some groups are more successful than others in mobilizing potential supporters, forming alliances with other groups, and appealing to the values and beliefs of the community to achieve their objectives. As Box 4.3, People Power, illustrates, mobilizing ordinary citizens around a popular cause can sometimes bring about fundamental changes.

BOX 4.2   THE TRAGEDY OF THE COMMONS

In a famous article Garrett Hardin (1968) asks us to imagine a situation where herders allow their flocks to graze on a common pasture (that is, a pasture available freely to all members of the community). To make more money, each herder may find it profitable to purchase more cattle to graze on the common land. Eventually, the pasture will be overgrazed and all will suffer. One solution would be to privatize the commons, with the owner then charging a fee to allow each head of cattle to graze there. This would, however, not necessarily lead to the common good, as only those who could afford the fee could then graze their cattle, or the owner might convert the pasture to another, more profitable endeavour. The alternative that Hardin favours involves a coercive government ensuring that the commons is not overused.

However, Elinor Ostrom (2000), looking at a variety of real-world situations, points out that under the right circumstances co-operation among the users of a common resource, such as water or pastures, can result in the proper management of that resource. These conditions include the development of a sense of community, shared values, and mechanisms to monitor and enforce the use of the resource to ensure that no cheating occurs. In contrast to Hardin's bleak outlook, which suggests that a dictatorial, overbearing global government is needed to solve global environmental problems such as overpopulation, Ostrom's analysis points to the possibility that co-operation to achieve solutions potentially can be arrived at even when individuals are concerned with their own interests, provided that there is trust and discussion among the members of the community. To what extent this can apply to global problems remains an open question, although Ostrom suggests that co-operative institutions in combination with governments and markets can be useful in dealing with global environmental problems (Dietz, Ostrom, & Stern, 2003).

TABLE 4.1   *The Three Faces of Power*

FIRST FACE	Ability to affect decisions
SECOND FACE	Ability to ensure that issues are not raised
THIRD FACE	Ability to affect the dominant ideas of society

The power of different groups is not only a product of their skill in mobilizing resources. Political institutions may be organized and operate in ways that advantage or disadvantage certain groups. For example, until recently the House of Lords, the upper chamber of the British Parliament, was designed to try to entrench the power of the aristocracy. Likewise, the method of allocating representatives to the provincial legislatures in some Canadian provinces deliberately overrepresents rural areas, thus giving the people of those areas greater potential power than if there was equal representation by population.

Analysts often disagree about how concentrated or dispersed power is in particular political communities. In part, these disagreements are a result of different perspectives about power, which can lead to different conclusions about the distribution of power and about who is powerful. Disagreements about how to analyze the distribution of power can be summarized as the **three faces of power** (see Table 4.1).

Three faces of power— the argument that looking at who affects particular decisions is insufficient to analyze power. Power can also involve the ability to keep issues off the political agenda and the ability to affect the dominant values of society.

The Three Faces of Power

One way to assess the distribution of power is to examine which groups or individuals are most successful in affecting a variety of decisions (the "first face" of power). If, for example, one group is usually successful in getting its way, then we would conclude that political power is highly concentrated. If, on the other hand, a variety of groups representing different interests had a significant influence on decisions, or if different groups influenced different decisions, we would conclude that political power is dispersed rather than concentrated.

However, some have argued that measuring political power in terms of who influenced particular decisions does not tell us the complete story. Bachrach and Baratz (1962) point out that power can be manifested not only by winning on contentious issues, but also by ensuring that certain issues are not raised in the first place. They call this deliberate avoidance of an important problem a "non-decision." For example, the owner of a polluting factory may be said to be powerful if discussion of the pollution problem is deliberately avoided by the political leaders of the community or by the media. In other words, this "second face" of power involves exercising control over the **political agenda**, that is, the issues that are considered important and are given priority in political deliberations.

Political agenda— the issues that are considered important and given priority in political deliberations.

Steven Lukes (1974) argues that there is a third face of power that is ignored when we focus on who influences specific decisions and "non-decisions." Those who are able to shape the dominant ideas in a society will have a general effect on the politics of that society and the decisions that are made. If those dominant ideas work against the interests of the weaker groups in society, and result in the weaker groups acting against their own "true" interests, then power has been exercised.

BOX 4.3   PEOPLE POWER

Those who control large corporations, occupy top government positions, or head major social organizations clearly have many resources that can be used to affect what the political community does. Occasionally, however, groups and individuals with seemingly few resources are able to bring about major changes.

The dictatorial Philippine government of Ferdinand Marcos was successfully challenged in 1986 when a very large number of people, including praying nuns, sat down in front of the army's tanks and refused to move. In Eastern Europe, peaceful demonstrations by ever-larger numbers of people helped to bring down communist regimes in 1989. Black South Africans, by engaging in a determined struggle against the white minority-controlled government and organizing international support for their cause, were eventually successful in challenging the system of apartheid that had suppressed them. Canadian Aboriginals, who in the past were ignored by the political system, have been able to make their voices heard through successful legal cases in the

People power. Citizens of Prague, Czechoslovakia, turned out by the hundreds of thousands in November 1989 to protest the Communist regime led by General Secretary Milos Jakes. Just one month later, the regime toppled peacefully, and the formerly Communist Assembly elected Václav Havel, leader of the pro-democracy Civic Forum, as the country's president.

courts, confrontation with Canadian authorities, and building a strong moral case that they have been treated unjustly. In each case, ordinary or disadvantaged people were able to challenge the powerful through determined and skilful action, even though serious personal risks and sacrifices were involved.

Of course, "people power" is not always successful. For example, in the People's Republic of China, student-led actions to support demands for democracy were brutally suppressed by the army on orders from the Communist party leadership in 1989. Despite the outrage in many parts of the world when news coverage revealed the suppression of peaceful protest, the Chinese government did not back away from its hard-line stance.

Take, for example, societies where women are expected to confine themselves to domestic responsibilities such as cooking, cleaning, and raising children, while men are involved in public activities, including politics. Ideas that these "separate spheres" are "natural" or that women do not have the qualities to participate in public life might lead many women to believe that the proper role of women is different from that of men, and thus not to challenge that system. Power, in this case, has been exerted through the dominant ideas that favour the interests of men, rather than through coercion or particular governmental decisions.

A problem with Lukes' analysis is that it is often difficult and controversial to determine what a person or group's true interests are. For example, are workers who vote for a party that favours policies that give tax breaks to promote business activity acting against their true interests? Further, the assumption that the leading ideas in a society necessarily reflect and serve the interests of the dominant groups in society is contentious. For example, the traditional ideas concerning the proper role of women that reflected male dominance have been challenged in Canada and a number of other societies in recent decades Likewise, the free-market capitalist ideas that work to the advantage of big business interests, although influential, have not been wholeheartedly accepted by a substantial proportion of the population.

Nevertheless, Lukes' analysis is useful in pointing out that power not only can be thought of as the ability to directly affect the behaviour of others, but also can operate indirectly by shaping people's ideas and preferences, which, in turn, affects how they act (Hay, 1997; Nye, 2004).

The Concentration of Power

Pluralist perspective— the freedom of individuals to establish and join groups that are not controlled by the government results in a wide variety of groups having an ability to influence the decisions of government, with no group dominant.

Studies of the distribution of power in terms of who influences the decision making in some American communities have suggested that power is not highly concentrated in a small number of hands (Dahl, 1961). In the **pluralist perspective**, a wide variety of groups has an ability to influence the decisions of government in democratic systems that allow groups the freedom to organize and take action. Some groups may have a greater ability than others to influence particular types of decisions, but no one group or set of groups has the dominant influence on most or all decisions.

Elitist perspective— the view that power in all communities is concentrated in a small number of hands, particularly in the elites that hold the top positions in the major institutions of the economy, society, and politics.

Others, however, have tried to show that power in all communities is concentrated in a small number of hands, particularly in the elites that hold the top positions in the major institutions of the economy, society, and politics (Panitch, 1995). Those who take this **elitist perspective** often focus on the interconnections among elite groups, their common backgrounds, and the extent to which they have a shared outlook that would bias their key decisions (Scott, 2001). For example, C. Wright Mills (1956) argued that a power elite, consisting of the top government, business, and military leaders, was crucial in setting the direction of the United States. In Canada, John Porter (1965) found that the political elite interacted with the economic elite and shared their conservative values. Power was, in Porter's view, largely concentrated in the hands of various connected elites. There was, however, disagreement from time to time, particularly between the economic and political elites.

Generally, the pluralist view sees democratic politics as working to satisfy (though not necessarily perfectly) the wishes of a wide variety of interests in society. The elitist view is more critical, suggesting that democratic procedures hide the reality that the "true" interests of much of society are not properly served. Elites are able not only to influence government decisions and "non-decisions," but also to influence the leading ideas of the society as a whole in ways that serve their own interests. Pluralists see government as open to influence from a wide variety of groups while elitists view the ruling elites as a group that is largely "closed off" from the ruled (Evans, 2006).

Authority and Legitimacy

Authority, the right to exercise power, is of special importance in understanding politics. Those with political authority claim that they have been *authorized* (whether by God, tradition, constitutional rules, election, or some other source) to govern. Political authority that is accepted by those being governed (or at least not challenged by a significant part of the population) can be described as legitimate. Although **legitimacy** may be established by legal procedures, legitimacy (as used in political science) refers more generally to the acceptance of the right to rule of those in positions of authority whether or not it was established by law.

Establishing and Maintaining Legitimacy

How is the legitimacy of a system of governing established and maintained? Why do most Canadians accept the right of a few people to make decisions for the political community, even though they may not agree with the decisions that are being made? German sociologist Max Weber (1864–1920) described three basic types of authority, each of which could try to establish its legitimacy in its own way:

* charismatic authority
* traditional authority
* legal–rational authority

Charismatic authority is based on the perception that a leader has extraordinary or supernatural qualities established through such means as performing miracles, issuing prophecies, or leading a military victory. The legitimacy of charismatic authority "rests upon the belief in magical powers, revelations and hero worship" by the followers

Authority—
the right to exercise power. Those with political authority claim that they have been *authorized* to govern.

Legitimacy—
acceptance by the members of a political community that those in positions of authority have the right to govern.

Charismatic authority—
authority based on the perception that a leader has extraordinary or supernatural qualities.

Charismatic leaders, such as Mao Zedong, leader of the Chinese Communist revolution, inspire intense devotion in their followers. Charismatic authority rests upon the belief of followers in magical powers, revelations, and hero worship. The Chinese media depicted an elderly Mao supposedly performing the heroic feat of swimming across the Yangtze River to maintain his charismatic image.

(Weber, 1958, p. 296). Charismatic leaders, such as Mao Zedong, leader of the Chinese Communist revolution, have inspired intense devotion in their followers.

Traditional authority, whether exercised through the elders of a tribe or a ruling family, is based on customs that establish the right of certain persons to rule. The traditional authority of monarchs who inherited their position was often buttressed with the idea that rulers had a divinely created right to rule that was sanctified by religious authorities. Japanese emperors, for example, claimed to be descended from the sun goddess. The legitimacy of traditional authority can be based on beliefs that a certain family has always ruled and that customs are sacred practices that will bring evil consequences if violated (Weber, 1958).

Modern societies, in Weber's view, are characterized by efficient management and bureaucratic organization. The **legal–rational authority** of modern societies is based on legal rules and procedures rather than on the personal qualities or characteristics of the rulers. Authority is impersonal in the sense that it rests in official positions such as prime minister or president, rather than in the individuals holding such positions. The right of those in governing positions to rule is based on being chosen by a set of established and accepted legal procedures. Those holding official positions are expected to act in accordance with legal rules and procedures. Thus, their authority is limited. The legitimacy of the system of governing is based on a belief in the legality of the procedures for selecting those who have official duties and the legal "correctness" of the procedures that are used in governing (Weber, 1958).

Holding free and fair elections involving all adult citizens to designate those authorized to make governing decisions is often considered to be the most effective way of establishing the legitimacy of government. Nevertheless, a "legitimacy crisis" can occur even in democratic systems (Habermas, 1975). Although an unpopular government in a democracy can be voted out, if governments are persistently ineffective in dealing with serious problems, citizens might question the legitimacy of the democratic institutions and processes in their country. For example, if the policies of successive governments led to widespread poverty and unemployment or to a collapse in the value of the currency, then the legitimacy of the system of governing might be challenged. Legitimacy can also be reduced if some groups feel that there is a long-term pattern of mistreatment by the government. In other words, legitimacy not only may require an acceptance of the procedures by which governing authorities are chosen and actions taken, but also may depend on the perceived rightfulness of how government (or more generally the system of governing) exercises its authority (Barnard, 2001). In particular, the governing authorities will have a higher level of legitimacy if their actions are perceived as being consistent with the general principles and values of the political community (Gilley, 2006).

In addition, a system of governing that is imposed on a country or on a part of the population without its consent might be viewed by as illegitimate, even if it establishes democratic procedures. For example, when a democratic system of governing was established in Germany after the First World War, some Germans doubted its legitimacy, partly because they viewed it as being imposed on the country by the victors in that war. The problem of legitimacy, combined with the failure of German governments

---

Traditional authority— authority based on customs that establish the right of certain persons to rule.

Legal-rational authority— The right to rule based on legal rules and procedures rather than on the personal qualities or characteristics of the rulers.

to deal effectively with the problems the country faced, eventually contributed to the demise of the democratic system and the takeover by Adolf Hitler and the Nazi party. Likewise, conquered peoples are often unwilling to accept the authority of the governing authorities regardless of how well the authorities govern.

The Significance of Legitimacy

Effective governing depends not only on governing institutions having the power to force people to act in certain ways, but also on their ability to establish and maintain legitimate authority. A government that is not accepted as legitimate by a significant proportion of the population will have to devote much of its energy and resources to persuading or coercing the population to obey its laws and maintain order. All governments rely on coercion and other forms of power to some extent, but generally people feel an obligation to obey a legitimate government. Thus, a government whose rule is considered legitimate can rely more on authority than on coercion to get people to obey the laws it adopts.

Having legitimate authority gives government a powerful resource to achieve its goals. People usually obey laws, even when they find those laws against their interests or values, because they view the source of those laws as legitimate. This can potentially allow the government to act for the good of the community as a whole, even when some may object to the policies adopted. However, even though most people would agree that political authority is a necessary and desirable feature of an orderly society, questions can arise concerning whether there are circumstances in which authority should be resisted or disobeyed. What would you do if you were drafted to fight in a war that you considered unjust? Would you resist the authority of a democratically elected government that was persecuting an unpopular minority, even if that persecution were done in a legal manner?

The Common Good

Political philosophers have often viewed politics as different from other activities in that it is concerned with what is common to the community as a whole. Ensuring the good functioning of the basic activities of governing—such as maintaining order and security, providing for a just settlement of disputes, and taking actions to promote a prosperous, sustainable economy—potentially benefits all members of the political community (Wolin, 1960). Ideally politics is about seeking the **common good** of a political community.

Common good— what is good for the entire political community.

On the surface, the concept of the common good (also referred to as the public interest) seems uncontroversial. Who would not agree that political activity should be directed toward the common good of the political community? However, in practice, determining and achieving the common good can be contentious.

The idea of the common good rests on the assumption that the members of a political community have some interests and values in common. However, contemporary political communities often feature considerable diversity such that a consensus on what is the common good may be difficult or impossible to determine. Even if there are a number of general values such as freedom, equality, order, and justice that are shared by people within the community, these values may be thought of in different ways and different people or groups may give these values different priorities. As well, the costs and benefits of actions to achieve the common good are often unequally distributed. For example, most people would agree that reducing air pollution would be for the common good of the Canadian political community. However, the costs of reducing pollution to achieve this objective may fall more heavily on some (such as factory owners and automobile users) than others. Likewise, a free school breakfast program primarily benefits those whose parents are very poor. Nevertheless, we might view such a program as being for the common good if we assume that being part of a community involves caring about others in the community and supporting policies that help others enjoy the benefits of the community.

However, in political communities where there are sharp divisions (based, for example, on economic inequality, religion, or cultural identities), the sense of being members of a shared community and a willingness to be concerned about others may be weak or non-existent. In such political communities, the notion of the common good may not be very meaningful.

Individualist perspective— a perspective that views human beings as acting primarily in accordance with their own interests.

Further, for those who have an **individualist perspective** on politics, the idea of the common good and how it can be achieved is rather different. This perspective assumes that human beings act primarily in accordance with their own interests—in other words, selfishly. A community is a collection of individuals each pursuing their own interests. Thus, it is naive or hopelessly idealistic to expect people (whether as voters, politicians, or government officials) to deliberately act for the common good, particularly when that involves sacrifices of their own interests. Those who hold the individualist perspective often argue that if each person is free to pursue their own interests, the result will lead to the best overall result for the members of the community. For example, as discussed in Chapter 3, many economic theorists suggest that if individuals pursue their own self-interest in a free marketplace system, the result will be the maximization of the wealth of society.

Are we concerned only with our own good? If individuals pursue their own interests, will the good of the entire community be served? Are the communities that we live in no more than a collection of independent individuals? Critics of the individualist perspective argue that humans are social beings who flourish through harmonious interaction with others. Connected to our social nature is the capability to care about others. This capability initially develops within our own family, but can extend to the social groups to which we belong, to citizens of our country, and potentially to the world as a whole. Further, the communities to which we belong—including political communities—help to shape our sense of ourselves, that is, our identity. A sense of belonging to and participating in a community (or a set of communities) could be considered an important part of a fulfilling and meaningful life. People do not only have an interest in their own material well-being, but also an interest in the quality of their community and the social relations that are a part of that community (Lutz, 1999). Individuals engage in political activity not only to advance their own interests, but also to pursue the values they think should guide the actions of government (Lewin, 1991).

Achieving the Common Good?

We often look to government to achieve the common good. But how can we be assured that government will pursue the common good rather than the particular interests of those in government? In *The Republic*, the ancient Greek philosopher Plato (c. 429–c. 347 BCE) sketched out an ideal of how the common good might be achieved. This involved placing political authority in the hands of a wise philosopher–king who had been thoroughly educated in the art of governing. To ensure that such a leader would rule for the common good rather than out of personal interest, leaders would be prevented from having a family or owning property.

What might this suggest for governments and their citizens operating in the real world and not a great thinker's utopia?

In the contemporary world, democracy is often seen as the form of government most likely to actually pursue the common good. Ideally, through discussion among citizens, an informed consensus can be reached about the policies that are desirable for the common good. However, meaningful discussion is often difficult to achieve outside of small groups and small communities. Instead, there is an expectation that decisions in a democracy will tend to reflect the opinions of the majority of the population. Even if this is the case, it does not ensure that the common good of the community will be achieved. The majority is not necessarily oriented toward the common good of all members of the community, and at various times majorities have supported policies that oppress minorities.

Some suggest that a pluralist system where a large number of interest groups put forward the demands of various groups of people will result in the common good. A potential problem here is that even if government is responsive to groups representing a wide variety of interests, this does not necessarily result in the common good. Providing particular benefits to various groups that are able to exert effective pressure may not be the same as acting for the common good. If each group pursues its own interests, the good of the entire community may be ignored.

Although seeking the common good is a worthwhile objective for political life, it should be kept in mind that the claim to be acting for the common good (or other ideals) can be deceptive. Ruthless leaders have tried to justify brutal actions in the name of the long-term good of the political community. For example, the Soviet leader Joseph Stalin tried to justify his actions, which resulted in the starvation of millions of peasants, with the ideal of creating a "classless society." Fascist leaders such as Adolf Hitler and Benito Mussolini used the appeal of the good of the nation to suppress dissent and justify wars of aggression. Even in those democratic countries where individual rights are valued, appeals to the common good are sometimes made to justify repressive government actions in order to fight terrorism, subversion, and crime. In general, there is a real danger that government leaders claiming to pursue the common good of the political community as a whole will act in ways that are oppressive to some members of that community.

A Question of Communities

The common good is often thought of in terms of the country that we live in. But the common good of the country may not necessarily be the same as the common good of the other political communities to which we belong, such as provincial or local communities. Indeed, some argue that we should be concerned about the common good of humanity. The processes of globalization (discussed later in this chapter) are creating increased interaction and interdependence among the peoples of the world. However, despite greater awareness of and concern about what happens in other parts of the world, for most of us our sense of being part of a global political community is much weaker than our sense of being Canadian. Major differences among the peoples of the world in culture and circumstances mean that there are fewer shared interests and values upon which a consensus about the common good of humanity could be based.

Some environmentalists suggest that the common good should include not only humanity (including future generations), but also the Earth as a whole, including plants, animals, and the ecosystems upon which life is based (Daly & Cobb, 1994). Protecting the environment is ultimately essential for humanity as well as for plants and animals. But, when faced with the issue of protecting the jobs of loggers or protecting the habitat of an endangered animal or plant, should the good of human beings be given greater priority than the good of other life forms? Or as parts of an interrelated whole, are all life forms, including humans, of equal inherent worth? (Devall & Sessions, 1998).

CITIZENSHIP AND THE POLITICAL COMMUNITY

Citizenship—
the idea that the permanent residents of a country are full members of the political community, involving various duties and rights.

Connected to the development of the modern nation-state is the idea of **citizenship**—that the permanent residents are full members of the political community with certain duties and rights. A citizen is not only subject to the laws passed by the governing institutions of that state, but also shares in the power of the sovereign state (Rousseau, 1762/1968).

Those who are born in a particular country are usually considered to be citizens of that country, as are those whose parents are citizens. Those who immigrate to a new country can usually apply for citizenship after a certain period of time.[4] They may have to pass an exam testing their knowledge of their new country, including its political system, and take an oath of allegiance before becoming citizens. Although we usually think of citizenship as involving an exclusive loyalty to one country, many persons are citizens of two countries (as discussed in Box 4.4, Who Is a Citizen?).

Is citizenship a matter of rights for individuals (such as the right to vote and hold elected office) or does it also involve obligations to the political community? Citizens may, for example, be expected to defend their country in times of war. Governments have used this argument to justify compulsory military service and to draft men (and likely women, in the future) to fight in wars, even those that are not strictly defensive in nature. As well, since citizenship is associated with being a member of the political community, some have argued that citizens have an obligation to become informed participants in politics. Indeed, it has been suggested that citizens should put aside their personal interests and act in political life for the common good of their country (Pierson, 1996).

The concept of citizenship is often based on the view that all citizens should be equal members of the political community regardless of social status, ethnicity, gender, wealth, or other characteristics. In the past, citizenship was limited to a small seg-

BOX 4.4   WHO IS A CITIZEN?

As Israeli planes bombarded Hezbollah strongholds in Lebanon in July 2006, the Canadian government attempted to bring its citizens to safety in Canada. To the surprise of many, this involved not just a relatively small number of tourists and business travellers, but up to fifty thousand persons, many of whom had dual Lebanese and Canadian citizenship and Canadian passports. Some argued that the Canadian government should not help persons who had, in some cases, never set foot in Canada or paid Canadian taxes (although many of those evacuated at government expense were tourists). Others argued that treating those with dual citizenship differently than other Canadians was discriminatory and would create two classes of citizens.

A more fundamental question is whether individuals should be required to have citizenship status in only one country or whether dual citizenship (as allowed by Canada's Citizenship Act, 1977) is an appropriate response to increased migration and the reality of globalization. Interestingly, when Michaëlle Jean (who came to Canada from Haiti as a child) was appointed as Canada's governor general in 2005, controversy erupted when it was discovered that she was a citizen of both France and Canada. The controversy subsided when she voluntarily gave up her French citizenship. A similar controversy arose when Stéphane Dion (who has French as well as Canadian citizenship) was elected as Liberal party leader.

ment of the population, such as males, property owners, and those born in the country. The struggles for equal political rights in the past century and a half have been successful in most countries in expanding citizenship to include most of the population of a country.

There has been increasing discussion about whether members of certain groups should have different citizenship rights because of their particular circumstances (termed "differentiated citizenship"), such as historic rights, a legacy of oppression and discrimination, or exclusion from the mainstream of society. For example, many Aboriginal tribes or nations in Canada have various rights established by treaties and other agreements between the British Crown or the Canadian government and Aboriginal chiefs. Although the nature of these rights is often in dispute and subject to lengthy negotiations, Aboriginal treaty rights are recognized in the Canadian constitution.

Some have argued that the special rights of Aboriginals eventually should be extinguished so that they can be treated the same as other Canadians (as was proposed by the Canadian government in 1969). Others have argued that Aboriginals should be self-governing nations within Canada. This could imply a form of dual citizenship in which Aboriginals are both citizens of their Aboriginal nation and citizens of Canada (Harty & Murphy, 2005). Political scientist Alan Cairns (2000) has tried to find a middle ground, termed "citizens plus," in which Aboriginal differences are recognized, but not at the expense of a strong common citizenship that would bind Canadians together.

Overall, the question of whether the conventional meaning of citizenship as equal membership in a particular political community with all persons having the same duties and rights has increasingly been raised, particularly in multinational states (Carens, 2000).

Identity Politics

A desire for recognition as members of a distinct nation within a larger country (such as Quebecers in Canada, the Scottish in the United Kingdom, and Catalans in Spain) could be considered as part of a broader phenomenon referred to as **identity politics**. Within a variety of groups that view themselves as oppressed or marginalized from mainstream society—including women, gays and lesbians, minority ethnic groups, the disabled, and Aboriginals—movements have developed seeking recognition and respect for their group identity and the values that they associate with their group. Instead of seeking to integrate into mainstream society, those involved in identity politics often seek to express their distinctiveness and gain a degree of autonomy from the rest of the community by such measures as developing their own institutions and services, obtaining recognition of their specific rights, and having their own means of political representation. In addition, various movements connected to identity politics often seek action by government and various social institutions to combat racism, sexism, and other social problems. Likewise, they may seek to ensure that there are positive portrayals of the diversity of society in the educational system and the mass media. Overall, rather than (or in addition to) being treated as equal *individual* citizens, those involved in identity politics often seek equality for their *group*, equal consideration of their particular needs and circumstances, and the ability to nurture their group's distinctiveness (Tully, 2003).

Identity Politics—
a perspective in which groups seek recognition and respect for their particular identity. Those involved in identity politics often seek to express their distinctiveness and gain a degree of autonomy from the rest of the community by developing their own institutions and services, obtaining recognition of their specific rights, and having their own means of political representation.

Identity politics is not just about achieving an equitable distribution of income and opportunities for each individual in the political community, but also about gaining respect, particular rights, political power, and autonomy for specific groups.

In recent decades, Canadian governments have officially recognized the diverse cultural heritage of Canadians through a policy of multiculturalism that provides support for different groups to retain their cultures. Critics have argued that multiculturalism might conflict with individual rights (for example, by protecting cultures that discriminate against women) and might interfere with the integration of immigrants into Canadian society. Similarly, while some gays and lesbians seek to be accepted as part of the mainstream society, with the same rights as heterosexuals, others act to promote and develop their own identity and culture.

GLOBALIZATION

Some analysts claim that the modern state is declining in significance. Globalization is making the boundaries of states less relevant, eroding state sovereignty, and reducing the ability of governments to determine the direction of their country. Indeed, one author predicted that by 2025 we will see the end of the nation-state, to be replaced by small units subordinate to a global economy (Ohmae, 1995).

Globalization is often described in terms of the processes that are, in effect, shrinking the world. The obstacles of space and time are being rapidly overcome by contemporary technology, such as high-speed, low-cost communications. This is increasing the interconnectedness of the world and creating a greater awareness of the world as a whole. American journalist Tom Friedman (2000, p. 9) describes globalization as

> the inexorable integration of markets, nation-states and technologies to a degree never witnessed before—in a way that is enabling individuals, corporations and nation-states to reach around the world farther, faster, deeper and cheaper than ever before, and in a way that is enabling the world to reach into individuals, corporations and nations farther, faster, deeper, and cheaper than ever before.

Three types of globalization are particularly important: economic globalization, cultural globalization, and political globalization.

The Globalization Website
www.emory.edu/ SOC/globalization

Globalization— the processes that are increasing the interconnectedness of the world.

Economic Globalization

A key aspect of globalization is the development of a global economic system. Such a development concerns manufacturing, trade, and finance. Many business corporations are becoming global in their activities; they move or contract out their production facilities to wherever goods and services can be produced at the lowest cost and sell their products and services in a variety of countries. Global trade has increased greatly in the past half-century (see Figure 4.1). The process of economic globalization has been most pronounced in the financial markets that provide a substantial proportion of the money and credit needed by business and government. Approximately $2 trillion is traded daily on the currency markets, much of it for speculative purposes (Harmes, 2004). Capital can flow instantaneously in and out of countries connected to the global financial markets. However, there is no

FIGURE 4.1 *The Increase in Global Trade, 1950 to 2005 (log scale)*

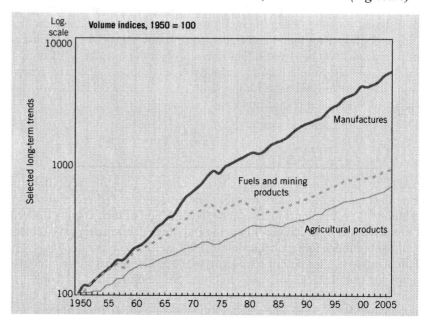

SOURCE: World Trade Organization, International trade statistics, 2006, retrieved July 15, 2007 from www.wto.org/english/res_e/statis_e/its2006_e/its06_longterm_e.pdf.

global free market in labour, as most workers in the poorer countries cannot easily move to countries featuring high wages and full employment.

Among the advantages of economic globalization are:

- *Efficiency.* Economic wealth is maximized when countries focus on those sectors of their economy in which they are most efficient, and then trade with other countries for those products and services that they cannot produce as efficiently. As well, the pressure of global competition encourages business to be more efficient and more attentive to the desires of their customers.

- *Access to money.* Easier access to global financial markets can help countries that are developing their economies to obtain the loans and investment capital they need.

- *Consumer prices.* Consumers benefit from the lower prices that can result from shifting the production of goods and services to areas where the costs of production are the lowest.

- *Wider variety.* Consumers enjoy access to a wider selection of goods.

Economic globalization, however, has come under considerable criticism because of several disadvantages:

- *Global inequality.* The increased wealth associated with economic globalization has gone more to the richest rather than to the poorest members of the global community. Although shifting production to some poor countries has created jobs in those countries, competition to attract those jobs has typically resulted in extremely low wages. Some countries (such as South Korea and Taiwan) have been successful in developing prosperous export-oriented economies, but many African countries have fallen behind.

* *Tax evasion.* The ease with which large amounts of money can be instantaneously transferred has resulted in wealthy individuals and corporations shifting their money to tax havens (jurisdictions that do not levy taxes) such as the Cayman Islands.

* *Concentration of power.* Globalization has substantially increased the power of the largest corporations. By threatening to shift production to other countries, they have been able to secure a variety of profitable concessions from governments, such as lower taxes and subsidies for their operations. Because of their power and mobility, it can be difficult for governments to try to ensure that large global corporations are operating for the common good. The enhanced economic power of business may result in increased pressure on governments to weaken or eliminate regulations, including those designed to protect the environment, ensure the safety of consumer products, and restrict the development of monopolies.

* *Weakening of labour.* Because many businesses can move their operations from location to location while workers are generally less able or willing to move to another country, business has generally been increasing its power at the expense of workers. The threat of a business "outsourcing" its operations to a low-wage country puts pressure on workers and unions to accept concessions such as lower wages and fewer benefits.

United Students against Sweatshops **www.students against sweatshops.org**

* *Challenges to the welfare state.* In order to increase the capability of national businesses to compete globally, governments may reduce or eliminate social benefits and programs (such as social assistance and unemployment insurance) in order to provide lower-cost labour to business, reduce taxes, or redirect government spending to programs that assist business competitiveness, particularly in education and research.

* *Economic crises snowball.* Globalization may increase the risk of serious global economic crises. Economic problems in one country can now quickly spread to other parts of the world because of the interdependence of economies, the instantaneous nature of contemporary communication, and the high level of speculation in global financial markets.

Cultural Globalization

Globalization also involves the spreading of cultural products and values around the world. Advances in communications, such as the Internet, have greatly increased the interaction of people, businesses, and other organizations worldwide. Leading brands such as Coke, Pepsi, McDonald's, Taco Bell, and Nike have become familiar to people around the world. American movies, television shows, and music videos are the leading sources of entertainment in many parts of the world. CNN and BBC World are major sources of news in many countries.

Cultural globalization is often viewed as a process in which Western (and particularly American) culture is spread globally. Although the transformation of communication has given us increased access to cultures in other parts of the world, the flow of cultural communication outward from Western countries is substantially greater than the flow in the reverse direction. How many movies and television shows have you watched lately that were produced outside of North America?

Cultural globalization may have some important political effects. The spread of democracy is often attributed, in part, to the information revolution that has both spread democratic values and presented challenges to the attempts of non-democratic governments to control information and ideas. The portrayal on television of the wealth of Western societies may have contributed to the collapse of communist regimes in Eastern Europe as people compared their situation to that of their Western neighbours. On the other hand, Islamic fundamentalists may have their negative views of Western societies reinforced by what they perceive as the decadence portrayed by Western-produced movies and television.

Political Globalization

A variety of contemporary problems, including the regulation of global business and finance, global climate change, international crime and terrorism, and the spread of diseases, cannot be dealt with effectively by individual states. A variety of institutions have developed to try to coordinate the actions of states, promote free trade, and deal with global problems. In a few cases, most notably the European Union, a level of governing above that of the state has been created. In other cases, such as the North American Free Trade Agreement involving Canada, the United States, and Mexico, countries have reached agreements that affect the policies they adopt. At the global level, the United Nations and its agencies have had some success in helping states deal with global issues, although only limited success in dealing with war and other forms of violence.

There are also a large number of groups that engage in political action on a global level. Greenpeace, for example, has grown from a small Vancouver organization concerned with nuclear weapons testing in Alaska to a large international organization involved in environmental causes around the world. A concerned American, Jody Williams, made extensive use of email to mobilize a wide variety of groups and individuals around the world that successfully pressed for an international treaty banning anti-personnel land mines (although forty countries, including the United States, Russia, and China, refused to sign the treaty). Growing networks of non-governmental organizations operate on a global scale seeking to influence the policies of states (and the actions of corporations) in such areas as human rights, the environment, the status of women, and peace. International business, labour, and religious groups are also important actors on the global political stage.

Is Globalization Inevitable?

There is little doubt that we live in an era of rapid change, and that the interconnectedness of the world's population is increasing. However, as discussed in Box 4.5, Is the Significance of Globalization Exaggerated?, some critics argue that the extent and consequences of globalization have been exaggerated.

BOX 4.5   IS THE SIGNIFICANCE OF GLOBALIZATION EXAGGERATED?

Is globalization a novel feature of human existence that is rapidly transforming the world? Or is the widespread discussion of globalization since the early 1990s largely an intellectual fad? The technological changes that have brought the world much closer together in the past few decades are truly amazing. But for millions of people, particularly those in poorer countries, computers and the Internet are unaffordable; for some, even telephones and televisions are beyond their financial reach. In addition, much of the world's trade and investment involves Europe, North America, and East Asia. Globalization is an uneven phenomenon with some parts of the world more closely interconnected than others.

Globalization is not entirely a new phenomenon. Trading is a very ancient occupation. Two thousand years ago, the Romans built a large empire, as did the Han dynasty in East Asia. Spanish, Portuguese, and Dutch explorers set up a global system of trading posts in the sixteenth century. A massive slave trade bringing Africans to the Americas developed in the seventeenth century. Britain built a global empire ("where the sun never sets") in the nineteenth century. Similarly, long before modern communications and transportation, religions spread across large areas of the earth. Christianity spread throughout the Roman Empire and continued to expand its geographical reach after the empire fell. And in a relatively short time after the death of its founder, Mohammed (632 CE), Islam spread through conquest from its home in Saudi Arabia as far as Spain and India. Likewise, large-scale migrations of people occurred well before the development of modern means of transportation.

Some features of globalization are new. In particular, the globalization of production—whereby a product (such as an automobile or a computer) is assembled from parts manufactured in many different countries—could be considered an important new feature of contemporary economic globalization (Harmes, 2004). Even so, most of the production of goods and services is still for domestic markets (Mann, 1997).

Questions have arisen as to whether a global "monoculture"—that is, a single global culture based on the cultural values of the Western world, particularly the United States—is developing. Certainly cultural diversity is diminishing and many traditional languages and cultures are endangered. American cultural products are widely distributed throughout much of the world. However, there are substantial cultural differences among various regions of the world that American movies, television shows, music, fast foods, and brand labels will not easily erase. Indeed, contemporary communications media, such as the Internet and satellite television, can help minority cultures that are spread across a variety of countries to maintain and develop their cultural values (Elkins, 1995).

Global Policy Forum
**www.globalpolicy.
org**

Although globalization is often described as an inevitable process, various circumstances, including the policies adopted by governments, can accelerate, slow down, or even reverse the trend. For example, the economic globalization that developed in the late nineteenth and early twentieth centuries was reversed by the First World War and later by the rise of economic and political nationalism during the Great Depression of the 1930s.

On the other hand, toward the end of the Second World War, there was an agreement among the Allied powers to prevent a recurrence of nationalism by promoting freer trade, establishing several international financial institutions, and creating a mechanism for managing currency exchanges, all of which came to be known as the Bretton Woods system. The system of basically fixed currency exchange rates collapsed in the early 1970s to be replaced by a system of floating (that is, market-determined) exchange rates, which, along with the removal of restrictions on the flow of capital, encouraged the development of a large global currency market. The tendency of governments since the early 1980s to reduce the regulation of their economies, privatize publicly owned enterprises, and reduce taxes has contributed to the acceleration of the growth of a global free-market capitalist economy.

International Forum
on Globalization
www.ifg.org

Globalization and the Nation-State

Is globalization seriously eroding the power of nation-states? The heightened pressures of economic competition may encourage countries to adopt policies that focus on removing barriers to the global free market, reducing the role of government in regulating the economy, and cutting the taxes that are needed to provide social benefits. The rules of trade adopted by bodies such as the World Trade Organization are aimed at trying to establish a "level playing field" in which government policies that protect domestic products and services and place barriers to trade and investment are expected to be eliminated.

Nevertheless, there is diversity among the policies adopted by different countries, reflecting continuing differences in cultures and circumstances. The relatively prosperous countries of Western Europe, for example, have generally continued to maintain a wider range of social benefits for their populations as well as higher environmental and health standards than other countries. The governments of the newly industrialized countries of East Asia are more heavily involved in directing their industries than is the case for the United States and Canada. Generally, countries have tended to adapt to globalization in different ways, and have chosen to integrate into the global economy to differing extents (Garrett, 1998).

It has been argued that globalization is eroding the power of the nation-state not only by shifting power upward to global institutions, global markets, and global corporations, but also by indirectly challenging the nation-state from below (see Box 4.6, Jihad versus McWorld). The decreasing importance of states in providing for the well-being of their people may have the effect of stimulating separatist movements. The development of organizations such as the European Union and the North American Free Trade Agreement makes it possible for some people in smaller areas, such as

---

BOX 4.6   JIHAD VERSUS MCWORLD

American political scientist Benjamin Barber describes the key forces in the contemporary world as "McWorld" (globalization) and "Jihad" (a term sometimes used to refer to war against the enemies of Islam that Barber uses more generally to describe the "retribalization" of different peoples opposed to global interdependence and homogenization).

These forces "operate with equal strength in opposite directions, the one driven by parochial hatreds, the other by universalizing markets, the one recreating ancient sub-national and ethnic borders from within, the other making national borders porous from without" (Barber, 1995, p. 6). Both undermine the nation-state and the ability of democratic nation-states to pursue the common good. In Barber's view, the success of either of these trends would lead to a bleak and undemocratic political future. McWorld involves imposing an unnatural uniformity based on consumerism and the pursuit of profit, while Jihad creates intolerant communities pursuing "a bloody politics of identity" (Barber, 1995, p. 8).

As an alternative, Barber advocates working toward a loose global confederation of democratic communities, smaller than existing states, in which citizens, active in a variety of voluntary organizations, work co-operatively toward the common good.

To what extent is Barber's interpretation of contemporary politics valid? The terrorist attack on the United States in 2001 by al-Qaeda extremists seemed to show the power of Jihad. However, al-Qaeda is not based on a particular tribe, nationality, or homeland, but rather a loose network of groups located in a large number of countries generally connected by an extreme interpretation of Islam and antipathy toward the West and Western-leaning governments of Muslim states. In addition, although movements seeking independence or autonomy have developed within several countries, such movements are not necessarily inward looking. For example, many Scottish and Catalan nationalists seek to develop stronger ties with other countries. Finally, powerful nation-states (such as the United States, China, and Russia) continue to pursue their national interests. Challenges to existing nation-states (such as the jihad against existing Muslim states by extremist Islamic groups) have often proved unsuccessful.

Scotland and Quebec, to think that belonging to such organizations will offset the disadvantages they would face by separating from a large country.

Finally, people's sense of identification with the nation-state may be reduced as an increasing proportion of people have multiple identities. This, however, is not an entirely new phenomenon, as religious, cultural, regional, local, and ethnic identities have often coexisted or competed with national identities. And although concern with human rights for all people and concern about global environmental problems may be challenging traditional notions of state sovereignty, it does not yet appear that a significant proportion of the world's population has developed a sense of global identity. Indeed, identity politics can lead to an expansion of the activities of the state. For example, although the women's movement has developed a significant global network, its demands, in various countries, have resulted in new state laws and programs such as child-care programs, laws dealing with abuse and sexual harassment, and programs to increase women's educational and employment opportunities (Mann, 1997).

LOCAL COMMUNITY

Democracy requires citizen participation, but usually, voter turnout at municipal elections is very low. On average, 30 to 40 per cent of eligible voters cast ballots in local elections, in contrast to the 70 or 80 per cent turnout at other levels. As a result, those who do participate can make more of an impact.

For democracy to work, people must participate and their opinions must be valued. This is particularly true at the local level, since this is where people have the greatest opportunity to voice their views and influence community decisions. Citizen participation benefits not only the people and the community, but also the decision-making process. Here are the reasons why.

Community participation is beneficial because:

- Citizens are most aware of their own needs, community problems, and available resources.
- Community organizations have more access to local information and local history.
- Citizens have most at stake. Commitment to a solution is greater and the chances of its success are strengthened when those who must live with the outcome are involved in making the decision.
- Programs and services are more appropriate, efficient, and effective.

Decision making in local government usually includes a stage for public input. There are several ways in which citizens can express their views:

- Municipal governments hold public consultations—meetings or surveys to find out what citizens think about a particular problem or proposal. Citizens can attend meetings to express their views.
- Citizens can be appointed to sit on municipal boards, commissions, and advisory councils.
- Individuals can get involved in local elections by working on a campaign.
- Individuals can run for elected office and vote for the candidates they prefer.

Expressing Your Views at the Local Level

As a citizen or a member of a community group, you can express your views in various ways. Many people participate locally without ever involving formal authorities. Involvement in social action activities in your school—such as an AIDS Awareness campaign, peer conflict resolution, Earth Week, a play that challenges stereotypes about street youth, or fundraising for a battered women's shelter—is an example of local participation. At the local level, even one person working alone can make an impact on the quality of life in the community—especially if she or he takes a leadership role.

We have all heard the phrase, "There is strength in numbers." When individuals collaborate and convince other local citizens to work with them, it is called **grassroots organizing.** The most effective opportunity for citizens to participate in the local decision-making process is when they work together. As a group, individuals with common goals can

grassroots organizing—
Organizing society at the local level, as distinguished from the centres of political leadership.

Grassroots organizations get involved in a wide range of community issues.

effectively research an issue, decide on a strategy, and set up a plan of action. Grassroots organizations often participate in civil society by educating the public, fundraising, providing services for needy groups, demonstrating, working for candidates in elections, and building links with other grassroots groups. Whether they are members of a neighbourhood or like-minded students in a high school class, a grassroots group can present forceful arguments and effective strategies to influence local government.

Contacting Your Municipal Officials

Some issues may require the involvement of a local representative. The job of a municipal representative is to protect the public interests—that is, the needs and wishes of the people they represent. If you have a problem that you wish to discuss with your municipal councillor, your school board trustee, or even the mayor, you will likely find him or her much easier to reach than your provincial or federal representative.

Municipal politicians are elected to serve community interests and resolve community problems. They generally live in the community they represent. As residents of the community, they are aware of local conditions and issues. A good municipal representative should be accessible, willing to listen to his or her constituents' views, and ready to act on their wishes.

Whether the issue is parking on your street or a threatened closing of your community centre, there are numerous ways for you to make your views known through the right channels.

Endnotes

1. In the years following the Summit, the goal of establishing the FTAA was not realized particularly because of dwindling support for the FTAA in several Latin American countries and the defeat of governments committed to that objective.

2. Some political scientists prefer to use the term *influence* for the general ability to affect behaviour, leaving the term *power* to refer to the use of coercion, inducements, or manipulation to get people to act against their own desires or interests (Dahl, 1984).

3. Power can be significant even when there is no intentional exercise of power. Political actors may change their behaviour because they *anticipate* that there will be negative consequences from those with greater power if they act in a particular way, even if no direct threat has been made. For example, knowing that the United States has imposed severe economic sanctions on Cuba, other Caribbean countries may be reluctant to act in ways that could result in similar consequences.

4. Some countries, however, connect citizenship to particular characteristics. Germany and Israel, for example, allow persons from other countries the right to become citizens based on their ancestry immediately upon taking up residence. In contrast, a number of European countries have been reluctant to grant citizenship to "guest workers" from North Africa and the Middle East, even when they have resided in the country for a lengthy period of time.

THINKING CRITICALLY

I t should now be clear to you that becoming a skilled thinker is like becoming skilled in basketball, ballet, or in playing the saxophone—it requires the development of basic intellectual skills, abilities, and insights. In this chapter we begin to focus on these skills.

The best thinkers recognize that there are parts to thinking, that the only way to ensure that we are thinking well is by taking command of these parts. This chapter focuses on how to take thinking apart—how to *analyze* it by examining its parts. The next chapter focuses on the *assessment* of thinking: how to apply intellectual standards to the parts of thinking to decide whether your thinking—or someone else's—is of high quality.

We begin with a brief discussion of *reasoning,* the mental process the mind uses to make sense of whatever we seek to understand.

THINKING IS EVERYWHERE IN HUMAN LIFE

The words *thinking* and *reasoning* are often used in everyday life as synonyms. *Reasoning,* however, has a more formal flavor. This is because it highlights the intellectual dimension of thinking.

Reasoning occurs whenever the mind draws conclusions on the basis of reasons. We draw conclusions whenever we make sense of things. So, whenever we think, we reason. Usually we are not aware of the full scope of reasoning in our lives.

We begin to reason from the moment we wake up in the morning. We reason when we figure out what to eat for breakfast, what to wear, whether to stop at the store on the way to school or work, whether to go with this or that friend to lunch. We reason while we drive, as we interpret the oncoming flow of traffic, react to the decisions of other drivers, and speed up or slow down.

EXHIBIT *Critical thinkers routinely apply the intellectual standards to the elements of reasoning in order to develop intellectual traits.*

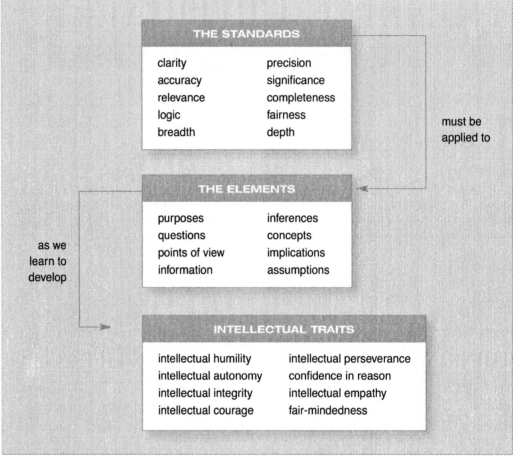

One can draw conclusions, then, about everyday events or, really, about anything at all: about poems, microbes, people, numbers, historical events, social settings, psychological states, character traits, the past, the present, the future.

To reason well, we must scrutinize the process we are using, by asking ourselves: What are we trying to figure out? What information do we need? Do we have that information? How could we check it for accuracy? The less conscious we are of how we are thinking, the easier it is to make some mistake or errors. To maximize your learning, try to approach your classes so that you are not only noticing but also analyzing and evaluating your reasoning.

Think for Yourself

BECOMING MORE AWARE OF THE ROLE OF REASONING IN YOUR LIFE

Make a list of all the things you did today. Then, for each act, figure out the thinking that led you to do, or guided you while doing, the act. (Remember that most of your thinking is unconscious.) For example, when you left your house this morning, you may have stopped at the store for food. This act makes no sense unless you somehow had come to the conclusion that you needed some food. Then, while at the store, you bought certain items. This action resulted from the tacit conclusion you came to that you needed some items and not others.

Realize that every time you make a decision, that decision represents a view or conclusion you reasoned to. For each action you identify, answer these two questions:

1. What exactly did I do?
2. What thinking is presupposed in my behavior?

Write out your answers or explain orally.

THE PARTS OF THINKING

The elements of thought also can be called the *parts of thinking* or the *fundamental structures of thought.* We will use these expressions interchangeably. The elements or parts of reasoning are those essential dimensions of reasoning that are present whenever and wherever reasoning occurs—regardless of whether we are reasoning well or poorly. Working together, these elements shape reasoning and provide a general framework for thought.

When you become adept at identifying the elements of your reasoning, you will be in a much better position to recognize flaws in your thinking, by locating problems in this or that part. This ability is essential to critical thinking. The ability to identify the elements of reasoning, then, is an important ability in critical thinking.

Reasoning is a process whereby one draws conclusions on the basis of reasons. On the surface, reasoning seems somewhat simple, as if it has no component structures. Looked at more closely, however, you can see that it is really a set of interrelated intellectual processes. Some of these may occur subconsciously, without your awareness. It is useful to practice making conscious what is subconscious in your thinking. Then you can better understand what's going on beneath the surface of your thought. In this chapter we introduce you to ways to make your thinking more conscious.

A First Look at the Elements of Thought

Let us begin by looking at the parts of thinking as they stand in an interrelated set. It is possible to name them in just one, somewhat complex, sentence:

Whenever you reason,

you do so in some circumstances,

EXHIBIT   *The parts or elements of reasoning are always present in human thinking.*

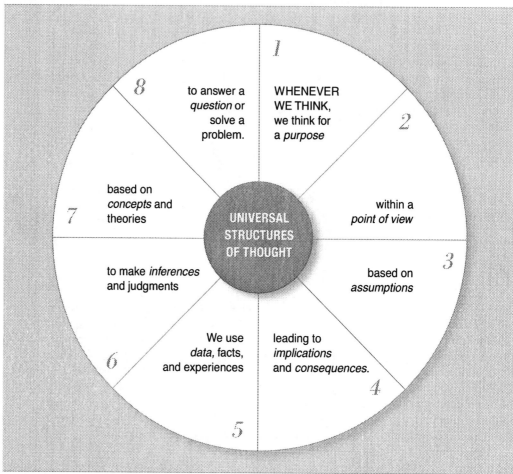

to answer a *question* or solve a problem.

WHENEVER WE THINK, we think for a *purpose*

based on *concepts* and theories

within a *point of view*

UNIVERSAL STRUCTURES OF THOUGHT

to make *inferences* and judgments

based on *assumptions*

We use *data*, facts, and experiences

leading to *implications* and *consequences*.

EXHIBIT   *Critical thinkers understand the importance of taking thinking apart in order to analyze it for flaws.*

Critical thinkers routinely ➤ take their thinking apart

making some inferences (that have some implications and consequences)

based on some reasons or information (and assumptions)

using some concepts,

in trying to settle some question (or solve some problem)

for some purpose

within a point of view.

If you like, you can put it in two sentences:

Whenever you are *reasoning,*

you are trying to accomplish some *purpose,*

within a *point of view,*

using concepts or ideas.

You are focused on some issue, *question,* or problem,

using *information*

to come to *conclusions,*

based on *assumptions,*

all of which has *implications.*

Let us now examine, at least provisionally, each of these crucial concepts. We will be using them throughout this book. It is essential that they become a comfortable part of your own critical thinking vocabulary. As you read these initial explanations, see if you can explain them in your own words and give examples from your own experience.

By *reasoning,* we mean *making sense of something by giving it some meaning in one's mind.* Virtually all thinking is part of our sense-making activities. We hear scratching at the door and think, "It's the dog." We see dark clouds in the sky and think, "It looks like rain." Some of this activity operates at a subconscious level. For example, all of the sights and sounds around me have meaning for me without my explicitly noticing that they do. Most of our reasoning is unspectacular. Our reasoning tends to become explicit to us only when someone challenges it and we have to defend it ("Why do you say that Jack is obnoxious? I thought he was quite pleasant."). Throughout life, we begin with a goal or purpose and then figure out what to do to achieve that goal. Reasoning is what enables us to come to these decisions using ideas and meanings.

By *reasoning having a purpose,* we mean that *when humans think about the world, we do not do so randomly but, rather, in line with our goals, desires, needs, and values.* Our thinking is an integral part of a patterned way of acting in the world, and we act, even in simple matters, with some set of ends in view. To understand someone's thinking—including your own—you must understand the functions it serves, what it is about, the direction it is moving, and the ends that motivate it. Most of the time, what we are "after" in our thinking is not obvious to us. Raising our goals and desires to the level of conscious awareness is an important part of critical thinking.

By *reasoning within a point of view,* we mean that *our thinking has some comprehensive focus or orientation.* Our thinking is focused *on* something *from* some angle. We can change either what we focus on or the angle of our focus. We often give names

EXHIBIT   *If you understand the parts of thinking, you can ask the crucial questions implied by those parts.*

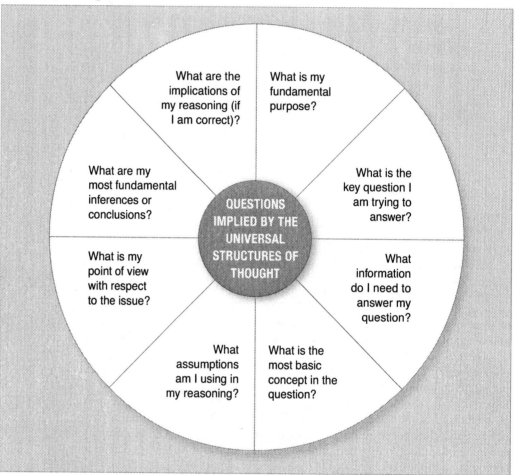

to the angle from which we are thinking about something. For example, we could look at an issue politically or scientifically, poetically or philosophically. We might look at a problem conservatively or liberally, religiously or secularly. We might view a question from a cultural or a financial perspective, or both. Once we understand how people are approaching a question or topic (what their comprehensive perspective is), we are usually much better able to understand the whole of their thinking.

By *using concepts and theories in reasoning,* we mean the *general categories or ideas by which we interpret, classify, or group the information we use in our thinking.* For example, in this book the concepts of critical thinking and uncritical thinking are important. Everything in this book can be classified as an attempt to explain one or the other of these two important ideas. Each of these ideas is explained, in turn, by means of other ideas. Thus, the concept of thinking critically is explained by reference to other concepts, such as "intellectual standards for thought." Each subject discipline (chemistry, geology, literature, math, and so forth) develops its own set of concepts or technical vocabulary to facilitate its thinking. Every sport requires a vocabulary of concepts that enables those who are trying to understand or master the game to make sense of it. Try to explain baseball to someone without using these ideas: *strike, ball, shortstop, inning, at bat, hit, run, safe, out, bunt.* To play the game, we must interpret everything we do in it by means of concepts such as these. The rules would not make sense without them; the game would be incomprehensible.

By *reasoning through some question, issue, or problem,* we mean that *when we think about the world in line with our goals, desires, needs, and values, we often face questions we need to answer, problems we need to solve, and issues we need to resolve.* Therefore, when we find ourselves confronting a difficulty, it makes sense to say, "What is the question we need to answer?" or, "What is the problem we need to solve?" or, "What is the issue we need to resolve?" To improve our ability to think well, it is important to learn how to phrase the questions, problems, and issues we need to deal with in a clear and distinct way. If we change the question, we change the criteria we have to meet to settle it. If we modify the problem, we need to modify how we are going to solve the problem. If we shift the issue, new considerations become relevant to its resolution.

By *using information in our reasoning,* we mean *using some set of facts, data, or experiences to support our conclusions.* Whenever someone is reasoning, it makes sense to ask, "Upon what facts or information are you basing your reasoning?" The factual basis for reasoning can be important. For example, in a newspaper ad (*New York Times,* November 22, 1999) the following pieces of information were used to support an argument against capital punishment:

* "Since the death penalty was reinstated by the Supreme Court in 1976, for every seven prisoners who were executed, one prisoner awaiting execution was found to be innocent and released."

* "At least 381 homicide convictions have been overturned since 1963 because prosecutors concealed evidence of innocence or presented evidence they knew to be false."

* "A study by the U.S. General Accounting Office found racial prejudice in death sentencing . . .: killers of whites were proportionally more likely to be executed than were killers of blacks."

* "Since 1984, 34 mentally retarded people have been executed."

Can you see how information such as this—if true—gives strength to the reasoning? People who hold the opposing position would, of course, advance information of their own to try to challenge or counter this information. Check your facts! Check your data! These are important critical-thinking axioms.

By *coming to conclusions* we mean *figuring out something new on the basis of something we believe we already know.* When we do this, we *make inferences.* For example, if you walk right by me without saying hello, I might come to the conclusion (make the inference) that you are angry with me. If the water kettle on the stove begins to whistle, I come to the conclusion (make the inference) that the water in it has started to boil. In everyday life, we are continually making inferences (coming to conclusions or making judgments about people, things, places, and events).

By *reasoning based on assumptions* we mean *using beliefs we take for granted to figure something else out.* Thus, if you infer that since a candidate is a Republican, he will support a balanced budget, you assume that all Republicans support a balanced budget. If you infer that foreign leaders presented in the news as "enemies" or "friends" of the United States are in fact enemies or friends, you assume that the news is always accurate in its presentation of the character of foreign leaders. If you infer that someone who invites you to her apartment after a party "to continue this interesting conversation" is really interested in you romantically or sexually, you might be assuming that the only reason for going to someone's apartment late at night after a party is to pursue a romantic or sexual relationship. All reasoning has some basis in the assumptions we make (but usually are unaware of).

By the *implications of reasoning* we mean that which follows from our thinking—*that to which our thinking is leading us.* If you say to someone that you "love" him, you *imply* that you are concerned with his welfare. If you make a promise, you *imply* that you intend to keep it. If you call a country a "democracy," you *imply* that the political power is in the hands of the people at large (as against in the hands of a powerful minority). If you call yourself a "feminist," you *imply* that you are in favor of the political, social, and economic equality of the sexes. We often test the credibility of people by seeing if they are true to the implications of their own words. "Say what you mean and mean what you say" is a sound principle of critical thinking (and of personal integrity, for that matter).

An Everyday Example: Jack and Jill

Let's now look at and then analyze a disagreement that might arise in everyday life—in this case, between lovers who come to different conclusions about a situation they both experienced. Suppose Jack and Jill, who are in a romantic relationship, go to a party, during which Jack spends most of the evening talking with Susan. On their way back, Jack, sensing that Jill is upset, asks, "What's wrong?"

After some hesitation, Jill says, "I didn't appreciate your spending the whole night flirting with Susan!"

Jack: Flirting . . . flirting, I was *not* flirting!

Jill: What would you call it?

Jack: Being friendly. I was being *friendly.*

Jill: When a guy spends the whole evening focused on one girl, sits very close to her, looks at her in a romantic way, and periodically touches her in supposedly casual ways, he is engaged in what can only be called *flirting.*

Jack: And when a girl spends her whole evening watching everything her boyfriend does, collecting evidence as if preparing for a trial, a boyfriend who has always been faithful to her, she is engaged in what can only be called *paranoia.*

Jill: Paranoid! How dare you call me that!

Jack: Well, how else can I describe your behavior? You're obviously distrustful and insecure. You're accusing me without a good reason for doing so.

Jill: Don't act like this is the only time you have ever flirted. I have heard that you played the field before we got together.

Jack: And I have heard about your possessiveness and jealousy from your friends. I think you need to deal with your own problems before you attack me. If you ask me, I think you need counseling.

Jill: You're nothing but a typical male. You gauge your manhood on how many girls you can conquer. You're so focused on getting strokes for that male ego of yours that you can't see or admit what you're doing. If you aren't willing to change, I don't see how we can have a relationship!

Jack: I don't see how we can have a relationship either—not because I am unfaithful, but because you are paranoid. And unless I get an apology, I'm out of here!

Analysis of the Example

Now let's analyze this exchange using the elements of thought.

- ▦ Purpose. Both Jack and Jill presumably seek a successful romantic relationship. That is their implied shared goal.
- ▦ Problem. They see a problem or issue standing in the way, a problem they conceptualize differently. To Jack, the problem is, "When is Jill going to deal with her paranoia?" To Jill, the problem is, "When is Jack going to take responsibility for his flirtatious behavior?"
- ▦ Assumptions. Jack is assuming that he is not self-deceived in his motivation with respect to Susan and other women. Jack also is assuming that he is competent to identify paranoia in another person's behavior. Further, he is assuming that a woman could not behave in the way that Jill is without being paranoid. Jill is assuming that Jack's behavior is not compatible with ordinary friendliness. Both of them assume that what they have heard about the other is accurate. Both assume themselves to be justified in their own behavior in the situation.
- ▦ Information. The information in the situation includes everything Jack actually said and did at the party. Other relevant facts include Jack's behavior toward other women in the past. Additional facts include Jill's behavior toward former boyfriends and any other facts that bear on whether she is acting out of insecurity or "paranoia."
- ▦ Concepts. There are four key concepts in the reasoning: *flirtation, friendliness, paranoia,* and *male ego.*
- ▦ Conclusions. Jack's and Jill's inferences (conclusions) about the situation derive from the same behavior in the same circumstance, but they clearly see the behavior differently. To Jack, his behavior is to be understood as merely "friendly." To Jill, Jack's behavior can be understood only as "flirtation."

- Implications. Both Jack and Jill imply by their reasoning that the other person is entirely to blame for any differences between them regarding Jack's behavior at the party. Both seem to imply that the relationship is hopeless.
- Point of view. Both Jack and Jill may be seeing the other through the bias of a gender-based point of view. Both see themselves as a victim of the other. Both see themselves as blameless.

Given what we know about the dispute, it is not possible for us to assess who is correct and to what extent. To decide whose interpretation of the situation is more plausible, we would need more facts. There are subtle but observable behaviors that might lead us to conclude that Jill is correct and that Jack was behaving flirtatiously—if we could verify them. Or, if we heard the conversation firsthand, we might decide that Jill's response is unjustified.

How the Parts of Thinking Fit Together

The trick to learning the elements of thought is to express them in a number of different ways until their interrelationships begin to become intuitive to you. For example, you might think of the parts of reasoning as analogous to the parts of the human body. They are all present, whether we are healthy or not. Like the parts of the body, the parts of thought function interdependently. One way to express those interrelationships is that

- our purpose affects the manner in which we ask *questions;*
- the manner in which we ask *questions* affects the *information* we gather;
- the *information* we gather affects the way we *interpret* it;
- the way we *interpret* information affects the way we *conceptualize* it;
- the way we *conceptualize* information affects the *assumptions* we make;
- the *assumptions* we make affect the *implications* that follow from our thinking;
- the *implications* that follow from our thinking affect the way we see things, our *point of view.*

Think for Yourself

THINKING THROUGH THE ELEMENTS OF YOUR REASONING

Select an important conclusion that you have reasoned to—for example, your decision to go to college. Identify the circumstances in which you made that decision and some of the inferences you made in the process (about the costs, advantages, etc.). State the likely *implications* of your decision: the consequences it has had, and will have, in your life; the *information* you took into account in deciding to go to college; the way you expressed the *question* to yourself; and the *way you looked at your life* and your future (while reasoning through the question). See if you can grasp the interrelationships of all of these elements in your thinking. Don't be surprised if you find this task difficult.

One of the fundamental skills of critical thinking is the ability to assess one's own reasoning. To be good at assessment requires that we consistently take apart our thinking and examine the parts (or elements) for quality. We do this using intellectual standards such as clarity, accuracy, precision, relevance, depth, breadth, logic, significance, and fairness. Critical thinkers recognize that, whenever they are reasoning, they reason to some purpose (element of reasoning). Implicit goals are built into their thought processes. But their reasoning is improved when they are clear (intellectual standard) about that purpose or goal. Similarly, to reason well, they need to know that, consciously or unconsciously, they are using information (element of reasoning) in thinking. But their reasoning improves if and when they make sure that the information they are using is accurate (intellectual standard).

Put another way, we assess our reasoning to find out how well we are reasoning. We do not assess the elements of reasoning for the fun of it, or just to satisfy some authority. Rather, we do so because we realize the negative consequences of failing to do so. In assessing reasoning, then, we recommend these intellectual standards as minimal:

▓ clarity	▓ breadth
▓ accuracy	▓ logic
▓ precision	▓ significance
▓ relevance	▓ fairness
▓ depth	

These are not the only intellectual standards a person might use. They are simply some of the most fundamental. In this respect, the elements of thought are more basic than the standards, because the eight elements are *universal*—present in *all* reasoning on *all* subjects in *all* cultures for *all* time. On the one hand, one cannot reason with *no* information about *no* question from *no* point of view with *no* assumptions. On the other hand, there is a wide variety of intellectual standards from which to choose in addition to those listed above—such as credibility, predictability, feasibility, and completeness—that we don't use routinely in assessing reasoning but that we sometimes use.

As critical thinkers, then, we think about our thinking with these kinds of questions in mind: Am I being clear? Accurate? Precise? Relevant? Am I thinking logically? Am I dealing with a matter of significance? Is my thinking justifiable in context? Typically, we apply these standards to one or more elements.

Think for Yourself

IDENTIFYING INAPPROPRIATE STANDARDS

Can you identify a class you have taken in which you think your work was graded, at least in part, by one or more inappropriate standards? What was the class? What was the standard? What was the result? Can you see the importance of basing all grades on appropriate intellectual standards? Write out or orally explain your answer.

TAKE A DEEPER LOOK AT UNIVERSAL INTELLECTUAL STANDARDS

Critical thinkers routinely ask questions to assess the quality of reasoning, questions that apply intellectual standards to their thinking. You want to become so familiar with these questions that you ask them automatically. Eventually they will become part of your "inner voice," guiding you to better and better reasoning.

Clarity

Questions you can ask yourself or another person to clarify thinking include:

- Could you elaborate on that point? *or* Do I need to elaborate on that point?
- Could you express that point another way? *or* Can I express that point differently?
- Could you give me an illustration? *or* Should I give an illustration?
- Could you give me an example? *or* Should I provide an example?
- Let me state in my own words what I think you just said. Tell me if I am clear about your meaning. *or* Please tell me in your own words what you think I just said, so I can be sure you understand me.

Clarity means the reader or listener can understand what is being said. Clarity is a "gateway" standard—the first assessment test that has to be passed. If a statement is unclear, we cannot determine whether it is accurate or relevant. In fact, we cannot apply any of the other standards to it, because we don't yet know what it is saying. For example, the question, "What can be done about the education system in America?" is unclear. To adequately address the question, we would need a clearer understanding of what the person asking the question considers the "problem" to be. A clearer question might be, "What can educators do to ensure that students learn the skills and abilities that help them function successfully on the job and in their daily decision making?" Because this question is clearer, it is a better guide to thinking. It lays out more definitively the intellectual task at hand.

Think for Yourself

CONVERTING UNCLEAR THOUGHTS TO CLEAR THOUGHTS

Suppose you are engaged in a discussion about welfare, and someone says, "Let's face it—welfare is corrupt!" What does this mean? What could it mean?

It could mean some very different things. It might mean, "The idea of giving people goods and services they have not personally earned is equivalent to stealing money from those who have earned it" (a moral claim). Or it might mean, "The welfare laws have so many loopholes that people are receiving money and services that were not envisioned when the laws were initially formulated" (a legal claim). Or it might mean, "The people who receive welfare often lie, cheat, and falsify the documents they submit, and they should be thrown in jail" (a claim about the ethical character of the recipients).

For practice in making thoughts clear, take this statement, "She is a good person." This statement is unclear. Because we don't know the *context* within which this statement is being made, we aren't sure in what way "she" is "good." Formulate three possible meanings of this statement.

Now take the statement, "He is a jerk." Again, formulate three different possible meanings of this statement.

When you become skilled in differentiating what is clear from what is unclear, you will find that much of the time we are unclear both about what we are thinking and about what we are saying.

Accuracy

Questions that focus on assessing thinking for accuracy include:

* Is that really true?
* How could we check to see if that is accurate?
* How could we find out if that is true?

A statement may be clear but not accurate, as in "Most dogs weigh more than 300 pounds." To be accurate is to represent something in accordance with the way it actually is. People often present or describe things, events, people, and ideas in a way that differs from the way they actually are. This often happens when people have a "vested interest" in defining things in a certain way. For example, advertisers often do this to keep a buyer from seeing the weaknesses in a product. If an advertisement states, "Our water is 100% pure" when in fact the water contains small amounts of chemicals such as chlorine and lead, it is inaccurate. If an advertisement says, "This bread contains 100% whole wheat" when the whole wheat has been bleached and enriched and the bread contains many additives, the advertisement is inaccurate. Good thinkers listen carefully to statements. When there is reason for skepticism, they question whether what they hear is true and accurate. They also question the extent to which what they read is correct, when asserted as fact. Critical thinking then implies having a healthy skepticism about information presented as fact (when it may well be questionable).

At the same time, because we tend to think from a narrow, self-serving perspective, assessing ideas for accuracy can be difficult. We naturally tend to believe that our thoughts are automatically accurate just because they are ours, and therefore that the thoughts of those who disagree with us are inaccurate. We often fail to question statements that others make that conform to what we already believe, while we tend to question statements that conflict with our views. But as critical thinkers, we force ourselves to accurately assess our own views as well as those of others. We do this even if it means facing deficiencies in our thinking.

Think for Yourself

RECOGNIZING INACCURATE STATEMENTS

Inaccurate statements are common, especially when people are praising or criticizing. People tend to make two kinds of inaccurate statements: false positives (untrue positive statements) about people they personally like and false negatives (untrue negative things) about people they personally dislike. Politically motivated statements tend to follow a similar pattern. Think of examples of inaccurate statements from your recent experience. Write them out or orally explain them.

Think for Yourself

SEARCHING FOR THE FACTS

One of the most important critical thinking skills is that of assessing the accuracy of factual claims. *Factual claims* are statements asserting that something is true. For example, in an ad in the *New York Times* (Nov. 29, 1999, p. A15), a group of 60 nonprofit organizations called the Turning Point Project accused the World Trade Organization (a coalition of 134 nation states) of operating in secret and undermining democratic institutions and the environment. The nonprofit group argued that the working class and the poor have not significantly benefited from the past 20 years of rapid expansion in global trade. They made the following factual claims, among others:

1. "American CEOs are now paid, on average, 419 times more than line workers, and the ratio is increasing."
2. "Median hourly wages for workers are down by 10% in the last 10 years."
3. "The top 20% of the U.S. population owns 84.6% of the country's wealth."
4. "The wealth of the world's 475 billionaires now equals the annual incomes of more than 50% of the world population *combined.*"

Discuss the probable accuracy of these claims. Do research to try to confirm or refute them. You might start with the Web site of the Turning Point Project, www.turnpoint.org, and that of the World Trade Organization at www.wto.org. You might find new information and arguments that provide a different perspective than that of the nonprofit coalition.

Precision

Questions that focus on assessing thinking for preciseness include:

- Could you give me more details?
- Could you be more specific?

It is possible for a statement to be both clear and accurate but not precise. An example is "Jack is overweight." We don't know how overweight Jack is—1 pound or 500 pounds. To be *precise* is to give the details needed for someone to understand exactly what is meant. Some situations don't call for precision. If you ask, "Is there any milk in the refrigerator?" and I answer "Yes," both the question and the answer are probably precise enough for the situation (though it might be important to specify how much milk there is). Or imagine that you are ill and you go to the doctor. He wouldn't say, "Take 1.4876946 antibiotic pills every 11.5692 hours." This level of specificity, or precision, would be beyond that which is useful in the situation.

In many situations, however, specifics are essential to good thinking. Let's say that your friend is having financial problems, and she asks you, "What should I do about my situation?" In this case, you want to probe her thinking for details. Without the full specifics, you could not help her. You might ask questions such as, "What *precisely* is the problem? What *exactly* are the variables that bear on the problem? What are some possible solutions to the problem—in detail?"

Think for Yourself

RECOGNIZING IMPRECISE STATEMENTS

Can you think of a recent situation where a lack of precision caused a problem? It might have been a situation where you needed more details to figure something out, or one where you experienced negative consequences because you didn't have enough details. For example, you might have been given directions to someone's house that caused you to get lost because they were not detailed enough.

Think of a situation in which the details were important (for example, in buying a computer, a car, or a stereo system). Then identify the negative consequences that resulted because you didn't get the details you needed to think well in the situation. Write out or orally explain your answer.

Relevance

Questions that focus on assessing thinking for relevance include:

- How is this idea connected to the question we are asking?
- How does this fact bear on the issue?
- How does this idea relate to this other idea?
- How does your question relate to the issue we are dealing with?

It is possible for a statement to be clear, accurate, and precise, but not relevant to the question at issue. For example, students often think the amount of effort they put into a course should contribute to raising their grade in the course. Often, however, effort does not measure the quality of student learning, and therefore it is irrelevant to the grade. Something is *relevant* when it is directly connected with and bears on the issue at hand. Something is relevant when it is pertinent or applicable to a problem we are trying to solve. Relevant thinking stays "on track." In contrast, irrelevant thinking encourages us to consider what we should set aside. People are often irrelevant in their thinking because they lack intellectual discipline. They don't know how to analyze an issue for what truly bears on it. Therefore, they aren't able to think effectively through the problems and issues they face.

Think for Yourself

RECOGNIZING IRRELEVANT STATEMENTS

Though we all sometimes stray from a question or task, we need to be sensitive to when this can have significant negative implications.

First, list some situations in which people tend to bring irrelevant considerations into a discussion (for example, in meetings, in responses to questions in class, in everyday discussions when they have a hidden agenda—or simply want to get control of the conversation for some reason). Then list some specific statements you have heard recently that were irrelevant. How did they affect the thinking process? Write out or orally explain your answer.

Depth

Questions that focus on assessing thinking for depth include:

- How does your answer address the complexities in the question?
- How are you taking into account the problems in the question?
- How are you dealing with the most significant factors in the problem?

We think *deeply* when we get beneath the surface of an issue or problem, identify the complexities in it, and then deal with those complexities in an intellectually responsible way. For some questions, even when we think deeply and deal well with the complexities, a solution or answer may still be difficult to find. Still our thinking will work better for us when we can recognize complicated questions and address each area of complexity in it.

It is possible for a statement to be clear, accurate, precise, and relevant, but superficial—lacking in depth. Suppose you are asked what should be done about the problem of drug abuse in America, and you answer by saying, "Just say no." This slogan, which appeared in anti-drug TV announcements for several years, is clear, accurate, precise, and relevant. Nevertheless, it lacks depth, because it treats a complex issue—the problem of drug abuse among people in our culture—superficially. It does not address the history of the problem, the politics of the problem, the economics of the problem, the psychology of addiction, and so on.

Think for Yourself

RECOGNIZING SUPERFICIAL APPROACHES

Look through a newspaper to find an article that contains a statement that is clear, accurate, precise, and relevant, but superficial with respect to a complex issue. For example, you might find a description of a law that takes a "Band-Aid" approach to a systemic problem such as drugs or crime.

State the problem at issue, then identify how the statement deals with the problem and why this approach is superficial. Think about the issue, trying to go deeply into its roots and complexities. State how the problem might be dealt with more effectively.

Breadth

Questions that focus on assessing thinking for breadth include:

- Do we need to consider another point of view?
- Is there another way to look at this question?
- What would this look like from a conservative or a liberal standpoint?
- What would this look like from the point of view of . . . ?

It is possible for a line of reasoning to be clear, accurate, precise, relevant, and deep, but still to lack breadth. Examples are arguments from either the conservative or the liberal standpoint that go deeply into an issue but show insight into only one side of the question.

Thinking broadly means considering the issue at hand from every relevant viewpoint. When multiple points of view are pertinent to an issue, yet we fail to give due consideration to those perspectives, our thinking is myopic or narrow-minded. We do not try to enter alternative or opposing viewpoints that could help us better address the issue.

Humans are frequently guilty of narrow-mindedness for many reasons: limited education, innate sociocentrism, natural selfishness, self-deception, and intellectual arrogance. Points of view that significantly contradict our own can seem threatening. We may find it easier to ignore perspectives with which we disagree than to consider them, because to consider them, in good faith, might mean reconsidering our own views.

Suppose, for example, that you and I are roommates and that I like to play loud music that annoys you. The question at issue is: "Should I play loud music when you are present?"

Both your viewpoint and mine are relevant to the question at issue. When I recognize your viewpoint as relevant, and then intellectually empathize with it—when I enter your way of thinking so as to actually understand it—I will be forced to see that imposing my loud music on you is unfair and inconsiderate. I will be able to imagine what it would be like to be forced to listen to loud music that I find annoying. But if I don't force myself to enter your viewpoint, I do not have to change my self-serving behavior. One of the primary mechanisms the mind uses to avoid giving up what it wants is unconsciously to refuse to enter viewpoints that differ from its own.

Think for Yourself

THINKING BROADLY ABOUT AN ISSUE

Take the question, "Is abortion ethically justified?" Some people argue that abortion is not ethically justifiable, and others argue that it is. Try to state and elaborate on each of these points of view in detail. Think about each point of view objectively, regardless of your personal views. Present each point of view in such a way that a person who actually takes that position would assess it as accurate. *Each line of reasoning should be clear, accurate, precise, relevant, and deep. Do not take a position on this issue yourself.*

Logic

Questions that focus on assessing thinking to determine whether it is logical include:

- Does all of this fit together logically?
- Does this really make sense?
- Does that conclusion follow from what you said?
- How does that inference follow from the evidence?
- Before, you implied this, and now you are saying that. I don't see how both can be true.

When we think, we bring together a variety of thoughts in some order. When the combined thoughts support each other and make sense together, the thinking is *logical.* When the combination is contradictory in some sense or the ideas do not make sense together, the combination is not logical. Because people often hold conflicting beliefs without being aware that they are doing so, it is not unusual to find inconsistencies in human life and thought.

Let's say we know, by looking at standardized tests of students in schools and the actual work they are able to produce, that for the most part students are deficient in basic academic skills such as reading, writing, speaking, and the core disciplines such as math, science, and history. Despite this evidence, teachers often conclude that there is nothing they can or should do to change their instruction to improve student learning (and in fact that there is nothing fundamentally wrong with the way they teach). Given the evidence, this conclusion seems illogical. The conclusion doesn't seem to follow from the facts.

For another example, suppose you know a person who has had a heart attack, and her doctors have told her she must eat more healthy foods to avoid problems in the future. Yet she concludes that what she eats really doesn't matter. Given the evidence, her conclusion is illogical. It doesn't make sense.

Think for Yourself

RECOGNIZING ILLOGICAL THINKING

Find a newspaper article that contains an example of illogical thinking—thinking that doesn't make sense to you.

1. State the issue that the thinking revolves around.
2. State the thinking that you believe is illogical and why you think it is illogical.
3. State some implications of the illogical thinking. In other words, what are some consequences likely to follow from the illogical thinking?

Significance

Questions that focus on assessing thinking for significance include:

- What is the most significant information we need to gather and use in our thinking if we are to address this issue?
- How is this fact important in context?
- Which of these questions is the most significant?
- Which of these ideas or concepts is the most important?

Thinking is most effective when it concentrates on the most important information and takes into account the most important ideas and concepts. Many ideas may be relevant to an issue, but not all of them are equally important. When we fail to ask important questions, we become mired in superficial questions, questions of little weight. For example, few college students focus on important questions such as, "What does it mean to be an educated person? What do I need to do to become educated?" Instead, they tend to ask questions such as, "What do I need to do to get an A in this course? How many pages does this paper have to be? What do I have to do to satisfy this professor?"

Think for Yourself

FOCUSING ON SIGNIFICANCE IN THINKING

Think about the way you spend your time. How much time do you spend on significant versus trivial things? Answer these questions:

1. What is the most important goal or purpose you should focus on at this point in your life? Why is this purpose important? How much time do you spend focused on it?
2. What are the most trivial or superficial things you spend time focused on (things such as your appearance, impressing your friends, chatting about insignificant things at parties, and the like).
3. What can you do to reduce the amount of time you spend on trivial things and increase the amount of time you spend on significant things?

Fairness

Questions that focus on assessing thinking for fairness include:

- Is my thinking justified given the evidence?

- Am I giving the evidence as much weight as it deserves?

- Are my assumptions justified?

- Is my behavior fair, given its implications?

- Is my selfish interest keeping me from considering the problem from alternative viewpoints?

- Am I using concepts justifiably, or am I using them unfairly in order to manipulate someone (to selfishly get what I want)?

When we think through problems, we want to make sure that our thinking is justified. To be justified is to think fairly in context. In other words, it is to think in accord with reason. If you are careful to meet the other intellectual standards covered thus far in this chapter, you will (by implication) satisfy the standard of fairness or justifiability.

We think it is important to target fairness in its own section because of the powerful nature of self-deception in human thinking. It is easy to deceive ourselves into believing that our ideas are fair and justified, when in fact we are refusing to consider significant relevant information that would cause us to change our view (and therefore not pursue our selfish interest). This is the natural state of the human mind. We often pursue unjustified purposes in order to get what we want even if we have to hurt others to get it. We often use concepts in an unjustified way in order to manipulate people. And we often make unjustified assumptions, unsupported by facts, that then lead to faulty inferences.

Sometimes the problem of unjustified thinking comes from ignoring relevant facts. Suppose that Kristi and Abbey live together. Abbey grew up in Vermont and Kristi is from Arizona. During the winter, Abbey likes to have the windows in the house open, while Kristi likes to keep them closed. But Abbey insists that it is "extremely uncomfortable" with the windows closed. All of the information Abbey is using in her reasoning centers on her own point of view—that *she* is hot, that *she* can't function well if she's hot, and that if Kristi is cold she can wear a sweater. But the fact is that Abbey is not justified in her thinking. She refuses to enter Kristi's point of view and to consider information supporting Kristi's perspective, because to do so would mean that *she would have to give something up.* She would have to adopt a more reasonable or fair point of view.

When we reason to conclusions, we want to check to make sure that the assumptions we are using to come to those conclusions are justifiable given the facts of the situation. For example, all of our prejudices and stereotypes function as assumptions in thinking. And no prejudices and stereotypes are justifiable, given their very nature. For example, we often make generalizations such as these:

- Liberals are soft on crime.

- Elderly people aren't interested in sex.

- Young men are only interested in sex.

- Jocks are cool.

- Blondes are dumb.

- Cheerleaders are airheads.

- Intellectuals are nerds.

- Learning is boring.

- School doesn't have anything to do with life.

The problem with assumptions like these is that they cause us to make basic—and often serious—mistakes in thinking. Because they aren't justifiable, they cause us to prejudge situations and people and to draw faulty inferences—or conclusions—about them. If we believe that all intellectuals are nerds, whenever we meet an intellectual we will infer that he or she is a nerd and act unfairly toward the person.

In sum, justifiability or fairness is an important standard in thinking because it helps us see how we may be distorting our own thinking in order to achieve self-serving ends—or how others are doing so at our expense.

Humans often engage in irrational behavior. We fight. We start wars. We kill. We are self-destructive. We are petty and vindictive. We act out when we don't get our way. We abuse our spouses. We neglect our children. We rationalize, project, and stereotype. We act inconsistently, ignore relevant evidence, jump to conclusions, and say and believe things that don't make good sense. We deceive ourselves in many ways. We are our own worst enemy.

There are two overlapping and interrelated motivating impulses behind human irrationality. These impulses are the focus of this chapter. They are:

1. *Human egocentrism,* the natural human tendency "to view everything within the world in relationship to oneself, to be self-centered" *(Webster's New World Dictionary)*

2. *Human sociocentrism,* most simply conceptualized as *group egocentricity.* To define sociocentricity, we might take Webster's definition of egocentricity and substitute *group* for *self.* Sociocentric thinking is the natural human tendency to view everything within the world in relationship to one's group—to be group-centered.

Human egocentricity has two basic tendencies. One is to see the world in **self-serving** terms, constantly to seek that which makes one feel good or that which one selfishly wants, at the expense of the rights and needs of others. The second primary tendency of egocentricity is the desire to maintain its beliefs. It manifests itself in **rigidity of thought.** It views its irrational beliefs as rational.

Sociocentric thinking is an extension of egocentric thinking. Humans are herd animals, largely influenced by and functioning within groups. And because most people are largely egocentric, or centered in themselves, they end up forming groups that are also largely centered in themselves. As a result of egocentrism and sociocentrism, most people are self-serving and rigid, they conform to group thinking, and they assume the correctness of their own beliefs and that of their groups.

Sociocentric thought, then, is a direct extension of egocentric thought in that it operates from the two primary tendencies of egocentric thought:

1. Seeking to get what it (or its group) wants without regard to the rights and needs of others

2. Rationalizing the beliefs and behavior of the group, regardless of whether those beliefs and behaviors are irrational

Sociocentric thought, then, presupposes the egocentric tendencies of the human mind. The selfish mind finds its natural home in the self-centered group. And virtually all groups operate with in-group advantages denied to those in the out-groups. The result is many forms of social conflict, punishment, and vengeance. Sociocentrism is also close to the root of most wars and war crimes. It enables some (advantaged) people to be comfortable in the face of the wretched suffering of masses of (disadvantaged) others. It enables some in a group (the elite) to manipulate others in the group (the non-elite).

Consider the similarity between street gangs and nations. Gangs collectively pursue irrational purposes and engage in violence against other gangs—behavior that can appear justified only in one-sided, group-serving thought. In a similar way, countries often attack other countries using equally one-sided, group-serving thought. The difference is often merely one of sophistication, not of kind. Gang violence is censured by society, international acts of war validated (at least by the attacking country).

In short, people are either born into or join groups. They then egocentrically identify with those groups. They rarely dissent. They rarely think for themselves. They rarely notice their own conformity and irrationality. Humans seek what is in their selfish interests and see the world from the perspectives of the (sociocentric) groups to which they belong. Both egocentric and sociocentric thought represent enormous barriers to the development of rational thought. This is true, in part, because these two tendencies in the mind *appear to the mind as perfectly rational.* Unless we fully understand these overlapping tendencies and fight to combat them, we can never fully develop as rational, autonomous, fair-minded thinkers.

CRITICAL, CREATIVE, AND PRACTICAL THINKING

To survive and to thrive in college and beyond, you will need to use your thinking power to do more than remember formulas for a test. When problems or decisions arise on the road toward goals large and small, how can you work through them successfully? The answer lies in how you combine your analytical, creative, and practical thinking skills—in other words, how you use your successful intelligence. Successful intelligence is "the kind of intelligence used to achieve important goals."[1]

Thinking, like note taking or car repair, is a skill that can be developed with practice. This chapter will help you build your ability to analyze information, come up with creative ideas, and put a practical plan into action. With these skills you can become a better thinker, problem solver, and decision maker, able to reach the goals that mean the most to you. This ability is emphasized by the Conference Board of Canada's Employability Skills 2000+ report in which employers underline the significance of being able to "assess situations, identify problems and then evaluate and implement solutions."

WHAT IS SUCCESSFULLY INTELLIGENT THINKING?

Robert Sternberg uses this story to illustrate the impact of successful intelligence:

> Two boys are walking in a forest. They are quite different. The first boy's teachers think he is smart, his parents think he is smart, and as a result, he thinks he is smart. He has good test scores, good grades, and other good paper credentials that will get him far in his scholastic life.
>
> Few people consider the second boy smart. His test scores are nothing great, his grades aren't so good, and his other paper credentials are, in general, marginal. At best, people would call him shrewd or street smart.
>
> As the two boys walk along in the forest, they encounter a problem—a huge, furious, hungry-looking grizzly bear, charging straight at them. The first boy, calculating that the grizzly bear will overtake them in 17.3 seconds, panics. In this state, he looks at the second boy, who is calmly taking off his hiking boots and putting on his jogging shoes.
>
> The first boy says to the second boy, "You must be crazy. There is no way you are going to outrun that grizzly bear!"
>
> The second boy replies, "That's true. But all I have to do is outrun you!"[2]

This story shows that successful problem solving and decision making require more than "book smarts." When confronted with a problem, using only analytical thinking put the first boy at a disadvantage. On the other hand, the second boy thought in different ways; he analyzed the situation, creatively considered the options, and took practical action. He asked and answered questions. He knew his purpose. And he lived to tell the tale.

Successfully Intelligent Thinking Is Balanced

Some tasks require only one thinking skill or ability at a time. You might use analytical thinking to complete a multiple-choice quiz, creative thinking to figure out how to get a paper done the same day you work a long shift, or practical thinking to put together a desk marked "some assembly required." However, when you need to solve a problem or make a decision, your analytical, creative, and practical thinking skills build upon one another to move you forward.[3] Envision it this way: Just as a pyramid needs

FIGURE 5.1   *Successful intelligence depends on three thinking skills.*

three sides in order to stand, successful thinkers need all three thinking skills to develop the best solutions and decisions (see Figure 5.1).

Each thinking skill adds an important dimension to accomplishing goals. Developing a balanced set of skills and knowing how and when to use each of them gives you more thinking power than having a strong aptitude in any one ability.[4] This kind of flexible thinking will help you connect your academic tasks to life goals—and show you where your hard work can take you (see Figure 5.2).

Successfully Intelligent Thinking Means Asking and Answering Questions

What is thinking? According to experts, it is what happens when you ask questions and move toward the answers.[5] "To think through or rethink anything," says Dr. Richard Paul, director of research at the Center for Critical Thinking and Moral Critique, "one must ask questions that stimulate our thought. Questions define tasks, express problems and delineate issues.... [O]nly students who have questions are really thinking and learning."[6]

As you answer questions, you transform raw data into information that you can use. A *Wall Street Journal* article entitled "The Best Innovations Are Those That Come from Smart Questions" relates the story of a cell biology student, William Hunter, whose professor told him that "the difference between good science and great science is the

FIGURE 5.2 *Successful intelligence helps you achieve goals in any discipline.*

Discipline	Analytical Thinking	Creative Thinking	Practical Thinking
Behavioural Science	Comparing one theory of child development with another	Devising a new theory of child development	Applying child development theories to help parents and teachers understand and deal with children more effectively
Literature	Analyzing the development of the main character in a novel	Writing alternative endings to the novel	Using the experience of the main character to better understand and manage one's own life situations
History	Considering similarities and differences between WWI and WWII	Imagining yourself as a German citizen, dealing with economic depression after WWI	Seeing what WWI and WWII lessons can be applied to current Middle East conflicts
Sports	Analyzing the opposing team's strategy on the soccer field	Coming up with innovative ways to move the ball downfield	Using tactics to hide your strategy from an opposing team—or a competing company

Source: Adapted from Robert J. Sternberg, *Successful Intelligence*. Plume: New York, 1997, p. 149.

quality of the questions posed." Later, as a doctor and the president and CEO of a pharmaceutical company, Dr. Hunter asked questions about new ways to use drugs. His questions led to the development of a revolutionary product—a drug-coated coronary stent that prevents scar tissue from forming. Through seeking answers to probing questions, Dr. Hunter reached a significant goal.[7]

You use questions in order to analyze ("How bad is my money situation?"), come up with creative ideas ("What ways could I earn money?"), and apply practical solutions ("How can I get a job on campus?"). Later in the chapter, in the sections on analytical, creative, and practical thinking, you will find examples of the kinds of questions that drive each skill.

Like any aspect of thinking, questioning is not often a straightforward process. Sometimes the answer doesn't come right away. Often the answer leads to more—and more specific—questions.

Successfully Intelligent Thinking Requires Knowing Your Purpose

In order to ask useful questions, you need to know *why* you are questioning. In other words, you need to define your purpose. Not knowing your purpose may lead you to ask questions that take you in irrelevant directions and waste your time. For example, if an assignment asks you to analyze the effectiveness of Canada's foreign policy during Jean Chrétien's tenure as prime minister, asking questions about his personal life may lead you off the track.

A general question can be your starting point for defining your purposes: "What am I trying to accomplish, and why?" Then, within each stage of the process, you will find more specific purposes or sub-goals that help you generate analytical, creative, or practical questions along the way.

Successfully Intelligent Thinking Is Yours to Build

You can improve your ability to think, now and throughout your life. Studies have shown that the brain continues to develop throughout your life if you continue to learn new things.[8] Puzzle master Nob Yoshigahara has said, "As jogging is to the body, thinking is to the brain. The more we do it, the better we become."[9]

The mini-assessments within this chapter will help you to get an idea of how you perceive yourself as an analytical, creative, and practical thinker. Every other chapter's set of *Get Analytical*, *Get Creative*, and *Get Practical* exercises then helps you to build your skills in those areas. Finally, the *Developing Successful Intelligence*: *Putting It All Together* exercises at the ends of chapters encourage you to both build and combine your skills. *Your work throughout the book is geared toward building your successful intelligence.*

Begin by exploring the analytical thinking skills that you'll need in order to solve problems and make decisions effectively.

HOW CAN YOU IMPROVE YOUR ANALYTICAL THINKING SKILLS?

Analytical thinking—also known as critical thinking—is the process of gathering information, analyzing it in different ways, and evaluating it for the purposes of gaining understanding, solving a problem, or making a decision. It is as essential for real-life problems and decisions as it is for thinking through the hypothetical questions on your chemistry homework.

The first step in analytical thinking, as with all aspects of successful intelligence, is to define your purpose. What do you want to analyze, and why? Perhaps you need to analyze the plot of a novel in order to determine its structure; maybe you want to analyze your schedule in order to figure out whether you are arranging your time and responsibilities effectively.

Once you define your purpose, the rest of the analytical process involves gathering the necessary information, analyzing and clarifying the ideas, and evaluating what you've found.

Gather Information

Information is the raw material for thinking. Choosing what to gather requires a careful analysis of how much information you need, how much time to spend gathering it, and whether the information is relevant. Say, for instance, that your assignment is to write a paper on rock 'n' roll music in Canada. If you gathered every available resource on the topic, it might be next semester before you got to the writing stage.

Here's how you might use analysis to effectively gather information for that paper:

※ Reviewing the assignment, you learn that the paper should be ten pages and cover at least three influential Canadian musicians.

※ At the library and on-line, you find a lot of what appears to be relevant information.

※ You choose Neil Young, Randy Bachman, and Joni Mitchell, and then select three in-depth sources on each of the three musicians and how they influenced the development of rock music in Canada.

In this way you achieve a sub-goal—a selection of useful materials—on the way to your larger goal of writing a well-crafted paper.

Analyze and Clarify Information

Once you've gathered the information, the next step is to analyze it to determine whether the information is reliable and useful in helping you answer your questions.

Break Information Into Parts

When analyzing information, you break information into parts and examine the parts so that you can see how they relate to each other and to information you already know. The following strategies help you break information down into pieces and set aside what is unclear, unrelated, or unimportant, resulting in a deeper and more reliable understanding.

Separate the Ideas.   If you are reading about Neil Young, you might want to break down his career and significant contributions to music as a solo artist, and as a member of The Mynah Birds, Buffalo Springfield, and Crosby, Stills, Nash, and Young. You might also want to separate his contributions as a performer and as a songwriter.

Compare and Contrast.   Look at how things are similar to, or different from, each other. You might explore how these three musicians are similar in style. You might look at how they differ in what they want to communicate with their music.

Examine Cause and Effect.   Look at the possible reasons why something happened (possible causes) and its consequences (effects, both positive and negative). You might also wish to examine which contemporary Canadian musicians were influenced by Neil Young or how the grunge movement of the 1990s was inspired by Young.

> If one wants to be successful,
> one must think; one must
> think until it hurts.
>
> Roy Thomson

Look for Themes, Patterns, and Categories.　Note connections that arise out of how bits of information relate to one another. You may choose to write about the theme of social and political consciousness in the lyrics of Neil Young. What category would Neil Young's music best fit into: rock or folk?

Once the ideas are broken down, you can examine whether examples support ideas, separate fact from opinion, consider perspective, and investigate hidden assumptions.

Examine Whether Examples Support Ideas

When you encounter an idea or claim, examine how it is supported with examples or evidence (facts, expert opinion, research findings, personal experience, and so on). Ideas that aren't backed up with solid evidence or made concrete with examples are not useful. Be critical of the information you gather; don't take it at face value.

For example, an advertisement for a weight-loss pill claiming that it allows users to drop a pound a day, quotes "Anne" who says that she lost 30 pounds in 30 days. The word of one person, who may or may not be telling the truth, is not adequate support. On the other hand, a claim that water once existed on Mars, backed up by measurements and photography from one of the Mars Exploration Rovers, may prove more reliable.

Distinguish Fact from Opinion

A *statement of fact* is information presented as objectively real and verifiable ("It's raining outside right now"). In contrast, a *statement of opinion* is a belief, conclusion, or judgment that is inherently difficult, and sometimes impossible, to verify ("This is the most miserable rainstorm ever"). Figure 5.3 defines important characteristics of fact and opinion. Finding credible, reliable information with which to answer questions and come up with ideas enables you to separate fact from opinion. Even though facts may seem more solid, you can also make use of opinions if you determine that they are backed up with facts. However, it is important to examine opinions for their underlying perspectives and assumptions.

Shifting your perspective helps you accept and understand different ways of living and interacting. Two students communicate via sign language while walking on campus.

Examine Perspectives and Assumptions

Perspective is a characteristic way of thinking about people, situations, events, and ideas.

FIGURE 5.3 *Examine how fact and opinion differ.*

Opinions include statements that . . .	Facts include statements that . . .
. . . *show evaluation.* Any statement of value indicates an opinion. Words such as *bad, good, pointless,* and *beneficial* indicate value judgments. Example: "Bob Geldof is the most socially consious rock star ever."	. . . *deal with actual people, places, objects, or events.* Example: "In 1985, Bob Geldof organized Live Aid, which raised money and awareness for famine relief in Africa. In 2005, Live8 helped push the G8 Summit agenda into the mainstream."
. . . *use abstract words.* Words that are complicated to define, like *misery* or *success,* usually indicate a personal opinion. Example: "The charity event was a smashing success."	. . . *use concrete words or measurable statistics.* Example: "The charity event raised $5,862."
. . . *predict future events.* Statements that examine future occurrences are often opinions. Example: "Mr. Maurin's course is going to set a new environment record this year."	. . . *describe current events in exact terms.* Example: "Mr. Maurin's course has set a new enrolment record this semester."
. . . *use emotional words.* Emotions are by nature unverifiable. Chances are that statements using such words as *delightful* or *miserable* express an opinion. Example: "That class is a miserable experience."	. . . *avoid emotional words and focus on the verifiable.* Example: "Citing dissatisfaction with the instruction, 7 out of the 25 students in that class withdrew in September."
. . . *use absolutes.* Absolute *qualifiers,* such as *all, none, never,* and *always,* often point to an opinion. Example: "All students need to have a job while in school."	. . . *avoid absolutes.* Example: "Some students need to have a job while in school."

Source: Adapted from Ben E. Johnson, *Stirring Up Thinking.* New York: Houghton Mifflin, 1998, pp. 268–270.

Perspectives can be broad, such as a generally optimistic or pessimistic view of life. Or they can be more focused, such as an attitude about whether students should commute or live on campus.

Perspectives are associated with *assumptions*—judgments, generalizations, or biases influenced by experience and values. For example, the perspective that there are many different successful ways to be a family leads to assumptions such as "Single-parent homes can provide nurturing environments" and "Same-sex couples can rear well-adjusted children." Having a particular experience with single-parent homes or same-sex couples can build or reinforce a perspective.

Assumptions often hide within questions and statements, blocking you from considering information in different ways. Take this classic puzzler as an example: "Which came first, the chicken or the egg?" Thinking about this question, most people assume that the egg is a chicken egg. If you think past that assumption and come up with a new idea—such as, the egg is a dinosaur egg—then the obvious answer is that the egg came first!

Examining perspectives and assumptions is important for two reasons. First, they often affect your perception of the validity of materials you read and research. Second, your own perspectives and assumptions can cloud your interpretation of the information you encounter.

Perspectives and Assumptions in Information

biased—
leaning in a
particular direction;
influenced by a
point of view.

Being able to determine the perspectives that underlie materials will help you separate **biased** from unbiased information. For example, the conclusions in two articles on federal versus provincial government control of education may differ radically if one appears in a politically conservative publication and one appears in a liberal publication. Comparing those articles will require that you understand and take into account the conservative and liberal perspectives on government's role in education.

Assumptions often affect the validity of materials you read and research. A historical document that originated on-line at a conservative blog may assume that liberal policies on health care are flawed, but may also leave out information to the contrary. Clearly understanding such a document means separating the assumptions from the facts.

Personal Perspectives and Assumptions

Your own preferences, values, and prejudices—which influence your perspective—can affect how accurately you view information. A student who thinks that the death penalty is wrong, for example, may have a hard time analyzing the facts and arguments in an article that supports it. Or in a research situation, he might use only materials that agree with his perspective.

Consider the perspectives and assumptions that might follow from your values. Then when you have to analyze information, try to set them aside. "Anticipate your reactions and prejudices and then consciously resist their influence," says Colby Glass, professor of information research and philosophy.[10]

In addition to helping you analyze accurately, opening yourself to new perspectives will help you build knowledge. The more you know, the more information you have to work with as you move through life and encounter new problems and decisions. Come to school ready to hear and read about new ideas, think about their merits, and make informed decisions about what you believe. Says Sternberg, "We need to... see issues from a variety of viewpoints and, especially, to see how other people and other cultures view issues and problems facing the world."[11]

Evaluate Information

You've gathered and analyzed your information. You have examined its components, its evidence, its validity, its perspective, and any underlying assumptions. Now, based on an examination of evidence and careful analysis, you *evaluate* whether an idea or

GET ANALYTICAL!

ASSESS ANALYTICAL THINKING SKILLS

How do you perceive yourself as an analytical thinker? For each statement, circle the number that feels right to you, from 1 for "least like me" to 5 for "most like me."

1. I tend to perform well on objective tests.   1   2   3   4   5

2. People say I'm a "thinker," "brainy," "studious."   1   2   3   4   5

3. I am not comfortable with grey areas—I prefer
   information to be laid out in black and white.   1   2   3   4   5

4. In a group setting, I like to tackle the details of a problem.   1   2   3   4   5

5. I sometimes over-think things and miss my moment of
   opportunity.   1   2   3   4   5

Total your answers here: _____

If your total ranges from 5–12, you consider your analytical thinking skills to be weak.

If your total ranges from 13–19, you consider your analytical thinking skills to be average.

If your total ranges from 20–25, you consider your analytical thinking skills to be strong.

piece of information is good or bad, important or unimportant, right or wrong. You then set aside what is not useful and use the rest to form an opinion, possible solution, or decision.

For example, you're working on a group presentation on the effects of television-watching on young children. You've gathered information that relates to your topic, come up with an idea, and analyzed whether the information supports this idea. Now you evaluate all of the evidence and present what's useful in an organized, persuasive way. Another example: In creating a résumé, you decide which information to include that will generate the most interest in potential employers and present you in the best light possible.

See Figure 5.4 for some questions you can ask to build and use analytical thinking skills.

Analytical thinking is only part of the picture. Pursuing your goals in school and in the workplace requires not just analyzing information but also thinking creatively about how to use it.

FIGURE 5.4 *Ask questions like these in order to analyze.*

To gather information, ask:	• What requirements does my goal have? • What kinds of information do I need to meet my goal? • What information is available? • Where and when is it available? Where and when can I access it? • Of the sources I found, which ones will best help me achieve my goal?
To analyze, ask:	• What are the parts of this information? • What is similar to this information? What is different? • What are the reasons for this? Why did this happen? • What ideas or themes emerge from this material? • How would you categorize this information? • What conclusions can you make about this information?
To see if examples support an idea, ask:	• What examples, or evidence, support the idea? • Does the evidence make sense? • Does the evidence support the idea/claim? • Is this evidence key information that I need to answer my question? • Are there examples that might disprove the idea/claim?
To distinguish fact from opinion, ask:	• Do the words in this information signal fact or opinion? (See Figure 5.3) • What is the source of this information? Is the source reliable? • How does this information compare to other facts or opinions? • If this is an opinion, is it supported by facts? • How can I use this fact or opinion?
To examine perspectives and assumptions, ask:	• Who is the author? What perspectives might this person have? • What might be emphasized or left out as a result of the perspective? • How could I consider this information from a different perspective? • What assumptions might lie behind this statement or material? • How could I prove or disprove an assumption? • What contradictory assumptions might be equally valid? • How might a personal perspective or assumption affect the way I see this material?
To evaluate, ask:	• Do I agree with this information? • Does this information fit what I'm trying to prove or accomplish? • Is this information true or false, and why? • How important is this information? • Which ideas or pieces of information would I choose to focus on?

Adapted from www.ed.fnal.gov/trc/tutorial/taxonomy.html (Richard Paul, *Critical Thinking: How to Prepare Students for a Rapidly Changing World,* 1993) and from www.kcmetro.edu/longview/ctac/blooms.htm, Barbara Fowler, Longview Community College "Bloom's Taxonomy and Critical Thinking."

HOW CAN YOU IMPROVE YOUR CREATIVE THINKING SKILLS?

ome researchers define creativity as combining existing elements in an innovative way to create a new purpose or result. For example, in 1970, 3M researcher Spencer Silver created a weak adhesive; four years later, another 3M scientist, Arthur Fry, used it for a hymnal marker. Post-it® Notes are now an office staple. Others see creativity as the art of generating ideas from taking a fresh look at how things are related (noting what ladybugs eat inspired organic farmers to bring them in to consume crop-destroying aphids).[12] Still others, including Sternberg, define it as the ability to make unusual connections—to view information in quirky ways that bring about unique results.

To think creatively is to generate new ideas that often go against conventional wisdom and may bring change. Consider how, in the 1940s, mathematician Grace Murray Hopper pioneered the effort to create computer languages that non-mathematicians could understand; her efforts opened the world of computers to a wide audience.

Creativity is not limited to inventions. For example, when she was in her first year of college, Meghan E. Taugher used her creative mind in two ways. First, she and her study group, as part of their class on electrical circuits, devised a solar-powered battery for a laptop computer. "We took the professor's laptop, put all the parts together, and sat outside watching it with a little device to see how much power it was saving. When it fully charged the battery, it was one of those times I felt that what I was learning was true, because I was putting it to use in real life."[13] Second, her experience led her to generate an idea of a new major and career plan—engineering.

Creativity forms a bridge between analytical and practical thinking. You need to think analytically to evaluate the quality of your creative ideas. You also need to think practically to implement them.

Where does creativity come from? Some people, through luck or natural inclination, seem to come up with inspired ideas more often than others. However, creative thinking, like analytical thinking, is a skill that can be developed. Creativity expert Roger von Oech says that mental flexibility is essential. "Like race-car drivers who shift in and out of different gears depending on where they are on the course," he says, you can enhance your creativity by learning to "shift in and out of different types of thinking depending on the needs of the situation at hand."[14]

These students, working through a problem for a course, demonstrate that successful problem solving often requires the input and teamwork of a group of people.

The following strategies will help you make those shifts and build your ability to think creatively. Note that, because creative ideas often pop up at random, writing them down as they arise will help you remember them. Keep a pen and paper by your bed, your BlackBerry or your Palm Pilot in your pocket, and a notepad in your car so that you can grab ideas before they fade from your mind.

Endnotes

1. Robert J. Sternberg, *Successful Intelligence*. New York: Plume, 1997, p. 12.
2. Ibid, p. 127.
3. Matt Thomas, "What Is Higher-Order Thinking and Critical/Creative/Constructive Thinking?" The Center for Studies in Higher-Order Literacy [on-line]. Available at: http://members.aol.com/MattT10574/HigherOrderLiteracy.htm#What (April 2004).
4. Sternberg, p. 128.
5. Vincent Ruggiero, *The Art of Thinking*, 2001, quoted in "Critical Thinking," Oregon State University [on-line]. Available at: http://success.oregonstate.edu/template/criticalthinking.html (April 2004).
6. Richard Paul, "The Role of Questions in Thinking, Teaching, and Learning," The Critical Thinking Community [on-line]. Available at: http://www.criticalthinking.org/resources/articles/the-role-of-questions.shtml (April 2004).
7. "The Best Innovations Are Those That Come from Smart Questions," *Wall Street Journal*, April 12, 2004, B1.
8. Lawrence F. Lowery, "The Biological Basis of Thinking and Learning," 1998, Full Option Science System at the University of California at Berkeley [on-line]. Available at: http://lhsfoss.org/newsletters/archive/pdfs/FOSS_BBTL.pdf (April 2004).
9. Ivan Moscovich, *1000 Playthinks*. New York: Workman Publishing, p. 7.
10. Colby Glass, "Strategies for Critical Thinking," March 1999 [on-line]. Available at: www.accd.edu/pac/philosop/phil1301/ctstrategies.htm (April 2004).
11. Sternberg, p. 49.
12. Charles Cave, "Definitions of Creativity," August 1999 [on-line]. Available at: http://members.ozemail.com.au/ྂcaveman/Creative/Basics/definitions.htm [subscription-based] (April 2003).
13. Elizabeth F. Farrell, "Engineering a Warmer Welcome for Female Students: The Discipline Tries to Stress its Social Relevance, an Important Factor for Many Women," *The Chronicle of Higher Education*, February 22, 2002 [on-line]. Available at: http://chronicle.com/weekly/v48/i24/24a03101.htm [subscription-based] (March 2004).
14. Roger von Oech, *A Kick in the Seat of the Pants*. New York: Harper & Row Publishers, 1986, pp. 5–21.

DEFINING AND APPLYING ETHICS

L ast Thursday, you went out for lunch with an acquaintance from biology class, a nice-enough fellow but not someone you consider a candidate for lifelong friendship. As you were wolfing down your last bite of cheeseburger, you suddenly gulped and flushed; you realized that you had forgotten your wallet. You were flat broke. Embarrassed, you entreated your classmate to lend you live dollars, which you would, of course, pay back on Tuesday. Today is Wednesday; you forgot.

Now you are doubly embarrassed, for having had to borrow the money in the first place and then for having forgotten to pay it back when promised. You are tempted, momentarily, to ignore the entire awkward situation, just to assume—what may well be true—that your classmate has forgotten about the loan. (After all, it is only five dollars.) But maybe he hasn't forgotten, or, at least, he'll remember it when he sees you. For an irrational instant, you consider dropping the class, but then you realize that would be ridiculous. It seems highly unlikely, since it would be very embarrassing (for him, that he would actually ask you for the money. Anyway, you aren't close friends and don't generally talk to each other. So what's the difference? You make up your mind not to repay the debt.

But now, small hints of large doubts start interrupting your day. You are convinced that no harm will come to you. The fellow knows none of your friends, and it is hardly likely that he will announce to the class or the world that you are a deadbeat. And yet, it's ruining your day, and it may well ruin other days. "If only I could get rid of this guilty feeling," you say to yourself. But it is not just a feeling; it is a new and wholly unwelcome sense of who you are. A voice inside of you (sometimes it sounds like your own voice; occasionally it seems to be your mother's) keeps whispering, "Deadbeat, deadbeat" (and worse). Already distracted from your work, you start speculating, "What if we all were to forget about our debts?" Your first response is that you would probably be washing dishes at the Burger Shoppe, since no one would ever lend anyone money. Your second response is that everyone doesn't forget, but this argument doesn't make you feel any better. It reminds you that in a world where most people pay their debts, you are one of the scoundrels who does not. You start rationalizing: "After all, I need the money more than he does." In a final moment of belligerence, you smash your fist on the table and say, within hearing distance of the people sharing your library table, "The only person I have to worry about is me!"

There is an embarrassed silence. Then you walk over to the bank of phones. You dial: "Hello, Harris? Remember that five dollars you loaned me?"

The point of this little scenario is to capture the day-to-day nature of ethics. Even such a simple situation involves conflicting interests, profound moral principles, and the nagging voice of conscience, culminating in a quiet but nevertheless telling conclusion concerning the sort of person you are. This case does not involve any of the more notoriously difficult social problems or life-or-death decisions so vehemently debated today, such as the abortion issue, the legitimacy of war, the plight of the homeless in a land of affluence, or starving children in a world awash with surplus food. But, ultimately, the considerations that enter into our debates on these global issues reflect our habits and opinions in the most ordinary circumstances. Our politics express who we are and what we believe, and even our most abstract ideologies reveal (although often in a convoluted and even reactionary way) the principles and prejudices of everyday llfe.

WHAT IS ETHICS?

Ethics is that part of philosophy that is concerned with living well, being a good person, doing the right thing, getting along with other people, and wanting the right things in life. Ethics is essential to living in society, any society, with its various traditions, practices, and institutions. Of course, those traditions, practices, and institutions can and must themselves be assessed according to ethical standards, but they themselves determine many of the rules and expectations that define the ethical outlook of the people living within them. Ethics therefore has both a social and a personal dimension, but it is not at all easy, in theory or in practice, to separate these. Moral judgment is both the product of society and one of its constitutive features. What we call our personal values are for the most part learned together and shared by a great many people. Indeed those values we consider most personal are typically not those that are most idiosyncratic but rather those that are most common, and most profound—respect for human (and animal) life, outrage at being the victim of a lie, compassion for those much worse off than yourself, and an insistence on personal integrity in the face of adversity.

The word *ethics* refers both to a discipline—the study of our values and their justification—and to the subject matter of that discipline—the actual values and rules of conduct by which we live. The two meanings merge in the fact that we behave (and misbehave) according to a complex and continually changing set of rules, customs, and expectations; consequently, we are forced to reflect on our conduct and attitudes, to justify and sometimes to revise them.

Why do we need to study ethics as a discipline? Isn't it enough that we have ethics, that we do (most of us, most of the time) act according to our values and rules? But part of our ethics is understanding ethics, that is, acting for reasons and being able to defend our actions if called upon to do so. It is not enough, after the age of eight or so, simply to do what you are told; it is just as important to know the reason why, and to be able to say no when you think an act is wrong. So, too, it is not enough to have strong political opinions on this or that controversial social issue. It is important to have reasons, to have a larger vision, to have a framework within which to house and defend your opinions. The study of ethics teaches us to appreciate the overall system of reasons within which having ethics makes sense. Understanding what we are doing and why is just as essential to ethics as doing the right thing.

We learn ethics, typically, a piece at a time. Our education begins in childhood, first and foremost, with examples, continuous demonstrations of "normal" behavior. We watch our parents and our older siblings, before we know what *we* are doing. Our education continues with a number of instructions and prohibitions, such as "Don't hit your little sister" and "You should share your toys with your friends." The recognition of authority is essential, of course, beginning with "You do what your father says" and culminating in "because it's the law, that's why." But it is also learning reasons, such as "because if everyone did that, there wouldn't be any left" or "because it will make her unhappy." Ultimately, we learn the specialized language of morality and the most abstract reasons for doing or refraining from certain actions, such as "because it is your duty" and "because it is immoral." By this time we have begun to learn that ethics is not just a varied collection of do's and don'ts but a system of values and principles which tie together in a reasonable and coherent way to make our society and our lives as civilized and as happy as possible. The study of ethics is the final step in this process of education—the understanding of that system as such and the way that all our particular values and principles fit into it.

CHANGE, CHOICE, AND PLURALISM

Our understanding of ethics is complicated enormously by the fact that, as a living system, our ethics is continually changing. Consider, for example, the tremendous changes that our society has experienced over just the past few decades in the realm of sexual morality; today, we accept behavior which would have been wanton immorality sixty years ago (for example, topless beachwear for men). Similar changes have taken place in our concept of personal roles and career options. Only twenty years ago, many people considered it unethical for a wife to work except in cases of dire family need, but it was perfectly acceptable—in fact, even commendable—for a husband to spend so much time working at his career that he virtually never saw his children or did anything but work. Today, many people do not find such behavior praiseworthy but, rather, akin to a disease (workaholism). Attitudes toward authority have also changed dramatically. Fifty years ago, the attitude of most young men, when drafted into the army (or invited to enlist) was unquestioning acceptance. Twenty-five years ago, those who refused to be drafted and otherwise resisted authority were praised by many people as moral heroes. What this means, and whether there are underlying values that support both obedience and disobedience, depending on the circumstances, are some of the most important questions of ethics.

We live in a society filled with change and disagreement, in which each generation tends to reexamine the values and actions of the older generation, in which doing what you are told or simply conforming to tradition is not necessarily a mark of moral goodness but may be considered cowardice or evidence of a lack of character. Our ethics, in other words, involves choice. In fact, having and permitting individual freedom of choice is itself one of the most noteworthy values of our ethics. To choose between alternative courses of action or opposed values requires intelligent deliberation and some sense of the reasons why we should choose one rather than another. Each of us must select a way of life, perhaps a career or a profession, perhaps a life of creativity or adventure. We might follow in our parents' footsteps or we might go off on a completely different path. But we must choose. Each of us must decide whether or not to get married, and when and to whom. We must decide whether or not to have children, how many, and how they will be raised; such decisions affect the lives of others in the most direct and dramatic sense possible. Every day, each of us decides whether or not to engage in a dozen small misdeeds and occasionally, whether to commit a misdemeanor, such as driving on a deserted highway at 80 miles per hour or taking a box of paperclips home from the office.

The importance of choice in ethics is often confused with a notion that we choose our values, or that values are merely subjective and that everyone has his or her own personal values. This assumption is misleading. Most of ethics involves decisions between already-established possibilities and already-available reasons. A student deciding between joining the Navy or going to law school does indeed have an important choice to make, but the alternatives and their values are provided by the society as a whole. (There must already be a military to join or a role for lawyers in society.) One does not choose the alternatives; one chooses among the alternatives. And once the choice is made, he or she is suddenly situated in a world of "objective" values—the iron-clad rules of the military or the stringent standards of the legal profession. In ethics we face choices, but the personal values we thereby endorse are virtually never one's own values alone. The very nature of values is such that they must be shared; they exist over and above those who embrace them.

Nevertheless, there is a sense, defended by the twentieth-century French existentialist Jean-Paul Sartre, in which we do choose our values, and ourselves, every time we make an ethical decision. By deciding not to take advantage of a loophole in the tax laws, for example, one personally affirms the priority of compliance over individual gain. By acting in one way rather than another, we support one value rather than another, one sense of who we are rather than another. For Sartre ethics is largely a matter of individual choice and commitment rather than of obedience to already-established authorities.

We live in an ethically *pluralist* society. This means that there is no single code of ethics but several different sets of values and rules in a variety of contexts, communities, and subcultures. Professional and business people in our society emphasize individual success and mobility; some cultural communities stress the importance of group identity and stable ethnic traditions. Some college and urban communities are notably more liberal in their tolerance for eccentricity and deviance than the more conservative suburban neighborhoods surrounding them. Even what would seem to be the most basic rules of morality vary from culture to culture, neighborhood to neighborhood, context to context. Thus, we find our Supreme Court, the ultimate arbiter of laws if not morals, insisting on "community standards" as the test for what is permissible, in the case of pornography, for instance.

Many people in our society insist that the ultimate value is individual freedom. But personal freedom has its costs, among them the possible inconvenience and deprivation of others. One person's freedom may well be an infringement of another person's rights, and many people thus argue there are issues of morality and justice that are more important than individual freedom. Such conflicts in ethics are not easily reconciled; in fact, they may be irreconcilable. But that makes it all the more important that we understand the nature of the conflicts and at least know how to try to reconcile our differences instead of intransigently shouting our views at one another, imposing them on others, or simply storming out of the room. Being reasonable in such situations is much of what ethical discussion and debate are about, and pluralism provides much of the motive. If one isn't clear about the nature and justification of one's own values, he or she won't be in a position to understand the nature and justification of other people's values. And if one doesn't understand other people's values, neither will one understand how they conflict or might be brought into harmony with one's own.

ETHICS AND ETHOS

The word *ethics* comes from the Greek word *ethos*, meaning "character" or "custom," and the derivative phrase *ta ethika*, which the philosophers Plato and Aristotle used to describe their own studies of Greek values and ideals. Accordingly, ethics is first of all a concern for character, including what we blandly call being a good person, but it is also a concern for the overall character of an entire society, which is called its *ethos*. Ethics is participation in, and an understanding of, an ethos; it is the effort to understand the social rules that govern and limit our behavior, especially those fundamental rules, such as prohibitions against killing and stealing, the commandments that one should honor thy parents, and respect for the rights of others, which we call *morality*.

The close connection between ethics and social customs, or *mores*, which shares its etymological root with the word *morality*, inevitably raises the question of whether morality is nothing but the customs of our particular society, our ethics nothing but the rules of our particular ethos. On the one hand, ethics and morality are very closely tied to the laws and the customs of a particular society. Kissing in public and making an enormous profit in a business transaction are considered immoral in some societies, not in others. On the other hand, some laws or customs endorsed by an entire society have more importance than others. The rules of etiquette may be merely a matter of local custom or taste, but the prohibition against cannibalism, for example, seems to have much more universal power and justification than the simple reminder, "That just isn't done around here."

One way of circumscribing the principles of morality—as distinguished from rules of etiquette and standards of good taste, for example—is to insist that these are not the province of only a particular society or subculture within society but, rather, rules which we apply to all people everywhere and expect them to obey. We might be happy to accept, and even be charmed by, the fact that people in another culture eat food with wooden sticks instead of forks or enjoy music based on quarter tones without a discernible melody. But when we consider the culture of gangland America, for example, or the satanic rituals of certain cults, our tolerance diminishes and we find ourselves quite willing to impose our own values and standards. Ethics provides the basic rules of an ethos, but those rules are not limited to that ethos. Ethics needs a culture in which to be cultivated, but that docs not mean that ethics consists of just the rules of that particular culture. Morality, according to many philosophers, is that set of rules which applies to all cultures, whatever their customs or traditions.

An ethos is that core of attitudes, beliefs, and feelings that gives coherence and vitality to a people (in ancient Greek, an *ethnos*, a word significantly similar to *ethos*). It may be spelled out explicitly in terms of laws, but much of an ethos resides in the hearts and minds of the people, in what they expect of one another and what they expect of themselves, in what they like and dislike, in what they value and disdain, hope and fear. An essential part of our ethos, for example, is that individual success, or "standing out in the crowd," is desirable. There is no law or moral principle that commands that this should be so, but our ethics very much depends upon the values of individualism and achievement. In some societies, by way of contrast, individual ambitions and eccentricities are unacceptable. "The nail that sticks out is the one that gets hammered down," reads a traditional Japanese proverb. We should not assume that all *ethé* (the plural of *ethos*) are the same, even in their most basic values and visions.

THE ADVANTAGES OF ETHICAL BEHAVIOUR IN THE WORKPLACE

Break into small groups. First, individually consider places you have worked in the past. Did employees treat co-workers with courtesy and consideration? Did managers treat the people they supervised fairly and ethically? Were clients dealt with honestly and respectfully? Did customers get value for their money when they purchased the products or services being sold? Next, discuss these questions as a group, and reflect on how the answers affected your employment. Try to list five or more benefits to an employee of working in an ethical workplace.

_____

_____

_____

_____

_____

_____

_____

_____

Now put yourselves in the place of your employers, or imagine yourselves as office managers or owners of a small business or practice. List five or more benefits to an employer of maintaining an ethical workplace.

_____

_____

_____

_____

_____

_____

_____

_____

CASE STUDIES

Case Study #1

You are the supervisor of a travel agency. All your agents work in a central office separated by dividers, which are only three feet high. One day your best agent, Sarah Recoskie, a long-term employee who brings a lot of business into the agency through loyal customers and word-of-mouth, complains that the perfume of one of the other agents who sits near her cubicle is making her sick.

You investigate but cannot smell any perfume. Sarah is pregnant and she says that unless the smell is removed, she cannot work in the room. She believes the employee responsible for the scent is Modela Tombe. Modela, a recent immigrant who joined the agency four weeks ago right after attaining her travel agent certification, does not have many clients yet and one of the walk-in clients you sent to her asked for another agent because he had trouble understanding her due to her strong accent. She has made two minor mistakes in booking holiday arrangements but you think she will be a good agent once she gets some more practice.

There is no space anywhere else in the building to set up a desk for Sarah or to separate her from Modela's office area. Furthermore, you are just at the beginning of the pre-winter travel booking period. You really need both agents to continue working through this season or you will lose business. What should you do?

What are the ethical issues involved?

....

....

....

What are the relevant facts?

....

....

....

Is there any missing information you should seek?

....

....

....

mensa!
sorry?

Initial Response:

_____

_____

_____

_____

Method of Resolution: _____

Case Study #2

Ayesha, a fellow employee and friend, repeatedly shows up late for work. You and others have covered for her in the past, but some people are beginning to resent her tardiness and several have made comments to her about it. However, she has not responded to peer pressure to correct her behaviour.

You are a union rep, and now Ayesha has come to you and asked you to be her union representative during a meeting with management to address a problem. As she describes the situation, you recall the event. One day Ayesha called in sick but was observed at a shopping mall having lunch with her sister. The two employees who were required to cover for Ayesha that day had to extend their shift for an additional four hours, and as a result ended up working for twelve consecutive hours. When employees work this long they are tired and more likely to make a mistake, which could have serious repercussions. People could get injured or cause an accident that hurts someone else.

The manager does not know about the restaurant lunch, but you do. Your duty as a union rep is to represent Ayesha; however, you are concerned that if you do so she may repeat her behaviour, which would result in unsafe working conditions and possibly an accident. If you tell on Ayesha, you will lose a friend, and employees might lose faith that their union will represent them. However, her behaviour is disrupting the morale at work and making things difficult for everyone.

What are the ethical issues involved?

_____

_____

_____

What are the relevant facts?

Is there any missing information you should seek?

Initial Response:

Method of Resolution: _____

Case Study #3

You are a managing director at the True North Credit Union (TNCU) branch in Nunavut. There are three other senior managers who work with you, and one of them is only a year away from retiring. The managers are all white males, two from Toronto, one from Montreal and one from Winnipeg. Recently a Native employee quit, accusing the company of racism when he was not promoted to a middle management position. Several newspaper articles and letters about this issue, most of them condemning your company, have since appeared in the *Nunavut Times*.

The TNCU has always been proud of its high standards in hiring middle management trainees, all of whom have a college or university degree in business or in finance and accounting. TNCU has managed to survive within the highly competitive banking community mainly because of the expertise of its managing directors. You like to promote from within, so mid-level managers are likely to advance to upper management in time, which is why the hiring criteria are so high. Unfortunately there are no Native

Canadians in Nunavut with the required level of education, since any who achieve this level are quickly hired by larger companies that can offer them more money.

You are concerned about losing customers due to the bad publicity and have decided to meet with the other TNCU directors to discuss hiring Nunavut Native Canadians into management positions. You are considering a number of options, such as lowering the required qualifications for Natives; offering an OJT internship in lieu of academic qualifications, for Natives only; increasing the salary to entice back Native Canadians who meet the current requirements; or offering them a one-time financial incentive. The TNCU cannot afford to increase all management salaries or make incentive pay universal. You are also open to any other options.

What are the ethical issues involved?

_____

_____

_____

What are the relevant facts?

_____

_____

_____

_____

Is there any missing information you should seek?

_____

_____

_____

_____

Initial Response:

_____

_____

_____

_____

Method of Resolution:_____

Case Study #4

Your office co-worker, Mary, has been coming into work for the past two weeks apparently often under the influence of alcohol or drugs. She is not violent or offensive, but the quality of her work has been affected. Mary has been off work in the past for this problem, so your supervisor knows about the situation but is not aware that the behaviour has begun again.

Mary is a single parent with three children to support and she is a friend of your sister. Your sister also had a drinking problem but has overcome it and put it behind her. You're very proud of your sister for doing so, and you know that if she had been fired from her job, she would probably not have been able to overcome her drinking problem. When Mary came back to work after her first leave of absence (to get her substance abuse under control), she told you that her supervisor had warned her that the company would be less lenient if she lapsed into abuse again. You are afraid that if you turn Mary in, she'll be fired before she has the opportunity to heal herself.

But her problem is affecting the company's clients. Last week she misplaced some documentation and had to ask the client to make another appointment. This week you noticed her typing incorrect information into two clients' files. The mistakes weren't serious and you were able to correct them, but you can't help wondering what other errors Mary may be making, or where the missing client files may turn up. You could be in trouble as well if you were caught checking her clients' confidential files for errors.

What are the ethical issues involved?

_____

_____

_____

What are the relevant facts?

_____

_____

_____

_____

Is there any missing information you should seek?

_____

_____

_____

_____

Initial Response:

_____

_____

_____

_____

Method of Resolution: _____

Case Study #5

While filling in for Sam, a vacationing colleague in your department, you come across one of his recent expense reports. You are surprised at the expenses listed on it. You have just returned from a training session at the same location, staying at the same hotel, which is within two blocks of the training facility. Not only is Sam's reported hotel bill significantly higher than what you were charged, but he has listed numerous "taxi trips to and from the facility" as well as several "client lunches." You are certain that at least one of those lunches did not occur because you were on the phone to that client the same day, and she was in another city.

The company is not doing well at the moment. Yesterday you received a memo stating that "overall expenses are up" and "cut-backs may be necessary." You remember hearing Sam complain at a staff meeting because there was no Christmas bonus last year and he "counts on that extra money." Sam's expense bill has already been paid. He's considered a good sales rep, and he's friends with two of the senior managers. However, the two of you have never hit it off. He has often made jokes at your expense including "humorous" comments about your size (you are short and somewhat plump). When you complained about this to your supervisor you were told that they were just harmless jokes and you should be "less sensitive." If you tell on Sam, you might be accused of trying to get back at him.

Your assistant, Sarah, was with you when you accidentally came across Sam's expense report, and is aware of the discrepancies because she accompanied you on the training session. Now she asks you what you are going to do.

What are the ethical issues involved?

_____

_____

_____

What are the relevant facts?

_____

_____

_____

_____

Is there any missing information you should seek?

_____

_____

_____

_____

Initial Response:

_____

_____

_____

_____

Method of Resolution: _____

Case Study #6

After graduating from a college marketing program, you and two friends started your own marketing agency. It's small, but it's growing rapidly. You've just received your first big account, from Canadian Pharmaceutical Company, to create an ad campaign for a new diet drug. They want to target young women from mid-teens to thirty-something with ads on billboards and in women's magazines. They want you to create a "hip," upscale and healthy image for their product. You and your two partners work on several ideas, and finally come up with a mother-daughter concept: a young woman and a middle-aged woman, both very slim, playing tennis while two smiling men of appropriate ages look on, and the diet aid promoted in the right lower quarter of the page. Subsequent seasonal ads will show the same women sailing, horseback riding and skiing. You are convinced the client will be pleased with the ad; it has everything—family ties, romance, healthy activities and the suggestion of wealth and leisure. When you test-market it, however, the reaction is mixed at best. Some women like it, but a substantial number complain that it reinforces a negative self-image for women, especially those who cannot achieve the desired slimness. "Ads like this," one woman says, "are responsible for illnesses like depression and bulimia." Others criticize the ad as misleading in nature, saying that it equates a slender female figure with romance, love and wealth. "It feeds into female insecurities, hitting the most vulnerable the hardest," is another comment.

You are shocked. You certainly didn't mean to make consumers feel inadequate. Do you and your company want to be linked to such ads if there is a negative backlash? One of your female partners says no, argues for dropping the account entirely and threatens to leave the company if you don't. The other partner protests that your company is not the only one selling products with images of romance and wealth. How can you compete with other agencies if you won't use such images? Furthermore, there isn't time to come up with a whole new concept; your client is coming in tomorrow to see your presentation. If you don't have anything to show, you will likely lose the account.

On the other hand, if the client sees the negative responses to your ad, you might lose the contract anyway, and you could be branded as amateurs. Should you offer the ad but withhold the negative feedback? You believe the client will like the ad. But what if it backfires and hurts product sales, and the client finds out that you didn't share your market test with them? What should you do?

What are the ethical issues involved?

What are the relevant facts?

Is there any missing information you should seek?

_____

_____

_____

_____

Initial Response:

_____

_____

_____

_____

Method of Resolution: _____

Case Study #7

You are the intake office administrator at a medical imaging lab. One of your tasks is to go over the general test procedures with patients and have them sign a consent form. Your manager has impressed upon you the importance of obtaining informed consent to avoid any lawsuits, and of keeping the flow of patients moving, since the tests are closely scheduled and getting behind costs the lab money. If patients have detailed questions or concerns, you are to refer them to the lab technician.

This situation is different, however. A middle-aged couple comes up to your desk assisting an elderly woman who is using a walker. The man explains that the old woman is his wife's mother. While you are explaining the procedure to the elderly woman, it is obvious that although the couple is listening to you, the elderly woman is not, and she is the patient. When you ask for her consent, the man says, "Yes, you have her consent," and reaches for the form to sign it. You explain that you need to hear it from the patient, whereupon the man's wife speaks rapidly in a foreign language to the old woman. While they are talking, the old woman repeatedly shakes her head, and when her daughter stops talking, the old woman speaks hesitantly in what sounds to you like an anxious tone of voice. However, she is speaking in a language you don't under-stand, and you could be misinterpreting her tone.

Suddenly, the son-in-law says something in a sharp voice, and the old woman is silent. "She gives her consent," the man repeats, "but she is illiterate. I'll have to sign for her." It is not against policy for a family member to sign on behalf of a patient who cannot do so herself, but in this case you're not sure what to do. You ask if they'd like to speak to the lab technician. "What for?" the man asks. He signs the consent form. This has taken a while and there is a line-up of people behind them waiting to be registered for their tests, and an orderly is waiting to escort the next patient to the change cubicles.

What are the ethical issues involved?

_____

_____

_____

What are the relevant facts?

_____

_____

_____

_____

Is there any missing information you should seek?

_____

_____

_____

_____

Initial Response:

_____

_____

_____

Method of Resolution: _____

COMMENTARIES

Current Controversy #1: Raising the Minimum Wage in Ontario

Article 1: "Minimum wage should rise to $10"

Toronto Star, September 20, 2006

In 1995, the new Ontario Conservative premier Mike Harris froze the legal minimum wage in the province at $6.85 an hour. The freeze remained in place for eight years. That move affected thousands of Ontario's lowest paid workers, many of them in unskilled and non-unionized jobs.

During the 2003 provincial election campaign, Liberal Leader Dalton McGuinty pledged to right that injustice. Once he became premier, McGuinty took the first steps toward fulfilling that promise by lifting the freeze and committing his government to increasing the minimum wage in stages over four years. The base now stands at $7.75 an hour. Next February, it is scheduled to jump to $8 an hour.

But while McGuinty deserves praise for moving on his promise, he needs to do much more—and soon. Specifically, he should raise the minimum wage to $10 an hour, not $8 an hour, effective Feb. 1, when the next increase is due to come into force. And he and opposition parties should pledge to boost rates in future years at least in line with inflation.

For Canada's second richest province, this would be a quick, responsible and fair way to help its poorest and most vulnerable workers who have failed to share, even to a limited degree, in the gains of a growing economy.

Since the beginning of 1995, the average hourly wage for employees in Ontario rose by more than 30 per cent. Had minimum-wage workers kept pace with the average Ontario worker over that period, they would be paid more than $9 an hour today. Instead, workers earning the minimum wage saw no increase from 1995 to 2004, a period when they lost 20 per cent of their purchasing power to inflation.

While a $10-an-hour minimum wage, which is advocated by many anti-poverty groups, would certainly help, it would lift only some, not all, of Ontario's working poor out of poverty.

Take the example of Maheswary Puvàneswaran, the mother of two featured Saturday in the *Star* as part of a series on the working poor. Working as much as she can in two low-wage cleaning jobs, she earns just over $1,000 a month. She would need to earn a minimum of $15 an hour working full-time to bring her family up to the generally accepted poverty line.

To some, raising the minimum wage to $10 from $7.75 an hour in one step might seem excessive. When McGuinty raised the rate in previous years, a number of business leaders complained, saying Ontario's economy would be hurt because it is already suffering from higher energy prices and more competition from lower wage countries, such as China.

While there might be some job losses because of raising the minimum wage to $10 an hour, such an increase is fully justified because the minimum wage needs to be more reflective of the real levels of income needed by Ontario's working poor to enjoy a decent standard of living.

So why aren't we calling for McGuinty to raise the minimum wage even higher, to a level that would truly be considered "a decent living wage"?

Such a wage would be at least $15 an hour, and possibly even higher in cities such as Toronto where the cost of living is high. This is particularly true for families with just a single wage earner. Unfortunately, rather than pay such a high minimum wage, many employers would opt to contract out the work, in effect replacing full- or part-time employees with self-employed contractors, who are not covered by minimum wage laws.

This growing trend toward contracting out work, which is being pursued more and more even by governments, worries anti-poverty activists, who fear the poor or those who are in low-wage occupations will lose their jobs. They say the best tool for increasing the incomes of all working poor, not just those earning the minimum wage, would be a new government-funded earned-income supplement. Among the many groups supporting the idea of such a supplement is the Daily Bread Food Bank in Toronto.

Ideally, both an income supplement and a hike in the basic minimum wage would occur at the same time. Together, they could go a long way in eradicating the term "working poor" from our vocabulary. Such a combination, moreover, would mean taxpayers would not have to bear the full burden of ensuring all working Canadians a decent income. With a higher minimum wage, employers would also have to foot part of the bill.

However, it is unlikely that both programs could be implemented together in a timely fashion because Ottawa would be responsible for the earned-income supplement and Queen's Park for raising the minimum wage. It is rare when the two governments act in unison.

That's why it is important for McGuinty to take the first step by acting now to raise the minimum wage to $10 an hour. The working poor should not have to wait until Ottawa gets on board with an income supplement. They need help now. They have waited long enough.

Article 2: *"The Injustice of the Minimum Wage"*

The National Post, Wednesday, January 10, 2007, p. A16

ANDREW COYNE

You have to admit the timing was awful. Two weeks after legislating a 25% pay increase for themselves, to more than $110,000 apiece, members of the Ontario legislature approved a 3.2% increase in the province's statutory minimum wage: from $7.75 an hour to $8.00.

The *Toronto Star* was properly appalled. Granted, it was the fourth increase in the minimum wage in as many years, and true, the paper was not actually opposed to the politician's pay hike, and no, the paper had not seen fit to raise its own workers' pay by 25% the last time they negotiated—they got roughly 8% over three years—but still: the optics. Eight measly bucks. When *everybody knows* the minimum wage should really be $10 an hour.

The paper has been campaigning for months for a $10 minimum wage, echoing an NDP private member's bill. Why $10? Why not $9, or $11? No one pretends that $10 an hour marks the difference between misery and happiness: even at 40 hours a week, that's still only $20,000 a year, and besides, hardly anyone works full-time for the minimum wage. (Indeed, hardly anyone works for the minimum wage at all: less than 5% of the province's workforce.) So what's so special about a $10 minimum?

If "because 10 is a nice round number" is the answer, why not $20? Or—an even rounder number—why not $100 an hour? If your answer to *that* is "because that would throw a lot of people out of work," then why should you not expect a $10 minimum wage to throw *some* people out of work? Or if an increase in wages has no effect on the demand for labour, then why stop at $10? Why not really do something for the working poor?

The whole point of a minimum wage is that the market wage for some workers—the wage that would just balance the supply of and demand for unskilled, transient, or young workers in highly unstable service industries—is deemed to be too low. If, accordingly, it is fixed by law above the market level, it must be at a point where the supply exceeds the demand. Economists have a technical term for that gap. It's called "unemployment."

Advocates of minimum wages either reject that elementary logic, or they don't care. The NDP is an example of the first: MPP Cheri DiNovo, the sponsor of that private member's bill, refers dismissively to "all those spurious arguments that this is somehow going to destroy the economy." But *The Star*, intriguingly, is in the second camp.

"While there might be some job losses because of raising the minimum wage to $10 an hour," the paper opined in a recent editorial, "such an increase is fully justified" by the need to make the minimum wage "more reflective of the real levels of income needed by Ontario's working poor to enjoy a decent standard of living."

Leave aside that the working poor will still not be enjoying anything like a decent standard of living, even at $10 an hour. What principle of social justice would suggest it was okay to toss some of the most vulnerable members of society on the scrap heap, forcing them out of their jobs altogether so that their still-employed co-workers could snag a raise?

The most influential philosopher of contemporary liberalism in fact prescribes the opposite. In *A Theory of Justice*, John Rawls argues we should measure our commitment to justice against how well the very worst off in society are faring, on broadly "there but for the grace of God" grounds. The aim of a just society should be to *maximize the minimum*—to improve the lot of those worst off, first off. That would suggest putting the interests of the unemployed ahead of those who already have jobs, rather than, in effect, locking the jobless out of the market.

The point is not that those struggling to get by on very low wages should be left to their own devices. The point is that wages, properly considered, are neither the instrument nor the objective of a just society. When we say their wages are "too low," we mean in terms of what society believes is decent. But that's not what wages are for. The point of a wage, like any other price, is to ensure every seller finds a willing buyer and vice versa, without giving rise to shortages or surpluses—not to attempt to reflect broader social notions of what is appropriate. That's especially true when employers can always sidestep any attempt to impose a "just" wage simply by hiring fewer workers.

Social goals should be socially financed. When we think about it, it's not a minimum wage we're really aiming for: it's a minimum income. If so, then the proper approach is to supplement the incomes of the working poor, through the tax-and-transfer system— not fix their wages and hope for the best.

Current Controversy #2:
The Ethics of The Wal-Mart Model

Article 1: "ROB Ranks Wal-Mart Among Canada's Best Employers"

Marketnews.ca, March 29, 2007

Report on Business Magazine has just released its annual *50 Best Employers in Canada* ranking, and Wal-Mart Canada was named among the list for the fifth time in the last six years. The retailer is the largest employer on this year's list with 70,000 employees: more than twice the number as the next closest company. The Best Employers list is assembled by global human-resources firm Hewitt Associates, and is based primarily on anonymous employee surveys. To participate in the ranking, an organization must have at least 400 permanent employees in Canada, and have operated in Canada for at least three years. In addition to employee questionnaires, a human resources practices survey is completed by HR personnel, and a leadership team survey is completed by top executives. Hewitt also assesses company policies and practices, and examines how closely employees' and leaders' goals are aligned, and whether workplace practices and programs reinforce that corporate vision.

"The overall measure used to identify and rank Best Employers is employee engagement, which quantifies how closely leaders and employees work together toward a common vision, as well as the collective energy that goes into making an organization a great place to work," read the report.

"It's always an honour when our associates proclaim Wal-Mart one of Canada's best employers," enthused Mary Alice Vuicic, Vice President, People, Wal-Mart Canada Corp. "This year, our number-one corporate goal has been to become Canada's favourite place to work. It's an ongoing process, but our associates tell us we're headed in the right direction. The best-employer lists recognize we've got a great foundation in place to meet our goal.

"Our company works hard to attract, train, support, and retain the best people we can," Vuicic continued. "In return, they have become our single best resource: the backbone of our operation."

Wal-Mart has taken many steps to promote diversity and equal opportunity within its organization and, as a result, says it has maintained one of the lowest staff turnover rates in the Canadian retail industry. The percentage of in-store female managers has doubled since 2004 to 40 per cent; and females now hold more than 30 per cent of senior executive roles. In 2006, more than 7,000 existing associates were promoted to senior roles. A "Tell Mario" program allowed any associate to communicate ideas to the firm's President and CEO Mario Pilozzi, and resulted in nearly 1,000 tangible suggestions. Further, approximately 40 per cent of Wal-Mart Canada's associates were enrolled in the company's shareholder program, taking advantage of subsidized stock purchasing.

Founded in 1994 and headquartered in Mississauga, ON, Wal-Mart Canada currently operates 273 Wal-Mart discount stores, three Wal-Mart Supercentres, and six SAM'S CLUB member warehouses.

So who was ranked Canada's best employer? According to the ROB results, it is Winnipeg, MB-based Wellington West Capital Inc., which ranked second in 2005. Wellington is a financial services company employing close to 500 advisers and other employees.

Article 2: *"The Costs of 'Walmartization'"*

Znet, January 16, 2005

SILVIA RIBEIRO

For the first time in history, demarcating the beginning of the 21st century, the biggest company in the world was not an oil concern or an automobile manufacturer, but Wal-Mart, a supermarket chain. The symbolic value of this fact weighs as much as its crushing implications: it is the "triumph" of the anonymous, the substitution of the traditional way of acquiring what we need to feed ourselves, take care of our houses, tools and even medicine, traditionally involving interpersonal relationships, for a new one which is standardized, "mercantilized," and where we know progressively less about who, where and how or under which conditions what we buy is produced. Now, we can theoretically buy everything under the same roof, and even though goods seem cheaper, which actually is an illusion, the whole paradigm can end up being very expensive. To buy today at Wal-Mart may mean losing one's own job or contributing to the loss of somebody else's in your family or community sometime down the line.

Wal-Mart's policy of low prices is maintained while there are other places to shop in the same community. When the other shops go under, not able to compete, nothing prevents Wal-Mart from raising their prices, which the company invariably ends up doing. Wal-Mart has had a devastating influence in those communities where it showed up, and according to Wal-Mart Watch, an organization of citizens affected by the company's policies, for every two jobs that are created when it moves into a community, three are lost.

Wal-Mart is 19th among the 100 most powerful economies in the world, only 49 of which are now countries. Sam Walton's widow and their four sons control 38 percent of its shares. In 2004 they were sixth among the richest people in the world, with about 20 billion dollars each. If Sam Walton was alive he would be twice as rich as Bill Gates, who is number one on the list with 46 billion. Both are a clear expression of the modern megamonopoly and the control that they exert over consumers. These monopolies are of course intent on increasing their control. Wal-Mart, it could be argued, has the biggest impact, as it sells such a wide range of products and it wields tremendous power over suppliers and politicians.

It is the biggest chain of direct sales to the consumer in North America. In the U.S. it has over three thousand Wal-Mart stores and 550 Sam's Club outfits. In Mexico it already possesses 54 percent of the market, with 687 stores in 71 cities, including Wal-Mart, Sam's Club, Bodegas Aurrera, Superama and Suburbia, aside from the restaurant chains Vips, El Porton and Ragazzi. It already controls very large sectors of the market in Canada, Great Britain, Brazil, Germany and Puerto Rico, and its influence is on the rise in many others, Japan, for example.

It is the biggest private employer in the United States and Mexico. In the few decades it has been in existence it has accumulated an amazing history of being sued for many reasons, including illegally preventing the unionizing of its workers, and just about every other imaginable violation of workers' rights: discrimination against the disabled, sexual discrimination, child labor, lack of health care coverage, and unpaid overtime. In the U.S., 38 percent of its workers are without health care, and the salaries it pays are, on average, 26 percent lower than the industry norm. In December 2003 there were 39 class action lawsuits pending against the company in 30 different states in the U.S. for violations of overtime laws. In a round up in October, 2003 the government found 250 undocumented foreign workers, who of course were operating in even worse conditions. In June 2004 Wal-Mart lost the largest class action lawsuit in history, where 1,600,000 women proved that they suffered gender discrimination as employees of the company since 1998.

But the company's low prices are not based only in the exploitation of its workers in the countries where it operates directly. The prices are the direct result of the systematic use of "maquiladoras" in conditions of extreme exploitation. A worker in one of these, located in Bangladesh, told the *Los Angeles Times* in 2003 that her normal workday was from 8 am to 3 am, 10 or 15 days in a row. This is what it took to be able to survive given the wages she was getting paid. But in the same article, the manager of the plant complained that they had to become even more efficient, as Wal-Mart was threatening to move the production to China, where it could obtain lower prices.

Though absolutely terrible, labor exploitation is not the only "Wal-Mart" effect. There are many others, including the use of new technologies to track people's purchases even after leaving the supermarket. Control seems to be the name of the game in the "Walmartization" of the world.

Feeding Big Brother

Supermarkets are the segment of the food chain that moves the most capital. According to certain analysts, their influence towers over and could devour every other previous link in the chain, such as food and beverage producers, distributors, and agricultural suppliers, and producers. Whether they end up getting involved in these parts of the chain will depend on the economics of the game, so that if it is cheaper to allow other companies to compete amongst themselves, they will not get involved. The effect, nevertheless, is the same: the concentration of control and power in fewer and fewer hands. This is not limited to Wal-Mart but also includes other giants such as Carrefour, Ahold, Costco or Tesco.

But Wal-Mart stands out particularly because, besides being the biggest company in the world, its income is four times that of its largest competitor, and larger than the next four combined. Because it is the biggest seller of food products on a global level it has tremendous influence over what and how food gets produced. It's already dabbling, for example, in agriculture by contract directly with the agricultural producers. It also is third in sales in medicines.

As if it was not enough to be such an economic power, largely due to its growing monopoly, Wal-Mart is beginning, as mentioned earlier, to utilize new technologies to obtain information over people's buying patterns. It is already testing, in three cities in the US, the substitution of bar codes for identification systems through radio frequency. This is a "labeling" system utilizing an electronic chip, no bigger than a grain of rice and potentially much smaller, containing information about the product, which is transmitted wirelessly to a computer. This chip is capable of storing much more information than the bar code. The problem is that its signal follows the purchaser outside of the supermarket doors. According to Wal-Mart, the consumer would have the choice of asking at the checkout that the chip be turned off, except it has no plans to advertise this possibility.

It has already experimented using products from Gillete and Procter & Gamble, and others such as Coca Cola, Kodak, Nestle and many others.

At the beginning of 2004, Wal-Mart told its 100 principal suppliers that they would have to be ready to provide this technology in January, 2005.

The system would start, at the beginning, only as a means to track wholesale shipments, that is to say, not necessarily directly related to the packaging that the consumer takes home. In November it announced that the majority of suppliers, plus an extra 37 added to the original list, would be ready. It is now only a matter of time until the cost of the chips goes down sufficiently before it is included in everything a consumer buys.

In practice, this means, for example, that consumers who register their credit cards on entering the store could conceivably pay for their purchase without having to go through a cashier, as the products would automatically register when exiting. But Wal-Mart and the others using the technology would have exact information regarding who, what, when, how much and where the products are used.

Though Wal-Mart is not the only one testing the technology—there's Tesco in Great Britain, and Metro, Carrefour and Home Depot in other places—it is the biggest force behind its development. It is important to know that the technology was first developed and implemented by the U.S. Defense Department.

Orwell must be spinning in his grave. These tiny systems of control, "little brothers," if you will, will go much further than the Big Brother he envisioned.

The paradigm of Walmartization towards a "happy world" trumpeted by the transnational companies needs our ignorance and passive indifference to succeed. Paradoxically, those remaining without access to credit or debit cards—in other words, the majority of the planet's inhabitants—will remain out of the reach of this control system. With all its power, Wal-Mart and the transnational needs us to survive. We don't need them.

Silvia Ribeiro is an investigator with Grupo ETC.
Translated from Spanish by Daniel Morduchowicz

EVALUATING
THE MEDIA

THE POLITICAL ROLE OF THE MASS MEDIA

In non-democratic countries, the media are generally expected to avoid any criticism of the ruling group. Publishers may be required to submit what they propose to print to government censors. Media outlets that are critical of government or spread "dangerous" ideas may be shut down and those responsible for "sedition" punished. The broadcast signals of foreign media may be jammed, Internet sites blocked, the sale of satellite dishes and short-wave radios prohibited, and those caught tuning in to foreign stations arrested. In totalitarian systems, the media are instruments of propaganda that are used systematically to promote the ideological perspective of those in control of the government and encourage the population to actively pursue ideological goals.

Index on Censorship
www.indexonline.org

Ideally, in liberal democracies the media should play a major role in encouraging the free discussion of ideas, providing the information citizens need to make an informed choice in elections, and preventing abuses of power. There are, however, different perspectives concerning how well the media actually perform these roles (Siebert, Peterson, & Schramm, 1956).

Perspectives

In the **libertarian perspective**, if the mass media are free from government control and regulation, individuals will be able to obtain and assess the information and ideas they want. With different ideas freely competing in the media, citizens can use their own judgment as to which ideas are good and which are bad. Freedom from government control also allows the media to hold government accountable for its actions.

The **social responsibility perspective** argues that a system of free media does not necessarily result in the public interest being served. In search of profitability, the media may resort to sensationalism rather than living up to its responsibility to be "truthful, accurate, fair, objective and

Libertarian perspective on the mass media—
the idea that if the mass media are free from government control and regulation, individuals will be able to obtain and assess the information and ideas they want.

Social responsibility perspective on the mass media—
The view that the media have a responsibility to the public. Freeing the media from government regulation and control does not necessarily result in the public interest being served.

The Internet is a communications medium that has, to a considerable extent, avoided both corporate and governmental control. Unfortunately, however, in comparison to the mainstream media, it falls short of the democratic ideal of informed discussion.

relevant" and to provide a "forum for the exchange of comment and criticism" by the public (McQuail, 1994, p. 124). In this perspective, the media should be viewed as a "public trust." This does not necessarily require substantial government regulation or control, but might be achieved by such measures as adopting codes of journalistic ethics, encouraging professionalism among journalists, and establishing press councils to hear citizen complaints about the media (McQuail, 1994).

Dominant ideology perspective on the mass media—
the view that the major media convey the values of the powerful and serve the interests of those who benefit from the status quo.

The **dominant ideology perspective** on the mass media is strongly critical. Those who hold this perspective argue that the major media in liberal democracies convey the values of the powerful and serve the interests of those who benefit from the status quo (see Box 7.1, Herman and Chomsky's Propaganda Model). Private ownership of the mass media is used to promote capitalist values and the global dominance of capitalist countries rather than to facilitate the free exchange of ideas. From the dominant ideology perspective, public ownership of the mass media, guaranteed access of community groups to the media, or the development of alternative media are some possible ways in which the dominance of capitalist values might be challenged.

OWNERSHIP AND REGULATION

In liberal democracies, newspapers and other print media have usually been privately owned and free of government regulation, except for censorship related to wartime and national security. Early newspapers were often connected to a particular political party; today, a number of European newspapers continue to be associated with a party

BOX 7.1   HERMAN AND CHOMSKY'S PROPAGANDA MODEL

A widely discussed version of the dominant ideology perspective is provided by Edward Herman and Noam Chomsky. They argue that "the media serve, and propagandize on behalf of, the powerful societal interests that control and finance them" (Herman & Chomsky, 2002, p. 5). Specifically, in their "propaganda model" of the mass media, they outline five filters that limit what American audiences receive (Herman & Chomsky, 2002):

- the ownership of the mass media by large media corporations
- the dependence of the mass media on advertisers
- the reliance of the mass media on government, business, and conservative think tanks for information and analysis
- the flak (negative responses or pressure) that the media receive if their presentations are received negatively by powerful groups and individuals
- the expectation that media take a strong stance against those deemed to be enemies of the United States and the American way of life

Although some of the specifics of Herman and Chomsky's analysis apply particularly to the United States, their general argument that the mass media do not challenge dominant ideological values has been applied to discussions of the media in other liberal democracies. The mass media's emphasis on conventional politics, including elections, party leadership races, and parliamentary debate, means that dissenting voices are often marginalized. Although some social movements, such as the feminist and environmental movements, have been skilful in obtaining media coverage, they do not receive the regular attention given to more conventional political organizations. As well, by focusing their attention on specific events (whether a murder, a hurricane, or the resignation of a Cabinet minister), the media often give little attention to ongoing problems such as poverty or the weak enforcement of environmental laws. The problems that the political community faces are portrayed more as a matter of individual defects or unusual circumstances, rather than as a result of the dominant values and structures of society.

or with the Catholic Church. North American newspapers are commercially oriented operations that seek to appeal to a mass audience, although many do support a particular candidate or party on their editorial page and may exhibit an ideological tendency in the balance of opinion pieces they publish.

In many liberal democracies, there is a mixture of private and public ownership of the broadcast media (radio and television). Fears that privately owned American broadcast networks would move into Canada led to the establishment of the Canadian Broadcasting Corporation (CBC) in 1936. Although the CBC is a government-owned Crown corporation and the recipient of substantial funding from Parliament, this network is expected to be non-partisan and independent of government control. In the United States, government ownership has been avoided; television and radio are almost entirely privately owned and profit-oriented. However, in 1967 the American Congress established the non-profit, non-governmental Corporation for Public Broadcasting that is responsible for the Public Broadcasting Service (PBS) and National Public Radio (NPR). These small networks rely primarily on private and corporate donations rather than government for their funding.

Until the early 1980s, almost all television broadcasting systems in Europe were publicly owned. Since then, many countries have opened up their airwaves to privately owned stations (see Box 7.2, Italy: Television and Political Power, for one example). Nevertheless, public broadcasting is still important in almost all European countries. Generally, an independent board appointed by government controls public broadcasting. In several countries, including Germany, Sweden, and the Netherlands, broadcasting is controlled by boards representing different political parties along with business, labour, religious, women's, and other organizations (Norris, 2000).

Publicly owned broadcasting outlets tend to devote substantially more attention to public affairs than the privately owned media that focus on profitable mass entertainment (Gunther & Mughan, 2000). In some countries the state-owned media are instru-

BOX 7.2   ITALY: TELEVISION AND POLITICAL POWER

The Italian government used to have monopoly control of television. However, each of the three public networks was, in effect, under the control of different political parties. Oversight boards helped to ensure that the public networks were generally impartial.

A 1976 ruling by the country's Constitutional Court changed all that by opening the way for private broadcasters. By the end of the 1980s, billionaire Silvio Berlusconi had gained control of private television, with his holding company Fininvest owning the three major private networks. In 1994, as the leading Italian parties collapsed as the result of a major corruption scandal, Berlusconi led his newly formed Forza Italia party to electoral victory. While the public networks were more balanced in their coverage, Berlusconi's television networks devoted much of their campaign coverage to his party's candidates, thus contributing to the victory of Forza Italia and its allies.

Subsequently, the management of the public networks was purged and replaced by Berlusconi supporters (Marletti & Roncarolo, 2000). This did not, however, result in a consolidation of Berlusconi's power. In 1996, his centre–right coalition lost an election to a centre–left coalition. In 2001, Berlusconi returned to power and resumed efforts to influence the direction of the public television networks—while continuing to own and control the major private television networks. During the 2006 election year, Berlusconi's television network was fined four times by the independent communications authority for being biased in favour of Berlusconi's party. The coalition he led narrowly lost the 2006 election.

Control of private television, along with expertise in media politics, undoubtedly helped Berlusconi's successful and rapid entry into politics. As well, it suggests that television may help to create a personality-oriented politics in which traditional party allegiances are of diminishing importance. However, control of the media and success in creating a popular image do not necessarily result in success in governing.

ments of government propaganda; in other countries public broadcasters are not afraid to criticize government actions. By placing control of publicly owned media in the hands of more or less non-partisan boards, democratic countries generally avoid the heavy-handed government control of the mass media that is characteristic of most non-democratic countries.

Regulation of the Media

The broadcast media are regulated, to varying extents in different countries, by government or a government-appointed agency. The initiation of regulation of radio and television was necessitated by technical considerations. Limited bandwidth meant that regulation was needed to allocate valuable licences and prevent stations from attempting to drown out their competitors. As well, governments wanted to ensure that the news media would act in the public interest, and thus typically required that broadcasting stations allot a certain amount of time to news and public affairs programming. The broadcast media have usually been required to be non-partisan and to provide balanced coverage of politics.

Freedom Forum
www.freedom forum.org

Despite being independent of government, the decisions of regulatory agencies can be controversial. In 2004, the decision of the Canadian Radio-television and Telecommunications Commission (CRTC) not to renew the licence of the most popular Quebec City radio station, CHOI-FM, led to a storm of protest, including a massive demonstration. The CRTC decision was prompted by complaints about the offensive comments of the morning show host (who was subsequently elected to the House of Commons as an independent) concerning women, the mentally ill, and African students. At the same time, the CRTC made a controversial decision to allow cable companies to carry Al Jazeera, the Qatar-based Arab-language television news network well known for broadcasting messages from al-Qaeda, while requiring these companies to modify or delete anything on Al Jazeera that could be considered abusive. Jewish organizations criticized Al Jazeera for propagating hatred against Jews; others worried about the precedent of requiring cable companies to act as censors. As it turned out, the CRTC requirements discouraged cable companies from carrying Al Jazeera.

There has been a trend toward reducing government regulation of the broadcast media. For example, the "Fairness Doctrine" in the United States, a policy that required broadcast outlets to devote time to important public issues and provide a "reasonable opportunity" for opposing positions to be aired, was repealed in 1987. President Ronald Reagan argued that with the large number of channels available on cable, regulation was no longer needed (Patterson, 2000).

The Internet has thus far generally avoided regulation (although some non-democratic countries including China, Iran, and Myanmar try to block access to many sites and prosecute those who post comments critical of the government). With an immense number of different sources of information and ideas, a highly decentralized structure, and the ability of any person to express and circulate his or her views, it could be viewed as the libertarian ideal.

Electronic Frontier Foundation
www.eff.org

Corporate Ownership

An important feature of the privately owned mass media is corporate ownership. Large corporations now own the majority of media outlets. There is a trend toward concentration and cross-media ownership, in which a few large corporations own a variety of different media and related industries. General Electric, Time Warner, Disney, National Amusements (through CBS and Viacom), News Corporation, Bertelsmann, and Vivendi have large holdings of television and radio networks and stations, cable TV outlets, Internet portals and websites, newspapers and magazines, as well as book publishers, music companies, film producers, theme parks, and professional sports teams. In Canada, CTVglobemedia, CanWest Global, and Quebecor control a substantial proportion of the media.

Media outlets that are part of large corporate empires may be less likely to report on problems occurring with other firms in the corporation. As well, there may be expectations that the media will promote other products of their corporate owners. Ownership of different types of media by the same corporation reduces the diversity of the media, and may result in a reduction in the number of journalists if resources are shared among the different media owned by the same corporation.

BIAS AND OBJECTIVITY

The Campaign for
Press and
Broadcasting
Freedom
**www.press
campaign.org**

The ownership of much of the mass media by large corporations may result in a bias toward defending and promoting the interests of big business and the values of the capitalist system. Media owners tend to be conservative and oriented to the dominant interests in society. Their choice of executives to run their media outlets will likely reflect, at least to some extent, their ideological orientation. On the other hand, as profit-oriented enterprises, media corporations will normally want to attract as large an audience as possible. This may involve avoiding taking political stances that offend segments of the public. As well, to attract large audiences, media outlets may find it necessary to allow the voices of different elements of the public to be heard.

Nevertheless, a number of prominent newspaper owners have used their position to promote their political views. For example, one of the reasons that Conrad Black established the *National Post* and purchased the largest chain of newspapers in Canada was to give voice to his strongly conservative views. (Under financial pressure, he later sold most of his Canadian interests.) CanWest Global has required that its newspapers cover some news stories in a manner consistent with the views of its owners, the Asper family. As well, CanWest Global required its local newspapers to carry some editorials prepared by the head office. The company, however, backed off after considerable criticism of this directive. Fox News, part of the News Corporation's media empire, is well known for its strong right-wing bias.

Advertising Influence

The extent to which the mass media are affected by their dependence upon advertising revenue is not easy to determine. Certainly, there have been cases in which advertisers have attempted to pressure the media, particularly to avoid negative publicity. Indeed, democratic governments have, at times, used their large advertising budgets to try to stifle negative coverage. For example, in the 1980s the Newfoundland government withdrew its advertising from an independent weekly newspaper that had been strongly critical of the government's involvement in a costly, unsuccessful effort to make the foggy capital of the province a major producer of greenhouse cucumbers.

To their credit, various media outlets have, on occasion, refused to submit to advertising pressure. However, it is possible that the power of major advertisers is relevant in a more indirect way. A media outlet may think twice before investigating a story that portrays a major advertiser in a negative way. As well, television stations may shy away from producing or carrying controversial programs with which advertisers would not want to be associated. For example, in 2003 the CBS network backed off from its plan to air the docudrama *The Reagans* amid concerns that conservative groups would pressure corporations to withdraw their advertisements.

Views of Journalists

Journalists and reporters are, on the whole, less likely to be conservative than most of the owners and managers of the mass media, although the question of whether they tend to lean in a leftist or socially progressive direction is contentious (Alterman, 2003; Croteau, 1998; Miljan & Cooper, 2003). However, it should be noted that editors and producers review and sometimes change the material that journalists submit, choose what stories are to be followed, and decide what stories will appear.

Even if journalists as a whole may tend to be critical of those in positions of power, this does not necessarily apply to most prominent journalists, such as TV news anchors, who earn high salaries and are treated like celebrities. They hobnob with the rich and powerful, and are often invited to high-paying speaking engagements arranged by business leaders. This raises questions as to whether leading journalists tend to lose their detachment from power and wealth and are therefore less likely to raise the concerns of ordinary people or criticisms of the powerful.

Fairness & Accuracy in Reporting
www.fair.org

Objectivity

When an independent commercial press that appealed to the mass public was developed in North America in the late nineteenth century, journalists began to view themselves as professionals conveying the objective truth to the public. Editors expected writers to report only the facts without exaggeration, interpretation, or opinion (Hackett & Zhao, 1998). A sharp distinction was made between fact and opinion, with opinions relegated to the editorial page.

However, the "facts" do not necessarily speak for themselves. Without background and interpretation, the facts may be largely meaningless for much of the public. Indeed, since the "facts" often come from official sources, the attempt to appear objective has been viewed by some analysts as reflecting a bias in favour of the dominant political forces (Hackett & Zhao, 1998). As well, since reporting inevitably involves selectivity in deciding what to report, objectivity may be impossible to achieve fully.

Columbia Journalism Review
www.cjr.org

The New Objectivity

The ideal of objectivity has not disappeared but, as Robert Hackett and Yuezhi Zhao (1998) point out, it has tended to be treated in the broader sense of allowing background and interpretation, provided that reporters attempt to be impartial, fair, and balanced. For example, to achieve the appearance of fairness, reporters are expected to seek reaction to a statement by a government leader from opposition party spokespersons. When an issue is considered controversial, both sides are often presented. However, this means that complex issues may be simplified into a "pro/con" format, ignoring the reality that there may be more than two sides to an issue. The media may only find it necessary to provide balanced treatment to issues that are matters of dispute among contending political parties. And viewpoints and positions that reflect the leading values of society may go unquestioned.

The media make considerable use of experts to provide comments and some background on issues. However, because most experts come from established institutions and organizations, challenging perspectives are not likely to receive much coverage. In particular, business-supported think tanks, such as C.D. Howe Institute and the Fraser Institute in Canada, often supply many of the experts who comment on a variety of topics.

Framing

Framing—
selecting and highlighting some facets of events or issues, and making connections among them so as to promote a particular interpretation, evaluation, and/or solution.

Instead of the traditional emphasis on the facts characteristic of newspaper reporting, television news typically uses a "story" format in order to make the news more interesting. Treating a news item as a story introduces a subtle form of selectivity known as **framing**. Framing involves "selecting and highlighting some facets of events or issues, and making connections among them so as to promote a particular interpretation, evaluation, and/or solution" (Entman, 2004, p. 5). Typically, a problem is defined, the cause of the problem is identified, a moral judgment is conveyed or implied, and remedies are suggested or endorsed in order to tell a consistent story (Entman, 2004). For example, during the invasion of Iraq in 2003, the media in the United States framed the story in terms of an effort to liberate Iraqis from an evil dictator who possessed weapons of mass destruction. Alternative interpretations were largely ignored.

Not all news stories carry a complete frame, but the metaphors and images that are chosen to depict a news story affect the way the news is described by journalists and the way it is perceived by the public. For example, election campaigns are often described in terms of a horse race, with great attention being given to public opinion polls (see Box 7.3, Public Opinion Polls). Questions of which party or candidate is ahead or behind and who is gaining or dropping back are often the frame within which specific events— a speech, a debate, or a rally—are discussed. The media tend to analyze the content of a speech or party policy positions in terms of the strategies adopted by a party or candidate for gaining power, instead of examining the feasibility and implications of the party's proposals.

The media typically frame politics in terms of the struggle among party leaders for power. In effect, a choice has been made to explain events and circumstances in terms of the qualities of leaders rather than in terms of broader social, economic, and political forces. This may exaggerate the power of a prime minister or president and create

BOX 7.3 PUBLIC OPINION POLLS

"Polls [poles] are for dogs," former Prime Minister John Diefenbaker once said. Many Canadians had similar thoughts after media coverage of the 2004 election heavily featured public opinion polls that wrongly predicted a Conservative party victory.

Properly done, a poll based on a random sample (one in which each individual has an equal probability of being chosen) of one or two thousand people can usually reflect quite accurately the opinions of a large electorate. The statistical laws of probability tell us that random samples of one thousand people, for example, will be accurate within about three percentage points nineteen times out of twenty. In other words, if a poll shows the Liberal party with the support of 40 percent of the population, we can be 95 percent certain that the actual support for the party is between 37 percent and 43 percent. A larger poll will have a smaller margin of error, but there is always a slight possibility that a poll will inaccurately reflect the opinions of the population.

In the 2004 election, several polls, all commissioned by media outlets and conducted near the end of the campaign, found that the Liberal and Conservative parties were virtually tied in popular support. Projections based on these results suggested that the Conservatives would win significantly more seats than the Liberals.* The media highlighted this conclusion and speculated about the nature of a Conservative government. Instead, the Liberals beat the Conservatives 36.7 percent to 29.6 percent, winning one hundred and thirty-five seats versus ninety-nine for the Conservatives.

Were the polls wrong? Not necessarily. Polls only reflect opinions at a particular point in time. There are indications that in the several days between the time the polls were conducted and election day there was a shift toward the Liberal party. Indeed, the extensive reporting of the polls could have contributed to this shift: some voters, concerned that the Conservatives might win the election, might have switched their vote to the Liberals. Instead of punishing the Liberals for their perceived misdeeds in office, these voters may have decided that electing a Conservative government was too risky.

Using poll results to predict election outcomes always holds some risks. A significant proportion of survey respondents say that they are undecided or only leaning toward one party. An increasing proportion of people refuse to be interviewed for polls. Many of those who do respond to a poll end up not voting. Finally, seat projections based on poll results are prone to substantial errors because they are based on a variety of assumptions. Small changes in the popular vote, for example, can result in substantial changes in the number of seats each party wins.

It is important to be aware of the limitations of polls and how they are interpreted. Indeed, political parties have, at times, presented false or misleading reports of the polls that they have conducted. During the 1968 election campaign, for example, PC strategists circulated an imaginary set of poll results showing their party in the lead in a desperate attempt to stem the groundswell of support for the Liberal party. Although the media focus on poll results is often criticized, it has also been argued that the media attention to poll results can provide some useful information to voters. For example, by drawing attention to the possibility of a Conservative victory in 2004, the reporting of poll results may have encouraged voters to consider whether they really wanted to elect a Conservative government.

*Polls conducted by four polling firms from June 21 to 24, 2004, found the two leading parties either tied or with only an insignificant difference of 1 percent. A poll conducted by SES Research for the Parliamentary Channel did indicate a Liberal lead of 34 percent to 30 percent for the Conservatives, but little attention was given to this result.

the impression that the leader is personally involved in all decisions. Further, the use of metaphors drawn from warfare and boxing, such as a candidate scoring a "knock-out punch" in a debate, may tend to reinforce the image of politics as a male activity (Gidengil & Everitt, 2002).

THE MEDIA AND GOVERNMENT: WATCHDOG OR LAPDOG?

Watchdogs

In a liberal democracy, the media are often expected not only to provide the political information needed by the public to choose among the contending parties, but also to play a watchdog role. By bringing to public attention abuses of power or the failure of governments to deal with important problems, the media can help to check the power of government and assist citizens in pressuring government to correct problems. For example, the media played a role in helping to uncover the sponsorship scandal (involving wasteful and undocumented payments made to Liberal-connected advertising firms) that rocked the Canadian government in 2004 and 2005.

Center for
Investigative
Reporting
www.muckraker.org

In some cases, the media dig out the abuses themselves; in others, they play the watchdog role by highlighting issues raised by the opposition parties, whistle-blowers (employees who go public when there has been wrongdoing within their organization), the Auditor General (an independent officer of Parliament), or anonymous sources within government who leak information.

Early commercial newspapers, particularly in the United States, engaged in some sensationalist exposure of corruption (known as muckraking) in both business and government. The development of the modern watchdog role and associated investigative reporting is often associated with the Watergate scandal of the early 1970s, as discussed in Box 7.4, Watergate: An Investigative Reporting Success. The watchdog role of the media has been aided by the access-to-information laws passed by many governments in recent decades. However, investigative reporting is time-consuming and costly and thus is not generally a major feature of the media's coverage of politics.

Attack Dogs

Some critics of the mass media have argued that the contemporary mass media, particularly in the United States, have turned from watchdogs into attack dogs. The media have sometimes mounted sharp personal attacks on politicians and other prominent persons. Political scientist Larry Sabato (1992) described American journalists as being like sharks, engaging in a "feeding frenzy" when they sense that a politician or a celebrity is in trouble. For example, massive media attention, national and international, was given to the arrest and trial of former football star O.J. Simpson for the alleged murder of his wife, to musician Michael Jackson for allegedly molesting children, and to celebrity Paris Hilton's jail time for alcohol-related reckless driving.

BOX 7.4   WATERGATE: AN INVESTIGATIVE REPORTING SUCCESS

Before the 1972 American election, operatives working for Republican President Richard Nixon's re-election committee broke into the Democratic Party offices in Washington's Watergate complex. Subsequently, the president's senior staff tried to cover up these illegal activities. Investigative reporting by journalists Bob Woodward and Carl Bernstein at *The Washington Post*, aided by an anonymous high-level source nicknamed Deep Throat (the deputy director of the FBI, who revealed his identity in 2005), unravelled the story. Eventually Nixon resigned in disgrace rather than face an impeachment trial.

Although the case of Watergate shows the potential significance of the investigative role of the media, questions can be raised as to whether the media take on this role regularly and consistently. In the case of the Watergate scandal, the publisher of *The Washington Post* was willing to devote considerable resources to allow reporters to pursue the story for a lengthy period of time. President Nixon had never maintained good relations with the press and his administration's failed attempt to prevent *The New York Times* from publishing the Pentagon Papers (a secret study of the decision making that led to the Vietnam War) turned the elite media against Nixon. In other circumstances, such as in the climate of fear that followed the 2001 terrorist attacks on the United States, the media have been more reluctant to conduct investigations that might reflect negatively on government leaders.

Reporters competed furiously to find juicy bits of information, rumours, and gossip to embellish the stories. Similarly, the media were obsessed with American President Bill Clinton's relationship with Monica Lewinsky in the late 1990s, obscuring important national and international issues.

More generally, the media have a tendency to take an aggressive, confrontational approach to political personalities, perhaps as a reaction to the efforts of governments and political parties to try to manipulate the media (Nadeau & Giasson, 2003).

The media often scrutinize the words and actions of leading politicians, more to ridicule them than to analyze their ideas. Canadian party leaders have, for example, suffered considerable media ridicule for losing their luggage, dropping a football, wearing a wetsuit to an election campaign kickoff, and wearing a required hairnet while touring a cheese factory. The media (particularly in the United States) have also often paid considerable attention to the personal lives of politicians: digging up or spreading gossip about their past marijuana usage, personal relationships, or sexual orientation.

Lapdogs

The prevalence of critical and negative journalism should not be exaggerated. The media can also be seen, to some extent, as lapdogs. There is often a cozy relationship between government and journalists, and much of what constitutes news originates from official sources. In the past, some politicians would hand out cash to journalists in order to encourage them to give favourable treatment to a press release. To this day, some journalists may be influenced by the hope of obtaining employment within government, receiving extra

"I'm so glad the media keeps us informed about politics."

income through speech writing or ghostwriting a book for a politician, or gaining access to gather material for a popular biography of a prominent political figure.

More importantly, journalists who are viewed as sympathetic to the government are more likely to be given the inside story, an exclusive interview with a leading political figure, or a "leak" of an impending government announcement. Even though contemporary journalists generally prefer to avoid too close a relationship with politicians, they rely on politicians and government officials for information to make sense of what is happening within government and to provide anecdotes and gossip for an inter- esting story. With pressure to report the news as quickly as possible and with the media trying to produce news at the lowest possible cost, journalists often lack the capability to properly research the news stories they are presenting.

Sleeping Dogs

Media watchdogs are sometimes asleep or muzzled. For example, the pattern of systematic physical, sexual, and cultural abuse of generations of Aboriginals forced to attend residential schools across Canada did not receive media scrutiny until long after the schools were closed. Likewise, in the case of physical and sexual abuse of boys by the Christian Brothers at the Mount Cashel Orphanage in St. John's, Newfoundland, the leading provincial newspaper apparently suppressed the story under influence from the hierarchy of the Catholic Church and other community leaders (Harris, 1991). American television networks have largely ignored the use of depleted uranium in U.S. military weaponry in the 2003 Iraq War, despite evidence of long-term, serious potential health consequences for both American soldiers and the Iraqi population.

Project Censored
**www.project
censored.org**

Walking the Dog: News Management

Governments and politicians often try to manage the news so as to avoid gaining negative treatment. **News management**—controlling and shaping the presentation of information—includes such techniques as issuing news releases close to news deadlines so that journalists cannot check the facts or obtain critical comments. Information that reflects negatively on government is often released when a more dramatic news event is occurring, or during summer or on weekends, when many journalists are not working and audiences are small.

**News
management**—
the controlling and
shaping of the
presentation of
news in order to
affect the public's
evaluation of news
stories.

   Politicians and their media advisers are often concerned with controlling the "spin" put on what they have said—that is, trying to ensure that a favourable interpretation is placed on information. For example, during a leaders' debate, "spin doctors" for each party will try to persuade journalists that their leader has won the debate and explain away any mistakes that their leader has made.

   To avoid unfavourable framing of their proposals and actions, governments spend large sums of money on advertising to carry their message directly to the public.

In April 2004, investigative reporter Seymour Hersh published articles in The New Yorker *magazine that included pictures illustrating the abuse and torture of Iraqis in the Abu Ghraib prison. This brought to public attention the evidence of abuse that had been largely ignored by the mainstream media.*

Although some government advertising is designed to increase awareness of government services and programs, governments have also mounted substantial advertising campaigns to promote their perspective on particular issues, boast about their accomplishments, and present themselves in a positive light. Similarly, political parties, interest groups, public relations firms, and think tanks often supply press releases, prepared newspaper articles, and television and radio clips that are distributed to media outlets free of charge. Such stories are sometimes incorporated into the news with little or no editing—particularly by media outlets that have limited resources.

News management by government is most clearly seen in times of war and, more generally, in much of the coverage of international affairs. The mass media often see it as unpatriotic to question their government's decision to go to war and feel obliged to support their country's troops. Government officials and military leaders usually try to control the media tightly during a foreign conflict. In the case of the 2003 invasion of Iraq, discussed at the start of this chapter, only carefully selected embedded journalists were allowed into Iraq and they were restricted in what they could report. During the 1991 Gulf War (involving the United States and its allies after Iraq's conquest of Kuwait), journalists were generally confined to the American military's Central Command headquarters in Qatar, a considerable distance from the war, and thus had to rely on military briefings and images supplied by the military. Canadian government and military leaders have tried to suppress information about the alleged torture by some authorities in Afghanistan of captured insurgents handed over to them by Canadian troops.